1956

Nick Richardson is an author, academic, and journalist who has written for a range of publications in England and Australia. He has a PhD in history from the University of Melbourne and is adjunct professor of journalism at La Trobe University. He lives in Melbourne.

Nick Richardson

1956

The year Australia
welcomed
the world

SCRIBE
Melbourne • London

Scribe Publications
18–20 Edward St, Brunswick, Victoria 3056, Australia
2 John St, Clerkenwell, London, WC1N 2ES, United Kingdom

First published by Scribe 2019

Cover images: Flags © shutterstock; 3000m steeplechase Olympic final,
1956 © Raymond Morris Collection, National Museum of Australia;
Dancers © George Marks; Mervyn Wood, source *Daily Telegraph*; Robert
Menzies © National Library of Australia from Canberra, Australia; Olympic
torch © imagedepotpro; Suez Crisis – Tank © PA Images/Alamy Stock
Photo; Betty Cuthbert © INTERFOTO/Alamy Stock Photo; TV © CSA
Images; ABC logo, source wikimedia commons.

Typeset in Bembo Book MT

Printed and bound in Australia by Griffin Press, part of Ovato

Scribe Publications is committed to the sustainable use of natural resources
and the use of paper products made responsibly from those resources.

9781925322910 (paperback)
9781925938081 (e-book)

A catalogue record for this book is available from the National
Library of Australia.

scribepublications.com.au
scribepublications.co.uk

To my mum

'Australia is only a young country and we are very proud of our achievements. But we are also fully conscious of our shortcomings.'

Victorian Governor Sir Dallas Brooks,
November 1956

'The Australian's enthusiasm for sport is a consuming passion and it gives him high marks for intelligence. He is smart enough to prefer playing to working: he is jealous of his leisure and he makes use of it.'

US sportswriter Red Smith,
December 1956

Contents

Preface   *xi*

Prologue: April 1949   1

Summer 1955–56

Chapter One   A Dame Is Born   25

Chapter Two   Rebels, Villains, and Heroes   40

Autumn 1956

Chapter Three   The Enemy Within   63

Chapter Four   The Bomb in the Outback   85

Winter 1956

Chapter Five   It's a Men's Game   105

Chapter Six   One-Armed Bandits   126

Spring 1956

Chapter Seven   With Open Arms   151

Chapter Eight   Clouds on the Horizon   173

Chapter Nine   Lighting the Way   188

Chapter Ten   The World Waits   208

Summer 1956–57

Chapter Eleven   Let the Games Begin   233

Chapter Twelve   The Worst of Times,
    the Best of Times   259
Finale   283

Acknowledgements   305
Notes   307
Select Bibliography   325

Preface

One of the hardiest clichés in Australian history is that the 1950s was a dull decade, when conformity settled on the nation's shoulders, not to leave until the dynamic 1960s. Yet even the slightest scratching of the historical record reveals that there was significantly more going on than this cliché would have us believe. The decade was distinguished by drama, innovation, social change, a loosening of British ties, a big boost in migration, and the rise of consumerism. Australia was already on the path to being a different country by the time 1960 arrived. And the pivotal year in the preceding decade was 1956, when a series of important events — some accidental, others years in the planning — were critical in shaping the nation.

Most people will nominate the Olympic Games in Melbourne and the arrival of television as the nation's best-known moments of the year, but, as important as these were, there were other events that revealed something else about Australia. There were the British atomic tests at Maralinga, the arrival of the Hungarian refugees in Sydney after the bloody uprising against Soviet rule, the success of *Summer of the Seventeenth Doll*, and the emergence of Barry Humphries' comic creation Edna Everage. While Prime Minister Robert Menzies capitalised electorally on the split in the Labor opposition, he also walked the international stage, trying to solve the impasse at the heart of the Suez Canal crisis. These were all elements contributing to a shifting perspective on Australia's place in the world — how we saw ourselves and how other nations saw us.

How Menzies' government handled Maralinga said much about our attitude to Indigenous Australians. How we embraced *The Doll* told us something about our cultural tastes and our desire to hear our own voices on stage. Our response to the Hungarian refugees affirmed our capacity to absorb others into what was an evolving multicultural society before the word was commonplace. And all of this was occurring during one of the most charged eras in world history, when the Cold War gave rise to suspicion and paranoia that inevitably spread to Australia. This is why the stakes were so high for many of the international events of 1956, and Australia's proximity to some of those events brought it to the world's attention.

There were subtle but distinct conflicts occurring across Australia by 1956: the rise of the energetic modernisers, who had a vision for the nation that elevated it to the international stage, and those who saw Australia as part of the Empire's rich continuum, stable and safe. There was also, in the broadest definitions of the word, the conflict between the 'amateurs', those who believed in the happy accident of talent, and those 'professionals' who saw the need for not only talent but also an organised and intelligent approach to sport, business, and the arts. And then there were those who felt that regulation and control was the right way for Australian society to proceed in an uncertain world, while some others saw the alternative as a means of freedom and a mark of maturity. All of them were caught up in the events of 1956.

This book has identified several characters who were part of the year's events. In some instances they were not the main figures but their story helps illuminate the bigger picture. They move in and out of focus as the year progresses, commenting on their circumstance, telling us how they got there and, in some cases, what happened next. The book's structure follows the chronology of the year, and culminates inevitably with the Olympic Games in Melbourne. The Games crystallised some of those shifts in Australian life, and underlined how the nation was in the world's sight like never before. This is a book about a year when Australia's gaze was pulled out-wards, beyond the Empire and the old world, and towards a different future.

Prologue
April 1949

The Pan Am aeroplane touched down at Honolulu airport at 11.20 pm on Friday 14 April 1949. On board was a neat, spare 72-year-old Japanese man who was embarking on a mission that required a unique set of skills: diplomacy, discretion, patience, and the detachment, or perhaps imagination, to put international opprobrium to one side. Matsuzo Nagai was on his way to Rome to lobby the International Olympic Committee to re-admit Japan to the Olympic movement. World War II had ended less than four years earlier, and under the terms of the peace Japan was still under US occupation.

Dr Nagai was a long-term and ardent advocate of Japan's return to the Olympic family. Before the war, he had been in charge of Tokyo's bid for the 1940 Olympics; it took Japan's war with China to end that dream. When the Games resumed in London after World War II, Japan and Germany were excluded, but later in 1948 Japan started organising itself for another tilt at hosting the Games. Dr Nagai told waiting reporters at Honolulu airport that he had been encouraged by a message from IOC vice president Avery Brundage that Japan's application to rejoin the Olympic movement might be received favourably. And General Douglas MacArthur, running the Allied occupation of Japan, had sanctioned the nation's participation in sports — so why not the Olympics, the greatest sporting

1

competition in the world? The time, Dr Nagai argued, was right for Japan to come in from the Olympic cold. 'I believe that through the medium of sports, nations can be brought closer to one another and a better spirit of understanding and friendship can be developed,' he said.[1]

This might have been the kind of soothing message that the IOC wanted to hear, but its neutral tone was no great surprise. Dr Nagai had a keen understanding of how to navigate the often dangerous waters of international politics: he had been Japan's ambassador to Finland and Sweden, and then Germany in 1933–35. It was a complex time to be a diplomat in Berlin, as the Nazi menace built its strength ahead of the 1936 Olympics. Now, Nagai was confident that his diplomatic skills would be rewarded in Rome with his nation's return to the 1952 Games, to be held in Helsinki. On Saturday 15 April Dr Nagai boarded his plane for the flight to Rome. What no one in the Olympic movement could have predicted was just how important his appearance at the IOC meeting would be for Australia.

The Hotel Excelsior in Rome was a grand testament to a time of European peace and glamour. It was close to the Via Veneto, and between the famed Spanish Steps and the Villa Borghese gardens and gallery. The US embassy was a short walk away. The famous and the infamous were regular guests, ranging from Mafia figure 'Lucky' Luciano to Hollywood star John Wayne to philosopher Jean-Paul Sartre. The staff wore starched uniforms, and patrolled the high-ceilinged dining rooms and lounges with crisp efficiency. It was a hotel of old-world elegance, and for a week in April 1949 the IOC executive and its members based themselves there to decide who would host the Summer and Winter Games of 1956.

*

One city that had thrown its hat into the ring to host the 1956 Games was Melbourne. The origins of this bid lay in the first year after the war, when a former boxer, POW, and newspaper sales representative, Edgar Tanner, convened a meeting of the Victorian Olympic Committee, where a resolution was made for Melbourne to apply to hold the Games. The resolution moved by Carlton & United Breweries' executive Ron Aitken, representing the Victorian Amateur Athletic Association, set in train what would become the first Olympics in the Southern Hemisphere. But that success had a complicated paternity: arguments went on for years among some Melbourne luminaries about just whose idea it was to launch the city's bid.

Chief among them was a former Olympian, former lord mayor, and prominent businessman, Sir Frank Beaurepaire. Sir Frank was a hard man to like but easy to admire. He had an outstanding Olympic career, having swum at the 1908, 1920, and 1924 Olympics, where he'd picked up three silver and three bronze medals. Short but powerfully built, Beaurepaire had strong shoulders and the physical confidence to match his self-belief. He had been desperate to enlist in World War I but was invalided out with appendicitis before he could see service. Beaurepaire hated the implied physical frailty. If he could not be in the Australian Imperial Force, he would do the next best thing: he joined the YMCA in a recreational role with the AIF.

He worked so assiduously at building the troops' morale through regular sport that Beaurepaire found himself as Sir John Monash's recreation officer of choice, and served with Monash's Third Division on the Western Front. Beaurepaire not only organised boxing tournaments for AIF servicemen but also established a theatre troupe of Pierrots: the soldiers dressed and performed in a disused stable behind the Western Front. Beaurepaire was also central to the organisation of the first overseas match of Australian Rules football, when two teams of AIF soldiers played at the Queen's Club, in London, in October 1916. Only a debilitating dose of trench fever ended his war. Monash wrote to him:

> As organiser of social work within the division, of comforts for the troops in the trenches and of sports and amusements, your

work has been on a uniform plane of excellence. I trust that
the gratitude felt towards you by all ranks will constitute some
measure of reward for your labours.[2]

These were qualities that augured well for a post-war business
career. In Sydney in 1920 Beaurepaire set up his own tyre retreading
business; two years later he returned to Melbourne to establish a
similar business under his own name in La Trobe Street. With the
motorcar growing in popularity, Beaurepaire established a tyre
manufacturing plant in West Footscray in 1933. Beaurepaire was well
aware of the sales power of his own sporting success, so he decided
to call the business the Olympic Tyre & Rubber Company. By 1940
he was lord mayor of Melbourne; he was knighted in 1942, and
then elected to the Victorian Legislative Council for, appropriately
enough, Monash Province. Conservative by nature, Beaurepaire
tried but failed to win a Senate seat for the United Australia Party
— the forerunner of Menzies' Liberals — at the 1943 federal election. In May 1947 he became president of the Victorian Olympic
Committee.

Beaurepaire's chief ally in Melbourne's bid was another former
lord mayor, Raymond Connelly, who had been campaigning for
years to break Melbourne out of its straitlaced ways. Connelly
collected newspaper stories about the grim entertainment options
in Melbourne, building his case for change when he became mayor.
'Young people could not be expected to sit around on Sunday and
twiddle their thumbs,' he told one council meeting in 1946, while
proposing Sunday sport, afternoon picture shows, and symphony
concerts as the antidote.[3] He wondered why Melbourne couldn't
have a month-long carnival in spring or autumn that involved
the Yarra River, a music festival, a band contest, a floral pageant,
and a bicycle race around the city.[4] This modernising bent made
him a perfect travelling companion for Beaurepaire: Connelly had
started his working life in the grains industry, but he was also the
managing director of LaTrobe Motors in the city, linking him, like

Beaurepaire, to the motor vehicle love affair that was becoming integral to Australian family life. (The other lord mayor on the bid team, James Disney, owned a 40,000-foot showroom in Melbourne for motorcycles and used cars.) Beaurepaire and Connelly, knighted in 1948, believed the Games would lift Australia out of its post-war slumber. 'From a commercial viewpoint, the possibilities are incalculable,' Beaurepaire assured Connelly.[5]

When the time came to launch his home town's bid to host the Olympics, Sir Frank put himself at its centre, even trying to ensure that his name was attached to the genesis of the idea. 'It has been obvious for some weeks that ... Tanner [is] trying to establish that the Victorian Olympic Council first mooted the Olympic Games for Melbourne,' Beaurepaire wrote in early 1949.

> This is far from true and I would propose that Sir Raymond Connelly not only release a statement ... but also prepare a statement for the archives. Sir Raymond and I first discussed this matter late in 1945 or early in January 1946 ... I personally do not much mind except that we should keep to factual things and not allow these chaps who have done so little to try and steer away from realities.[6]

Except that Sir Frank did actually mind who took credit for the idea, and in the years to come it was a theme to which he frequently returned: he and Sir Raymond were the parents of the bid, not the creaking, groaning old gentlemen's club that was the Victorian Olympic Committee.

The battle for ownership of the idea was of course second to actually securing the Olympic bid, though, so from the moment it was clear that the 1948 London Olympics were going ahead, the Melbourne bid focused on lobbying for the Games to be held eight years later. The planning was initially built around the premise that the people Melbourne needed to impress would be in London for the 1948 Olympics. The intelligence they had gleaned from the IOC's decision about the 1952 Games revealed that the successful city — Helsinki — was a clear winner, by 10 votes, from Minneapolis and Los Angeles, and then Amsterdam. Helsinki had been awarded the 1940 Games when Tokyo had pulled out, so it was no surprise that the IOC honoured its pre-war commitment to the Finnish capital. The IOC doubled down on Europe, awarding Oslo the 1952 Winter Games.

Melbourne understood that its biggest challenge was general ignorance about the city and the nation, which was exemplified by its distance from everywhere else. The city was not a metropolis like Los Angeles or Detroit. It wasn't at the centre of the world, as London was, nor was it part of a broader continent of nations, like Finland, which was accessible to practically everyone in Europe. Melbourne was at the other end of the world, in a country few people knew anything about.

A closer look revealed a city aspiring to be cosmopolitan but not quite reaching the mark. City cafes were stuffy and drab, offering unappetising food chosen from dirty menus and served in chipped crockery, according to one newspaper survey.[7] Arts and culture were only available overseas, unless delivered by seasoned artistes who had braved the journey from the Old Country. Even local businessman and Australian IOC delegate Sir Harold Luxton could see the city's problems. 'I love Melbourne and I have lived here all my life, but it is still deadly dull,' he said.[8]

It was a difficult sell. Compounding the problem was the Melbourne bid team's determination to stick to what it knew — in the months ahead, there would be trips across Europe, handshaking, meeting and greeting. But there would be no mission to the United States, nor to central or southern America, nor to Asia. For a team bidding to host an international event, it sure lacked a global strategy. The Melbourne bid decided early on that it would source its support from the old Empire, the Commonwealth of Nations, who at least had a nodding familiarity with Australia and Melbourne. Not surprisingly, the final bid team — plus Sir Harold Luxton — contained four knights of the Commonwealth, and two who would be subsequently honoured with the same title. They might have been modern in their outlook, but these were Empire men embarking on an international task that was already limited by where they came from and who they knew. But if their effort came off, the world might finally take notice.

Initially, a team of Melbourne's great and good was established under Connelly's supervision to prepare the invitation document for the IOC. Connelly followed this up in January 1948 with an invitation book that was sent to IOC members. The grand publication – some copies of which were covered in lambs' wool, some in suede – documented Melbourne's appeal and preparedness to host the Games. Later that year, in London for the Olympics, a special lunch for 300 officials was held at Mansion House. It was nominally hosted by the lord mayor of London, but it was acknowledged during the banquet that the actual host was his Melbourne equivalent. Food and wine from Australia had been shipped to London for the event, and, for a city still in the grip of post-war rationing, the Australian largesse suggested a land of plenty on the other side of the world. Prince Bertil, the president of the Swedish Olympic Committee, was so taken with the Lindeman's burgundy that he asked Sir Raymond where he could get more. In fact, the wine was so popular that cases were sent to IOC members around the globe. In Tokyo Dr Nagai and two colleagues received a case each.

Plans were put in place to generate positive stories about the bid in the Melbourne press, with the intention that IOC president Sigfrid Edström's business representative in Melbourne would dutifully send them on to his boss. Every visiting notable was identified and lobbied. Prince Axel, Denmark's IOC delegate, came to Melbourne on business and was lobbied by Luxton and the Victorian-born governor of New South Wales, Lieutenant General John Northcott, to vote for Melbourne; the prince promised he would.

Following the London Games, Sir Raymond went on a European tour, distributing bid books and reminding the IOC committee members he met of Melbourne's desire to host the Games. At a meeting in London with the Earl Mountbatten and his wife, fresh from their time presiding over Indian independence in 1947, Sir Raymond extracted a promise of Indian support for Melbourne. It was a peculiar demonstration of the lack of Indian independence that the Mountbattens felt they could make such a promise, but Sir Raymond did not linger to debate the diplomatic niceties.

The next leg of his tour was to Europe's Catholic nations. It was the former Xavier boy's Olympic pilgrimage. He spoke to the Italians, who told him they were supportive of Melbourne; the mayors of Paris and Rome, neither of whom had a vote at the IOC, were also given a bid book. So too was Pope Pius XII, whom Sir Raymond saw at the Vatican, ostensibly to help engage some Latin members of the IOC but perhaps also because Sir Raymond was seeking some spiritual balm. It appeared to be a trip with no strategy, other than to cover territory and fly the Melbourne flag. Sir Raymond confessed, with a mixture of pride and fatigue, that he had covered some 7,000 miles in the Melbourne cause. 'In every country we have visited, I have seen as many as possible of the members of the International Committee,' he wrote to Beaurepaire, 'and they were all very pleased at the visit, particularly coming — as we did — from so far away.'[9]

Distance was the acknowledged issue, and Melbourne decided to tackle it head-on. The bid team enlisted the help of the federal minister for the air, Arthur S. Drakeford, to write a letter to the IOC outlining that distance, in the aircraft era, was not such a big issue. Drakeford pointed out that Australia was indeed linked to the world by airlines:

[T]hese services ensure that Australia can be conveniently reached at present in a matter of a few days from anywhere in the world. Australia's progress in air travel is such that planes are already being envisaged for stratosphere travel in pressurized jet-propelled aircraft and these will reach Australia from London in 24 hours.

Distance, the minister concluded, was no longer an obstacle to coming to Australia.[10]

There was some optimism behind Drakeford's forecast — in the immediate post-war transport world, the big problem was actually finding enough ships to transport soldiers, refugees, and travellers to where they needed to go. For quick and effective transport, everyone had to hope that jet airlines would be sufficiently reliable by 1956 to make coming to Australia appealing. Drakeford's other implied point was that airline travel was really the best way to come to Australia, and to cross the vast continent: two of the nation's airlines ranked among the top 14 biggest operators in the world, he told the IOC, proof of the nation's acceptance of airline travel.[11]

But how many IOC delegates found this crystal-ball gazing reassuring, a kind of Jules Verne forecast of the future? It did look difficult. The distance was even an issue for the Melbourne bid team: airfares to Rome with Qantas were over £300 each, a hefty fare, considering the average price of a five-roomed cottage was about £3,000.[12] So an approach was made to Prime Minister Ben Chifley for financial support. Reluctantly, Chifley agreed that the government would give £1,000 to help cover the travel costs.[13] The PM knew that the grant was also a demonstration of the federal government's support for the Games coming to Australia.

There was another key issue related to Australia's remoteness: the athletic season in the Northern Hemisphere was held in the summer. An Olympic Games in Australia would likely be scheduled in late spring or early summer, out of season for the Northern Hemisphere athletes. (It was, of course, a clear demonstration of the Games' historical focus on the Northern Hemisphere that this out-of-season competition was not an issue worth contemplating for Southern Hemisphere athletes who had to compete in London, Paris, Amsterdam, Los Angeles, or Berlin during their home winter months.)

A related consideration went to the 'amateur ethos' at the heart of the modern Olympics: many of the athletes were students at universities and colleges, and used their summer break to compete. An Olympics in Australia would effectively mean the athletes were compromising their education. Professional athletes were never worried by such prosaic considerations — they were paid to compete whenever and wherever they could — but professional athletes were not welcome at the Games. Melbourne's answer to this issue was vague: because a date had not been finalised to hold the Olympics, there was a suggestion that the Games could actually be held in early spring in Australia, eliminating the need for a significant break after the Northern Hemisphere competition. The Melbourne Olympics would become an extension of the Northern Hemisphere season. The secondary response was that the students would not miss much of their academic year because the competition would last only two weeks, and they could return home quickly because of the wonder of air travel.

The trickiest part of the bid was trying to convince the IOC that the Games could go south of the equator for the first time, without letting the perceived impediments of that move overwhelm the novelty of Melbourne playing host. A sophisticated approach was needed.

In the end, the Melbourne team at the 43rd IOC Session, in Rome in April 1949, comprised Lord Mayor James Disney, the Australian Olympic Federation chairman Harold Alderson, Victoria's agent-general in London Sir Norman Martin, and Sir Frank Beaurepaire. Australia had two votes. One was held by the Melbourne-based businessman — and former state political ally of Robert Menzies — Sir Harold Luxton. The other belonged to Hugh Weir, who had been involved with athletics, boxing, and wrestling for two decades, and was a stalwart of the Victorian Olympic Committee. He had become the manager of a Sydney-based shipping company two years earlier and couldn't make it to Rome because of competing business and family interests. Weir hoped to lodge a postal vote.

Sir Frank was confident, boldly predicting several months before the vote that Melbourne had an even-money chance of securing the 1956 Games. There were two other main contenders, he argued: Buenos Aires ('6/4 against') and Detroit ('2/1'). All the others had 'Buckley's chance', Sir Frank forecast.[14]

Being in the Southern Hemisphere, Buenos Aires had the same appeal and the same impediments as Melbourne: it was hard to get to, and it was out of season for Northern Hemisphere athletes. Unlike Melbourne, it had the appeal not just of being exotic but also of having strong links to Spanish-speaking communities across the IOC network. Detroit had emerged as the favourite of the United States Olympic Association, largely because of the city's wealth, built on the thriving automobile industry. But there were long-term festering racial issues; they would finally erupt 20 years later. In an inexplicable repeat of the strategic error of the 1952 bids, a number of other US cities decided to effectively cannibalise Detroit's bid — Los Angeles, Minneapolis, and Philadelphia added their bids to the ticket, and then San Francisco and Chicago came on board. Mexico City, Buenos Aires, and Melbourne were the only non-US cities to offer themselves as hosts. By the time the IOC delegates gathered in Rome, the bid resembled a confused assemblage of US Olympic interests and some hopeful participants from the new world.

Just four days before the IOC met, a report was lodged in the Filipino parliament that created a furore which threatened to undermine Melbourne's bid. The report centred on a debate against non-discriminatory immigration policies, but it led to a discussion of Australia's position on race — and the shadow of the White Australia policy was never far away. The critique was set against the role the Philippines had played in halting the Japanese advance on Australia during the Pacific War. 'Were it not for the heroism and patriotism of the flower of our manhood on the battlefields in Bataan and Corregidor in delaying enemy operations,' one Filipino MP said, 'Australia would have been invaded by the Japanese, and would now not be a land of white people but of coloured people.' He pointed out too that Australia was originally a country of black men that had been 'usurped' by the whites. The language was strong, and motivated largely by Australian immigration minister Arthur Calwell's decision to prevent a Filipino and naturalised American sergeant, Lorenzo Gamboa, from entering Australia.

Calwell's decision spurred the Filipino parliament into delivering a pointed rebuke to Australia at its most vulnerable point — the Olympic bid. It came when the Filipino MP linked the situation to an approach from the Melbourne bid team asking for Filipino support in Rome:

> Australians are the biggest hypocrites in the world. When it comes to propagandising their country, they want coloured people to do it, but when it comes to equality they do not accept coloured races because they are inferior. I believe we would be doing a grave injustice to the Philippines if we consented to Melbourne as the seat of the 1956 Olympics.[15]

The Filipinos took the matter seriously enough to invite an Australian parliamentary delegation to Manila to sort out the situation, although the likelihood of such a dialogue taking place was remote. The Australian government was not inclined to participate.

What the Melbourne bid team thought of this outburst is not recorded, but it was a powerful demonstration that Australia did not come to the Olympic vote without political baggage. Australia had a reputation, especially in the Asia-Pacific region, for its commitment to the racist White Australia policy, which had been in place for years with the aim of fostering the growth of a white, homogenous population. The policy was dismantled in stages, with the first significant change occurring in 1950 when the Menzies government allowed 800 non-European refugees to stay in Australia, followed by the approval for some Japanese war brides to migrate to Australia in 1952.

Calwell might have opened Australia to a steady stream of post-war European migrants, but there was still little affection for Asians, officially or otherwise, especially after Japan's role in World

War II. And it was wilfully naive of the Melbourne bid team to expect that such political concerns would not have an impact on the final vote in Rome. Equally, there was nothing the bid team could do to mollify the Filipinos or induce the federal government to arrive at a diplomatic solution.

*

Since the conclusion of World War II, Japan and Germany had excluded themselves from IOC meetings. But Dr Nagai's appearance in Rome changed all that, and put the IOC in something of a cleft stick — what to do now about Germany? The IOC decided to alert Germany to Dr Nagai's presence and leave the German delegate to make his own decision. Germany, though, was not quite a nation anymore; in the aftermath of the war, it was being divided between east and west. It was logically impossible to have a German delegate.

Dr Nagai's determination to have his country back in the IOC's embrace was partly an echo of Japan's pre-war disappointment at having to withdraw from hosting the 1940 Games. Japan had wanted the Games to restore its place in the world after it was expelled from the League of Nations in 1931 for invading Manchuria. The IOC was won over to the Japanese bid in 1936, but within a year the nation's claim to the Games was imperilled by its aggressive penetration deep into China, brutalising Nanjing and Shanghai. But the world's hostile reaction to the incursions initially failed to dent Dr Nagai's confidence that the Games were destined for Tokyo. 'People abroad have the false impression that the Japanese were no longer interested in anything pertaining to peaceful attainments of mankind, but ordinary life, including sport, was going on as usual,' Dr Nagai told the West in 1938.[16]

The war with China, however, told another story. Five months after his statement, Dr Nagai was forced to concede the Olympics could not happen. He went on radio in July 1938, in his role as the head of the Tokyo bid, to explain to listeners in the United States why

Tokyo could no longer host the Olympics. In English, he explained that the 'protracted warfare' with China meant Japan had to concentrate its national resources on the conflict, but added that Japan wanted to make an application to host the Games in 1944, so that 'the torch of Olympia will then burn in the eastern sky brilliantly'.[17]

Japan's decision actually pointed to something potentially more dangerous: its general withdrawal from the world, and its increasing nationalism. This proved a toxic and tragic signifier of the abandoned Olympics.[18] Dr Nagai's appearance in Rome in 1949 was an indication that some in Japan now wanted to re-engage with an international community that had made it a pariah. Just as they had used the Games as a means of rebuilding their international reputation in 1936, so the Games again became a 'safe' way of showing Japan had changed. It was classic soft diplomacy.

*

The US Olympic Association president (and IOC vice president), Avery Brundage, was a former Olympic pentathlete and decathlete with a fat wallet and a skill for tactless candour. No one was ever in any doubt what Brundage thought about anything, especially his wholehearted embrace of amateur sport: it was his raison d'être. But spreading the word put many people offside. Not for nothing was he called 'Slavery Brundage' or 'Avery Umbrage'. He was also parochial when required: before leaving for Rome, he told the US press that Detroit was the favourite to win the Games. The voting was a secret ballot, so there is no way of knowing how much vote-counting took place before the final ballot. And there is no telling what role Brundage played in assembling or directing votes to any of the bidders. What did happen in Rome was that the IOC spent some time trying to reduce the number of US bids. It was a sensible approach, but the Americans wouldn't have it.

The Melbourne bid team hung out its shingle in a suite that displayed large tinted images of a proposed stadium, the new swimming pool, and the stadium for boxing and wrestling. The drawings also emphasised the stadium's proximity to the athletes' village, considered an advantage over the Detroit bid, which had proposed a village some distance from the main stadiums. Beaurepaire approached as many undecided delegates as he could find, joining some for breakfast, extolling Melbourne's charms, reminding Iron Curtain countries that they had nothing to fear from a secret ballot, which apparently relieved one delegate, who had instructions from his national Olympic committee not to vote for Melbourne.[19] Others in the bid team were more obvious about their tactics. 'We were perfectly friendly with everybody,' Harold Alderson said, 'and told them what we were going to do. No one ever asked anyone to vote for us. We just went around and made friends.'[20]

On the day, the Melbourne message was explicit: Australia had taken part in every Games dating back to 1896, and no nation had had to travel further, every four years, to demonstrate its commitment to the Olympic movement. This was the obverse of the distance argument against Melbourne, a plea for returning the Antipodean favour that had been racked up over half a century of Olympic participation. Alderson also put the somewhat unusual case that Melbourne had successfully prepared for two world wars, so why not a sporting event?[21] Melbourne's final presentation to the IOC concluded with a short film that traversed the cityscape, its beaches, the sporting arenas, and deliberately tried to inject Melbourne with an air of glamour and sophistication.

Beaurepaire had his fingerprints all over it, having advocated for the inclusion of footage of a 'Learn to Swim' campaign with which he had been intimately involved. He was even cautious of the language used. 'I would suggest that you are particularly careful to avoid the use of the word "workers", which has such unpleasant associations, concentrating rather on as many variations as possible of "Australians" and "Melburnians",' he said.[22] It was a wise point — 'workers', with its echoes of communist terminology, might well have spooked some of the finer political instincts of the IOC delegates. But the film's end result was a melange of exaggeration and cultural envy, describing Collins Street as 'the Regent Street, Fifth Avenue, Rue de la Paix of Melbourne'.[23] And the film highlighted Melbourne's dining and entertainment scene, an odd choice given that the city was still firmly in the grip of the notorious 'six o'clock swill'.

Ultimately, 41 IOC delegates voted. Hugh Weir's application for a postal vote was rejected, so Australia could bank on only Sir Harold Luxton's vote. Inevitably, the US vote was split in the first round of voting, and several of the US cities dropped out. Mexico City was a casualty of the second round. The final preliminary ballot had Melbourne on 19 votes, Buenos Aires on 13, Los Angeles on 5, and Detroit on 4. That left a final ballot between Buenos Aires and Melbourne, the two first-time hosts and also both in the Southern Hemisphere.

On the numbers, Buenos Aires needed to pick up at least eight of the nine votes that had been shared between the two US cities to win the bid, assuming Melbourne retained all its votes in the final round. Prince Axel, of Denmark, who had been lobbied with such success in Melbourne months earlier, was the official scrutineer for the final ballot. He kissed the ballot paper and announced: 'Melbourne.' The city had got over the line by one vote, 21 votes to 20, the smallest margin in Olympic history. Buenos Aires had moved seven votes, but Melbourne had picked up two from the penultimate ballot.

Whose vote made the difference? Some suggested that it was the Philippines, but that seemed unlikely, given its anger with Australia over the Gumbao incident.[24] In fact, as was revealed six months later, the vote that secured the Olympic Games for Melbourne came from the Japanese delegate, Dr Nagai. This extraordinary development only became known when Sir Harold admitted that, to his 'utter amazement', Dr Nagai had told him Japan had supported the Australian bid.[25] Japan had probably voted for either Los Angeles or Detroit in the early ballots, and when it came to the final vote Dr Nagai shifted to Melbourne. Why he did so remains a mystery.

Detroit's mayor, Eugene Van Antwerp, blamed his city's loss on the IOC's determination to ensure the Games went to the Southern Hemisphere. 'Spanish nations of Latin and South America lined up solidly for Buenos Aires, while the British Empire nations voted solidly for Melbourne,' he said.[26]

The Detroit bid boss, Fred Matthaei, was less diplomatic, claiming the city could not compete with rival bidders who, he said, had offered money and gratuities to IOC members. He claimed the Argentine dictator, Juan Perón, had backed the Buenos Aires bid with US$30 million, a huge amount that would have dwarfed any other city's bid. He also believed the Australian bid had effectively bribed IOC voters:

Melbourne is paying the complete expenses of all members of the International Olympic Committee and a companion to the Games. The complete spirit of amateurism for which the Olympics are supposed to stand has been violated. Instead of following an orderly procedure, the award of the Games has been made the occasion of an international auction, with the site chosen being the highest bidder.[27]

This sounded like the whine of sour grapes and was quickly rejected in Melbourne, where a level of bemusement at the implied riches of the bid was the dominant theme. 'The Melbourne delegation so far as I know had neither the authority to guarantee payment of any money for fares, nor the money with which to back it up,' Hugh Weir responded.[28]

Avery Brundage might have looked sceptically at the mention of Melbourne's financial health. The most persuasive element of Melbourne's bid for the IOC vice president's vote had been its assurances about the investments it would make in Olympic-standard facilities.[29] These would haunt Melbourne during the next seven years, and drive Brundage's nagging about the city's lack of progress.

Back in Melbourne, Sir Raymond Connelly lit a replica of the Olympic torch that was at the Town Hall to celebrate the successful bid. Just a few days later, he collapsed on Swanston Street and died in hospital. He was 53.

*

Immediately following the IOC decision, Australia's ambassador to Japan, Patrick Shaw, was sent a series of questions by the United Press of America, including:

> In Hong Kong and other places in the Far East the question has been raised whether or not the so-called White Australia Policy will prohibit Asiatics from participating. Will Japanese be permitted to enter Australia and participate in the Olympic Games providing Japan's participation in the Olympic Games is approved?

Shaw cabled the question to Canberra and included his proposed reply:

> I am sure the teams of athletes from Asiatic countries, as from all Nations affiliated with the Olympic Games, will be hear[t]ily welcome[d] in Melbourne in 1956. In regard to such visits no question of our immigration policy is involved. With reference to Japan it is hoped that Japan's status in international spheres and the Olympic Committee will be clarified by that time. There again it would be [no] question of applying the Australian immigration policy.

The approach to Shaw was a smart piece of journalism: at least one overseas reporter had realised that the White Australia policy could pose a problem for Asian athletes travelling to the Melbourne Games.

A day after receiving Shaw's cable, Don Rodgers, Prime Minister Chifley's press secretary, told Shaw to not make any response. But it was too late; Shaw's statement had already been sent to United Press. Shaw was contrite, up to a point:

I regret any possibility of embarrassment but consider the statement factual and non-controversial. It seemed the least that could be said in the face of increasing comments and criticism regarding Australia's alleged discrimination against Asiatics which is now coming from both American and Asiatic sources here and in Hong Kong.[30]

Rodgers had a fine nose for potential pitfalls, and his instincts about the dangers of commenting on the issue were correct. But Shaw was equally seasoned, being a diplomat with a skill for not saying too much. His response didn't add any fuel to a debate about Japan competing in the Games, even though the issue was becoming more heated in Australia.

The Returned Sailors' Soldiers' and Airmen's Imperial League of Australia had written to Chifley stating that its federal executive had resolved that 'in view of the inhuman acts committed by the Japanese during the 1939–45 War ... such a race is not worthy of the honour and privilege of competing in the Olympic Games'.[31]

Immigration minister Arthur Calwell didn't want any Japanese entering Australia either; the recent history was overwhelming. 'I think the feelings of those relatives of men who were butchered fiendishly are more worthy of consideration by a Minister of State than the profits to be made from trade and the laurels to be won from sport,' he said in November 1949.[32] He was reported even to support Australia losing the Games rather than allowing Japanese athletes to compete.

Australian nurse Sister Vivian Bullwinkel, the only survivor of a Japanese attack on a group of nurses off a Bangka Island beach, didn't want any Australian athlete to look like they supported what Japan had done during the war. '[S]urely no Australian sportsman can condone the actions of the Japs a bare five years ago,' she said, 'in their machine gunning of defenceless women, their calculated fiendish bashing of our men and the withholding of medical supplies.' Sister Bullwinkel saw a similarity in the way the Japanese went about war and the way they competed: 'If anyone wants to see if the Japs are in sport for sport, go and see the newsreels of their swimmers in America. Just look at the swimmer's [sic] eyes. You will see they are out to do only one thing — to win at all costs.'[33]

Despite US approval, Australia opposed Japan's return to Davis Cup tennis in 1949. One Japanese tennis official commented: 'We remember Australian sportsmen as generous and goodhearted. How long will this Australian quarantine continue?' At the heart of the conflation between Japan's behaviour in the war and sport was Australians' belief that sport was a privileged place where excellence was equated with virtue. Fraternising with Japan on the sporting field, it was thought, could offend the idealism many Australians still had about the purity of sport, and stir their memories of the Pacific War.

Japan, though, saw sport as a way of addressing the hostility, and its Olympic Society secretary, Masaji Tabata, invited Australia to take part in the 1950 Asian Games in New Delhi. The ostensible reason for the invitation was to affirm Australia's place in the region. 'Our plan to have Australia invited to the games is not turning the other cheek,' Tabata explained. 'Geographically and politically Australia is just as much part of Asia as is Indonesia. Australian participation would greatly improve goodwill between Australia and Asia, besides adding immeasurably to interest in the games.'[34]

As a statement of fact — and as an expression of goodwill — this move had a lot going for it. But no Australian athlete went to New Delhi for the 1950 Asian Games. As one US occupational officer in Japan remarked, 'Your Aussies are sure good haters!'[35]

Sir Frank Beaurepaire and Wilfrid Kent Hughes — a former Victorian deputy premier, Olympic sprinter, World War I hero, and World War II prisoner of war — both spoke out against stopping Japan from attending the Games. Sir Frank argued that Italy, one of Japan's Axis partners, had been allowed back into the fold, and had been granted the 1956 Winter Games (in Cortina), so why penalise Japan? The final decision about Japan's participation in the 1952 and therefore the 1956 Games would be made at the 44th IOC Session, to be held in Copenhagen in 1950.

In the meantime, there was plenty of international speculation about what Calwell's stance would mean for Australia's reputation. Kent Hughes didn't like it one bit. 'The matter of vital importance to Australia is the legacy of reciprocal hate that some "Nip-happy" people, who should know better, are building up against us in the Far East,' he said. 'These "frantic boasts and foolish words" do us no good and a lot of harm.'[36] The post-war politics had inevitably infiltrated sport. The old notion — and the hardy determination to maintain the pretext — that sport and politics somehow existed in separate universes was a fallacy.

Japan tried to remain above the debate. Its athletics coach talked about the team already preparing for the Melbourne competition. Dr Nagai's IOC colleague Chingoro Takaishi took it upon himself to respond to Calwell:

> We are quite harmless now and it is most surprising to hear such remarks from a man of Cabinet rank. The Japanese are all sick of war and really believe in peace. We are going through a bloodless revolution … and Japan is becoming a democratic peace-loving nation without any thought of aggression.

Lest Calwell think Japanese athletes would miss out on this 'bloodless revolution' and come to Melbourne with their imperial aims intact, Takaishi added: 'Our purpose would be to show how the Japanese can swim … and run as an expression of goodwill.'[37] There was no word from Dr Nagai. After the Rome vote, he had been confined to bed because he felt 'feeble', and took his time returning home.

*

The war that occupied everyone's mind in 1949 would, by the time the 1956 Olympics arrived, be replaced by a different, distinctly chillier form of conflict that would frame international relations, and Australia's place in the world, for the next generation. But for the meantime it was sufficient to dream about what it meant to be an Olympic city. Sir Frank told the Victorian parliament in November 1949 that the benefits of hosting the Olympics extended beyond Melbourne, to the nation:

> Every aspect of city, state and commonwealth life can benefit from this great occasion. It will focus for all time, greater attention upon this country. It is up to us to make the Olympic Games of 1956 memorable, not alone in the annals of the Olympic movement, but in the furthering of world appreciation of our country as one of the leading nations in hospitality, in stature and in the graciousness of modern civilization.[38]

Sir Frank had lifted the bar of expectation as high as anyone could have imagined. Several weeks later, Robert Menzies led the Liberal–Country Coalition to victory at the 1949 federal election, establishing a personal hold on power that would last for 16 years. Middle Australia — the 'forgotten people', as Menzies had dubbed them years earlier — would sustain and nourish the new prime minister in the years ahead. They would be the beneficiaries of the nation's new prosperity and take comfort from Menzies' determination to shelter them from an uncertain world. A new era was about to begin.

Summer
1955–56

Chapter One
A Dame Is Born

Every night, whether it was at a town hall, a local cinema, or a mechanics' institute, the troupe of actors would be thanked for their performance of Shakespeare's *Twelfth Night*. The vote of thanks would often come from a prominent local woman — a headmistress, a lady mayor, a representative of the Country Women's Association or the Ladies' Auxiliary — before a supper feast would be unveiled. The next day, on the bus that would take the actors to their next Victorian town, a young Barry Humphries, with his distinctive flop of dark hair and his pitiless capacity for capturing the character of middle Australia, was improvising a routine that sounded just like the vote of thanks from the night before, deploying 'a flutey falsetto' to echo the 'speech of gratitude'. The actors, including Zoe Caldwell and director Ray Lawler, loved the parody. Humphries was just 21 and in his first year of acting. He was a university dropout and an employee of record company EMI, where he occasionally shattered old 78 rpm records with a hammer. In 1955, in regional Victoria, cultural performances — whether Shakespeare or opera — were of great moment, received with a kind of yearning for what many patrons believed were the sounds of England and Empire. Shakespeare in particular was the high-water mark of culture, a night's entertainment that was highbrow but familiar, epic but appropriate.

Humphries rejoiced in being miscast as Duke Orsino in the

production, but his work at the back of the bus was evolving into something more substantial. As the tour progressed, Humphries' character became more nuanced and more absurd. Several months later, the actors were preparing the end-of-season revue and Humphries was searching for inspiration. Lawler, soon to become famous with his drama *Summer of the Seventeenth Doll*, which featured working-class characters in an unashamedly Australian setting, urged Humphries to give a shape and a name to the 'woman' he heard at the back of the bus. Humphries decided to call her 'Edna' after a kindly nanny he once had.[1] Humphries was reluctant to play the part and suggested to Lawler that Caldwell play Edna and Humphries could even do the voice off-stage. 'No, you be Edna,' Lawler replied. 'Do it like a pantomime dame ...'[2]

The time and place for Edna's debut was fixed for 19 December 1955, at Melbourne's Union Theatre. The subject was the Olympics, and the need for Melbourne householders to open their suburban homes to the expected thousands of visitors who would come to the city during the Games. Thousands of Victorian households had already volunteered to host visitors, but 'Operation Hostess' was still short of its 30,000-bed target. One panicky Olympic official had urged all housewives to offer hospitality as soon as possible.[3] Lawler nudged Humphries: 'Wouldn't [Edna] be just be the kind of person who would offer her spare bedroom to a Latvian pole-vaulter, provided of course, that he was spotlessly clean and didn't hang his jockstrap on her rotary clothes-hoist in full view of the neighbours?'[4] So Mrs Norman Everage, of 36 Humoresque Street, Moonee Ponds, volunteered to do her bit.

The stage direction describing Mrs Everage was explicit: 'She is a middle-aged, middle-sized woman wearing a charcoal grey suit embellished with a large chartreuse cabbage rose in her revere. She wears "Mrs Trabert" earrings in appropriate 1956 formation.'[5] That was a statement of Mrs Everage's style. The reality of opening night was somewhat different — Humphries wore his own shirt under a blue cardigan and floral skirt, and a pointed yellow felt hat. There was no make-up, no stockings, and the shoes were black brogues. Mrs Everage tells the Olympic Games officer Leslie Hopechest (originally played by Noel Ferrier) that she has several bedrooms and could accommodate three athletes comfortably, 'counting Valmai's sleep out'. All of Edna's family gets a mention — husband Norm, daughter Valmai, and sons Bruce and 'little' Kenny, who wants the family to host a 'Red Indian'. There is much to-ing and fro-ing between Mr Hopechest and Mrs Everage about which nationality would be most appropriate for Moonee Ponds, and Edna asks to use Mr Hopechest's telephone to check with her mother about what she thinks. Edna's mother reminds her that it might not be suitable to host an athlete after all. Edna confesses to Mr Hopechest:

> You really are going to be *cross* when I tell you this, but Mother's just remembered that Fran and Tom are coming from Tassie to do the Games and she says if we've got to have anyone in the house, Aussies will do her. And you've got to admit she's right, you know, remember the [White Australia] policy!

Edna was, in this early stage of her 'life', a unique way of revealing middle-class Australia to itself. As Humphries later acknowledged, 'Edna's simpering genteelisms and her post-war, house-proud rhapsodies had a thrilling novelty'[6] for local audiences. Her first appearance provoked 'the whoosh of laughter' that denoted recognition and understanding. Edna was also a means of exploring what Humphries saw as the dull hand of Australian suburbia, where homes on quarter-acre blocks represented a noble ambition that was, as Edna portrayed it, a succession of acquisitions and effects. In particular, it was the interior decorating — 'sand-blasted reindeers on the glass', 'the genoa velvet couch ... the burgundy Axminster squares' — that captured a way of life for many Australians in the 1950s. Most importantly for Humphries, he had found something that was uniquely his: 'I found that I'd discovered something I could write about, not by putting the telescope to my eyes and trying to write something in the manner of [Noël] Coward or Alan Melville but by just looking through the venetian blinds on to my own front lawn.'[7] This was new territory: Humphries could make audiences laugh but also feel uncomfortable at seeing something so recognisable. Edna was a breakthrough on the eve of Australia's momentous year. She would be back before 1956 was finished.

*

The national mood at the start of 1956 was more than the usual cheery expectation of better days ahead. There was a determination to be optimistic and make the most of the nation's growing prosperity. *The Australian Women's Weekly* made it clear to its thousands of readers that the year was going to be different:

> Materially, Australians of 1956 can hardly fail to have a good New Year. The long years of plenty show no signs of ending. Though there are individual failures and disasters, the country as a whole is flourishing. Business is good. Jobs are plentiful. Wages are high. Opportunity is practically banging on the door for anyone who cares to grasp it. All of these things are very good. No one could wish them otherwise or want a return to the lean years of poverty and depression. For no matter what the gloomy prophets of doom may say, poverty and happiness rarely go hand-in-hand.[8]

The message from the soon-to-be Olympic host city was equally sunny. 'So here's to us,' *The Argus* trumpeted, while predicting that 1956 would be Victoria's most exciting '12 months ever'. Ten new skyscrapers were scheduled for Melbourne, a continued greatest share of the migrant stream would make its way to Victoria, there would be a successful referendum to end the six o'clock swill, and some brand-new electric trains and 'a forest of TV aerials' signalling the arrival of television were forecast to be part of the Olympic year.

'We are in for a year of great progress,' the paper declared.[9]

As it is for every optimist on New Year's Eve, the reality of the 12 months ahead would not match the expectation. What did happen was a more challenging, heady, confronting, and illuminating 12 months than anyone could have predicted.

Nine days before Mrs Everage made her theatre debut, Robert Menzies won his fourth federal election as Liberal leader. The pretext for Menzies' calling the 1955 election just 18 months after the previous poll was to bring the two houses of parliament back into alignment. The timing enabled Menzies to take advantage of a deeply divided Labor opposition that was caught between the evils of communism and the salvation of Catholicism. Menzies had been on the communist case for years, trying to ban the party and narrowly losing a referendum on the issue. But the defection of Soviet diplomat and spy Vladimir Petrov in 1954 had caused an uproar that was still echoing 18 months later. For much of the 1950s Menzies' domestic politics were shaped by the shifting international situation: national security, defence, trade, and Australia's economic wellbeing were fundamental considerations that Menzies turned into vote-winners. At the 1955 election the Coalition increased its majority by 11 seats, to 28, and effectively condemned the bitterly split Labor Party to another two terms in opposition. It also gave Menzies an iron grip on the parliament and the nation's political life.

The young Menzies had fallen in love with a Britain that filled the books he read and studied. His first trip, in 1935, brought the words to life, filling Menzies with a deep regard for what he believed made Britain what it was: its law, its parliament, its institutions, its cricket, its Commonwealth leadership, and the royal family. As prime minister, Menzies adopted a more pragmatic approach, recognising the importance of the United States to Australia's defence, especially as communism became a greater regional threat. Even so, he never surrendered the prime place Britain held in his affections to any other nation.

Menzies came to believe that another world war was possible, and with the encouragement of his two best diplomats — Percy Spender and Richard Casey — he supported regional initiatives that were designed to build Australia's regional alliances. In 1951 Australia initiated the Colombo Plan with Sri Lanka to strengthen ties across Asia and deliver aid to other nations needing help, with the goal of providing political and economic stability to the region. The Southeast Asia Treaty Organization was born in September 1954, and brought together the United States, France, Britain, New Zealand, the Philippines, Thailand, Pakistan, and Australia as a regional buffer against communism. Menzies had signed the ANZUS Treaty with the United States and New Zealand, sent Australian troops (and ships) to the Korean War, and been part of the armed response to the Malaya insurgency. Part of the anxiety driving these commitments were the memories of World War II, and the lingering concerns that Japan may well re-arm, but more important was the threat of China, which became communist with Mao Zedong's victory in 1949. The Empire was shifting and breaking, and Australia could no longer rely on Britain alone for help with regional threats.

The end of the war had provoked a crisis of faith in capitalism and imperialism among many Australians. About 23,000 joined the Communist Party, believing that the new world promised more than could be found in the ruins of the old.[10] Some would retain their hopes for a communist-led revolution, but many others found that the steady drip of information about Stalin's atrocities in the Soviet Union was enough to end the flirtation. By the time Menzies returned from a trip to England in 1950, it was clear that the Soviet Union and the spread of communism were the biggest threats to the peace in the Western world. The Korean War was underway, and the course of events was unpredictable. Menzies made sure Australians were under no illusions about the seriousness of the situation. 'If we are to be involved in a third world war in the next few years, it will be as the result of attack by international Communism ... Korea is a sort of preliminary: a test out of our strength,' he said.[11]

Menzies had an opportunity to demonstrate the practical response to such fears in September 1950, when British prime minister Clement Atlee approached Menzies with a request for the United Kingdom to use some of the supposedly uninhabited areas of Australia as a testing ground for its nuclear weapons. Canada had turned Atlee down, but Australia wouldn't: without consulting his cabinet, Menzies agreed. His elevated sense of secrecy underlined the suspicious mood of the times. Leaks were tantamount to betrayal. The fewer people who knew, the better. Trust was a priority. Silence was priceless.

The British government was keen to develop its nuclear arsenal, especially after the Soviets released their own nuclear bomb in 1949. Menzies' agreement to allow British testing might have given Australia the opportunity to develop its own nuclear capability, but that turned out to be a false hope. It did, however, provide the Australian government with some leverage, should it need to get under the United Kingdom's security blanket in a time of need.[12] For Menzies, the United States might be the new acquaintance he needed to cultivate, but sometimes old friends were still the best.

In the flush of his dominant electoral victory in 1955 Menzies commanded the Australian political landscape like no one before him. He had identified his core constituency — the 'forgotten people' — in his wartime radio broadcasts, and now he relied on their good sense and innate conservatism to support him. Menzies characterised them as noble, altruistic, family-focused Australians who were the backbone of the nation. 'I do not believe that the real life of this nation is to be found either in great luxury hotels and the petty gossip of so-called fashionable suburbs, or in the officialdom of the organised masses,' Menzies said in the broadcast in which he first discussed these Australians.

It is to be found in the homes of people who are nameless and unadvertised, and how, whatever their individual religious conviction or dogma, see in their children their greatest contribution to the immortality of their race. The home is the foundation of sanity and sobriety; it is the indispensable condition of continuity; its health determines the health of society as a whole.[13]

Recognising the unrecognised, identifying their wisdom and diligence, and celebrating their contribution to the nation was a powerful political tool for Menzies. Perhaps the most successful element of his appeal to the middle class was Menzies' timing: out in the suburbs, the nation was starting to wake from its wartime slumber and feel the benefits of prosperity and security. The Cold War was a potent threat to this new view, and Menzies was determined to prevent the changing world order from disrupting his still fragile and evolving vision of modern Australia.

On 7 January 1956 Robert Menzies summoned his old confrere and cabinet colleague Wilfrid Kent Hughes to a meeting in Canberra. It would not end well for Kent Hughes. He had spent the past three years wrestling with Menzies, Sir Frank Beaurepaire, Victorian Labor premier John Cain, various influential Melbourne civic identities, and Avery Brundage about the state of Melbourne's Olympic preparations. Kent Hughes was chairman of the Melbourne Olympic Organising Committee, a role that demanded patience, foresight, and, unfortunately for Hughes, a decent dose of diplomacy, mixed with an inexhaustible optimism that Melbourne would be ready. Brundage had bullied Kent Hughes about Melbourne's lack of progress, taunting him with the threat of taking the Games away, even suggesting he had a telegram in his pocket from another city pleading for the chance to replace Melbourne as the host city. There was some relief from the badgering when Menzies pledged that the federal government would pay half the overall cost of the Games, and the Victorian government and Melbourne local council a quarter each. The deal, struck almost three years earlier, had eliminated any residual fears about Melbourne being able to afford the Games but did little to reassure Brundage that Melbourne could deliver the Games. Menzies, though, wasn't interested in talking to Kent Hughes about the Olympics.

The careers of both Menzies and Kent Hughes grew out of the Young Nationalist group, which had brought about dynamic change in Victorian state politics. Menzies was senior by only six months, and both had been eligible to enlist in World War I. Menzies didn't, and it became a criticism that dogged his public life.

Kent Hughes, who was known to his friends as Billy, was more likely to speak his mind, rather than surrender to strategic silence or political expediency. Often, his statements took on the flavour of a man trying to protest about the march of progress. Despite being a 1914 Rhodes scholar, Kent Hughes lacked Menzies' gravitas and his willingness to display his intellectual horsepower. And then there was Kent Hughes' dalliance with fascism, which in 1933 he described as capturing the 'spirit of the age'. He even admitted he was a fascist 'without the shirt'. It was illustrative of a man who had passing enthusiasms, plus a propensity to speak his mind, neither of which endeared him to Menzies. Both men started their political careers in the Victorian parliament. Kent Hughes, having become deputy premier, resigned in the lead-up to the 1949 federal election in order to move to Canberra, with Menzies as prime minister.

For all of that shared history, Menzies and Kent Hughes never became firm friends. Part of the reason was that Kent Hughes had a habit of making political faux pas, and his time as the minister charged with developing Canberra — a task close to Menzies' heart — was routinely disparaged in the capital. At one stage Kent Hughes had to deny claims that he disliked Canberra, while adding: 'If to dislike a system of subsidies to individuals and clubs who can well afford to be ordinary Australians is to dislike Canberra, then I plead guilty.'[14] It was hardly an iron-clad denial. Kent Hughes' cabinet colleague Paul Hasluck observed some years later that his colleague was an inefficient administrator:

At times it seemed to me that he found some satisfaction for himself at being 'a voice crying in the wilderness'. The tragedy of his political life, however, was that he was not a 'voice' crying in the wilderness to foretell the coming of a new era but a 'voice' that was nostalgic for an era that was disappearing.[15]

Menzies meeting with Kent Hughes in January had all the hallmarks of trying to deal with the consequences of Kent Hughes' ministerial failings, including his continued inability to get on top of his portfolio and his comments on a recent trip to Japan, during which he had contradicted Menzies' position on Formosa (now Taiwan). The meeting was destined to end in only one way. Menzies' dispatch of Kent Hughes from his cabinet was ruthless if a little imprecise. Menzies began the meeting by outlining his need to enact a reshuffle that would inject some younger talent into his Cabinet. 'I am very sorry, but you are one of those who has got to go out,' Menzies told him.

Kent Hughes pressed for reasons why, but Menzies demurred.

'I feel I am definitely entitled to something more than has been said,' Kent Hughes replied. 'I have given you all the loyalty I could. Do you consider my work has been unsatisfactory?'

Menzies attempted candour: 'I do not consider your administration has been very efficient.' When Kent Hughes asked for details of his deficient administration, Menzies declined.

Not surprisingly, Kent Hughes felt he was entitled to more than that from a man he had known for almost 30 years. 'I go out without a word of thanks. I know exactly where I stand,' Kent Hughes told Menzies as he left the room.[16]

There was a subsequent exchange of letters, but nothing assuaged Kent Hughes' anger and disappointment. In a parting shot, he let the prime minister know that the Australian Olympic Federation had approached him to become its president, but he had insisted Menzies was 'the logical and proper choice'.[17] Menzies accepted the role.

*

Robert Menzies didn't particularly like television. In 1952 he had grumbled to the BBC: 'I hope this thing will not come to Australia within my terms of office.'[18] Perhaps his suspicion had something to do with his earlier treatment by US television journalists. He had been approached to appear on a US current-affairs program, *Meet the Press*, and was politely asked before the show was recorded what questions he would not like to answer. When the time came to do the interview, the questions Menzies didn't want to answer turned out to be the only questions he was asked.[19]

Australia was giving Britain 20 years and the United States almost a decade when it came to introducing television. The BBC began broadcasting high-definition programs in 1936, although by the time television shut down because of World War II there were only 20,000 sets in the country. The United States waited until after the war, and by 1947 commercial TV was up and running.

Menzies' tardiness on television might also have had something to do with his suspicion that the technology was not going to have a civilising or culturally enriching influence on Australia. He also remained wedded to the power of the radio. He had delivered more than 80 radio broadcasts during the war, when he was opposition leader, reaching directly into the nation's lounge rooms and kitchens as families gathered around the wireless. There were no filters, and no one trying to interpret or second-guess his messages. Underlying Menzies' embrace of ABC radio was his view that it had an important public function to perform, and so could mirror the BBC's role in British public life to entertain, stimulate, and engage.[20] But perhaps Menzies' most practical consideration about introducing television to Australia was that the post-war world posed a myriad of complex challenges for any government; television was, in comparison, a secondary issue. But whatever Menzies' priorities, there was one man who was determined that the prime minister would commit, sooner rather than later, to bringing television to Australia. His name was Colin Bednall.

Bednall was a mercurial character, a gifted journalist, and one of Sir Keith Murdoch's protégés. Bednall's wife, Marion — the daughter of Charles Abbott, former administrator of the Northern Territory and home affairs minister in the Stanley Bruce Coalition government — later described life with her husband as 'difficult ... but never dull'. Bednall started his working life as a journalist, becoming a copyboy at *The Adelaide News* at the age of 14. He left St Peter's College, one of Adelaide's oldest establishment schools, to take up the job. In a vivid glimpse of the man he would become, in 1932 the teenage reporter secured a spot for himself on an anthropological expedition in search of Indigenous Australian communities in the red heart of Australia. But the expedition leaders threw him off the trip when Bednall's newspaper rivals, *The Adelaide Advertiser*, underwrote the expedition.

Undeterred, Bednall hired an Indigenous tracker called Albert, a Swedish tourist, and a haycart, and followed the expedition to the MacDonnell Ranges. Albert kept Bednall informed about what the local Indigenous communities thought of the expedition and the academic assortment who crossed their path. Miles from anywhere, without any form of communication, and instructed by his Adelaide bosses to send his stories to Alice Springs, Bednall decided to write the story on toilet paper and attach it to carrier pigeons. All was going well until Bednall released the pigeons: out of the vivid blue sky a peregrine falcon emerged, swooped down on the neat quartet of pigeons, and turned them into a cloud of feathers.[21]

Bednall's career prospered and he became one of a famous group of Australian war correspondents that included Chester Wilmot, Osmar White, Alan Moorehead, and Noel Monks. Bednall was the aviation correspondent for London's *Daily Mail*, where his reputation was burnished by surviving the notoriously dangerous raids over Europe in Lancaster bombers.

'I flew only when the top brass saw a need for publicity, which was often enough,' Bednall said. 'I did have myself trained as an air gunner. I found it better to have control of a turret or a waist gun than just to sit miserably contemplating the prominent possibility of death.'[22] Bednall understood why his newspaper gave his stories prominence: 'Probably because no other paper, British or American, had a flying reporter who survived.'[23] It was a bleak analysis and too self-deprecating.

Bednall was justifiably highly regarded in the centre of British journalism, Fleet Street. Bednall had another admirer, though, closer to home: the proprietor of The Herald and Weekly Times, Keith Murdoch, with whom Bednall had developed something of a filial bond when he had worked for Murdoch before the war. It was to Murdoch that Bednall turned when he took the Daily Mail job. 'Hope you approve,' Bednall telegraphed.

'Certainly. Splendid. Regards Murdoch,' came the reply.[24]

And it was Murdoch who provided Bednall with a post-war job back home, running the Brisbane Courier-Mail. It was there that Bednall started to get a feel for the new medium of television.

Bednall had no desire to actually be on television. He understood that he was not cut out for a visual medium: his mop of curly hair and his thick, black-framed glasses were, even in the 1950s, not the best attributes for an on-screen career. But behind the scenes was another thing. Bednall saw television's potential and began a systematic campaign to bring it to Australia.

His Damascene experience happened during a trip to New York during Bednall's Brisbane tenure. Bednall was on an early-morning train trip when he looked out the window and saw 'weird designs in hardware on house roofs'. When he asked what these were, Bednall was told they were television antennas. Not only that: sometimes, if a family couldn't buy or hire a TV, they put up something resembling an antenna to suggest they weren't missing out.

The newspaperman in Bednall saw beyond the obvious story of a new consumer entertainment option. Here was something else altogether. 'As far back as I can remember a fear that some new media of mass communication might arise as a threat to newspapers had lurked in the minds of newspapermen and a consuming interest in television began for me,' Bednall explained.[25] He gleaned something else about television during that New York trip: its ability to reach a broad audience. 'Then I began to notice that the poorer and the more densely populated the district, the more the television antennas. This suggested a medium of communication truly for the masses, and reaching the masses was my business.' The Americans told him the new medium not only brought families together, but 'brother, does it sell soap!'. It would even find out lying politicians, because it was impossible for anyone to lie on television.[26] Bednall was converted. He began lobbying the government with unstinting fervour.

The Courier-Mail was under Bednall's management when Menzies was campaigning ahead of the 1949 election. The paper's support for Menzies was so pronounced that Labor's Arthur Calwell bitterly promised to send Bednall to Korea when Labor next won an election.[27] Menzies was delighted with the paper's continued support some years later, and wrote to Bednall: 'No government could have asked for its case to be better or more enthusiastically presented.'[28]

Bednall leveraged that support to invite Menzies to a meeting at the Lennon Hotel, in Brisbane, to discuss how television should be introduced to Australia. Bednall talked with a mixture of urgency and passion, outlining the need for the Menzies government to show some initiative and establish a commercial television service. There were dangers aplenty in Labor's state monopoly television service that Chifley had promised in 1949.

Menzies listened but knew there were would be debates within his cabinet about television. Harold Holt's father was a cinema manager, and there was concern in that sector about the impact television would have on audiences. The Country Party needed to know how its constituents would access a technology that looked to be designed only for city folk. And how would you structure the television industry in Australia? What role would the newspaper moguls play? How would the interests of radio stations dovetail with those of television stations? And where would the ABC fit in? It all needed thought, tact, and political acumen. Menzies tried to counsel Bednall that if he felt so strongly about television, he should write about it. But Bednall was not satisfied with that, and warned

Menzies that Australia would become 'a hill-billy country' without television.

There was no doubt that Bednall's goals were commercially self-interested. If television was going to come to Australia, the content providers, such as *The Courier-Mail* (and, by extension, The Herald and Weekly Times), needed to have a presence on the landscape. Bednall was a vigorous prosecutor of his case and made sure the interested parties knew of his efforts. He even wrote to Keith Murdoch's son, Rupert, then at Oxford, to let him know his plans: 'For the last two years I have been fighting hard behind the political scenes for recognition by the Federal government of the right of existing newspaper-radio interests to participate in T[elevision] …'

Rupert, ever sensitive to the opportunity of building a bridge to a potential influencer, let alone his father's protégé, responded: 'The government's television proposals seem to be in large part a great personal triumph for you … We have a great chance here and I pray that we will be able to take it.'[29]

On Friday 16 January 1953 the Menzies cabinet decided to hold a royal commission into the introduction and operation of television in Australia. A few weeks later, Prime Minister Menzies announced that there would be six royal commissioners. One was Colin Bednall. His course to the arrival of television in 1956 was set. Bednall would be there when the lights went up.

Chapter Two
Rebels, Villains, and Heroes

In March 1956 a parcel of books arrived at Melbourne from an address in Indianapolis, in the United States. The parcel was addressed to a young married man in a small Victorian town. There was, on the face of it, nothing untoward about the parcel, with one exception: it contained a novel entitled *The Catcher in the Rye*, by J.D. Salinger. An eagle-eyed customs official in Melbourne detected a whiff of subversive intent about the book and promptly confiscated it. It was passed on to the Book Censorship section of the Customs and Excise office for review. The novel, which centred on the 16-year-old Holden Caulfield, was first published in July 1951. It had been an instant commercial success, but for the next few years it languished. There was little critical discussion of its content: Holden seemed to have had his moment.[1] The book had been available in Australia for some time, but suddenly, without anyone really knowing why, it appeared to have become notorious.

The customs clerk, Mr E.F. Dixon, observed:

This book attempts, not without success, to express the intimate thoughts of a young man of sixteen who has been expelled from school and who decides to spend a few days 'lying low' in New York. It is an extremely readable novel written in a refreshing style and punctuated with humour, pathos and wise commentaries on our society.

So far, so good. In many ways, Mr Dixon had done a fine job of providing a brief review of the central character and the novel itself. But then: 'However, it contains references which, it is thought, are indelicate, indecent and almost blasphemous, not to mention others that are merely crude.' Mr Dixon went on to make a point about literature itself: 'While these references may have a basis in reality, that is, that people really do think such things but perhaps do not always say them, nevertheless, there is a limit to their expression in literature. In the present case it is submitted that this limit has been exceeded ...'[2] The book was held 'for review', and its intended recipient notified. America's most famous literary teenager was banned in Australia.

Book banning was something of a feature of the Australian literary scene. Many publishers tried to circumvent an anticipated ban by getting to contentious international titles and making discreet changes before they were released in Australia. The books were then called 'Australian editions'. Many of the titles banned were the pulp detective magazines or racy murder mysteries, including *Hotel Wife*, *Road Floozie*, and *The Housekeeper's Daughter* ('She was curvy and careless and lived down the hall ...'). The banning wasn't just pulp titles: Aldous Huxley's *Brave New World*, Kathleen Winsor's *Forever Amber*, and Vladimir Nabokov's *Lolita* were off the shelves too. Australian censors apparently felt they had some responsibility to uphold a morality they perceived to be at the heart of the Empire, a kind of common understanding of what was obscene and prurient among the world's more civilised types. There was also an old-fashioned sense of social control about the decisions, an implied anxiety that no one could be sure of the consequences of such material finding its way into Australian society.[3] Inevitably, this enthusiasm extended to magazines, such as *Playboy*, which was banned from 1955 to 1960, but not to Alfred Kinsey's major works on sexuality, on men (1948) and women (1953).

The 1953 Kinsey Report marked a generational shift in attitudes to sex between older and younger Australian women. 'The problem of married life with so many disappointments and frustrations are to be expected if we understand the vows we make on our wedding day, and we do not want any help from Dr Kinsey's nonsensical reports and misleading statements,' one Manly housewife wrote to her local newspaper.[4] But for younger Australian women, the report became a resource for changing attitudes to intimacy. Now was the time when Australians could actually concentrate on their private lives — the wars were over, the Depression a fading memory, and there was a sense that, finally, relationships had the time to develop and flourish.[5] On a four-month tour of the nation in 1956 the National Marriage Guidance Council of Australia (in association with *The Australian Women's Weekly*) identified a marked change in Australian women's attitudes to sex, and some of it was attributed to the Kinsey Report.

The tour revealed that many young women believed the idea of chastity was no longer desirable. (The contraceptive pill was still five years away.) 'The case against chastity, I was informed is being presented to young people much more forcibly than the case in favour of it,' wrote Dr David Mace, the British academic with an expertise in human relations who ran the tour. 'If there is a case in favour of it, said some young people, those who should be putting it are strangely silent.'[6]

This change in attitude was also captured in the nation's marriage numbers: there had been a steady decline in marriage from 8.25 per 1,000 population in 1951 to 7.92 per 1,000 in 1956. Possible reasons for the decline were many and varied: some said it was inevitable after the wartime and post-war peak in marriage. Others claimed it was to do with the increased number of women in the workforce, many of whom were reluctant to leave their position for marriage and a potentially diminished income. And then there was the cost of buying a home and filling it with the consumer goods that were becoming the basic family requirements.[7]

The number of working Australian women had steadily increased from 717,200 in 1947 to 845,400 in 1954. And single or separated working women outnumbered married working women in 1954 by more than two to one.[8] In 1956 the Victorian Education Department made news when it allowed married women to continue their careers as teachers. Twenty years later, the Commonwealth Public Service followed suit.[9] There was, however, a consequence for all these working mothers, according to society's moral guardians: 'latch-key children'. These kids, whose parents both worked, had no one at home to look after them at the end of the school day, the argument went, so they went out to make their own fun — or cause mischief. They were, in fact, a little like Holden Caulfield.

*

Nobody could be sure what impact the new medium of television would have on newspapers. The overseas experience suggested newspapers remained an essential part of people's lives when TV came along, but there was no telling if that would hold true in Australia. Newspaper owners felt the hot breath of new competitors on their necks. What no one knew was that by 1956 Australian newspaper circulation had reached its high-water mark. Newspapers were buoyant during the bad news days, such as during the war and its immediate aftermath. But as Australia drew away from its days of austerity, circulation relative to the size of the newspaper-buying population went south. It became more pronounced as the suburbs, especially in Sydney, spread out, and as motorcars, rather than public transport, became the preferred means of getting to and from work.[10]

The Herald, an afternoon broadsheet in Melbourne, was selling well over 439,000 copies a day in 1955. Melbourne had three daily papers — *The Argus*, *The Age*, and *The Sun* — but it was *The Herald* that was preferred by commuters hurrying home from work, or sports fans keen to check the football, racing, or cricket results. Every state had afternoon papers — Sydney had two, *The Daily Mirror* and

The Sun — but none came close to *The Herald*'s circulation or reputation with its readers. It was also the newspaper at which a young Bruce Howard believed he could fashion a career.

Howard's family had seen the impact of the Great Depression up close. His father, Tom, had experience in the milk delivery business and decided in 1932 to set up a dairy, at the bottom end of Ascot Vale, just over the Maribyrnong River. Tom Howard was optimistic that the worst of the Depression was over — after all, the Wall Street Crash was three years in the past. He believed the milk business was the key to a prosperous future for his family. Within a year, though, the business was broke, a victim of the Depression's long reach. It took Tom Howard nine years to find a full-time job, finally securing a role at a Maribyrnong munitions factory in 1941; in the interim he'd survived on a combination of three part-time jobs.

The difficult circumstances meant that everyone in the family — Bruce Howard's sister, older brother, and him — had to contribute, and that meant earning pocket money. Bruce washed a car in Moonee Ponds once a week and sold *The Herald* outside the train station when races were held at the Moonee Valley track. In time, Bruce became a messenger boy at *The Herald*, and for a time dreamt of being a journalist, until a particularly savage assessment of his writing skills from his school English teacher convinced him otherwise.

Howard switched to photography, and by 1952 he was a cadet photographer learning the trade. He spent most of his daylight hours in *The Herald*'s darkroom, mixing developing chemicals, watching the pros, and learning what he had to do to take publishable photographs for the biggest-selling afternoon daily in the country. Three years later, Howard, just 19, was on the road, a handsome young man with dark, wavy hair and a gentle demeanour that hid a determination to find his niche in an industry full of seasoned older men.

Just as he was starting to make inroads, Howard was called up for national service. The decision to introduce national service in 1951 was another reminder of Australia's vulnerability, and of Menzies' desire to make sure the nation was prepared for any eventuality. Most 18-year-olds had to register for 14 weeks of national service training and 42 days in the citizen military force over three years. 'I hated the idea in advance. I thought it was going to cost me my career,' Howard said.[11]

After one stint without his camera, Howard returned to the Puckapunyal training camp with his gear. He noticed that his former Essendon High School mate Ron Clarke was in another battalion. Clarke was a champion teenage athlete whom Howard had already photographed at University Oval. This time, Howard took some photos of Clarke on the rifle range, and sent them back to *The Herald*. One picture was published, confirming to Howard's bosses that he could spot a news picture with popular appeal. More importantly, it demonstrated the young man's initiative.

Sport was vitally important to the newspapers, especially in Melbourne, where the pink twice-weekly *Sporting Globe* provided additional coverage of local and national events. Newspapers that didn't give sport prominence were not catering to their audience's interests. In the days before television, the newspaper photographer's images became the moment in time that framed thousands of sporting memories. Howard had been a promising footballer and cricketer at Essendon High, and now he was about to become a recorder of the vast sporting dramas that unfolded throughout the Olympic year. As he explained:

> I felt I had to have a great interest in sport. As the lowest photographer [in the hierarchy], I'd get the lowest job. On Saturdays, it was football, cricket, horseracing. I had to show an interest in sport. [But] it didn't just stop at the major sports. There had to be an interest in all sports — soccer, hockey — I had to have an understanding of the Games if I was going to cover it. I just thought it was essential.[12]

On Saturday 10 March Howard was at Olympic Park in Melbourne for the men's national athletic championships. The meeting would help decide the Australian men's Olympic track team. The venue was full, with 22,000 spectators, many of them enticed along to see the men's mile race between Clarke, the precocious junior world record holder at the distance, and John Landy, one of the greats in the event. Landy had broken the fabled 'four-minute mile' and been a world record holder for the distance. He was a role model for the sport, supremely talented and without ego. As a boy, Clarke had also been inspired by the first man to break the four-minute mark, Roger Bannister, to take on what had become a glamour event, as the world's best milers duelled to shrink the time it took to run four laps. Here was a contest that pitted the legendary Landy against the youthful Clarke.

Howard, like most press photographers, took up a spot near the finishing line. It meant that he was as far away as he could have been when one of the most extraordinary moments in Australian sport occurred.

A lap and a half into the race, and with some of the runners starting to break from the pack, Clarke lost his balance momentarily, and Landy, immediately behind him, clipped his heels. Landy leapt over Clarke as the younger athlete fell to the ground, but his spikes collected Clarke's arm. Landy stopped, jogged back to help Clarke and apologised for what had happened. Clarke yelled at him that he was all right. 'Get going, John!' he shouted. Landy thought he had 'half-killed Clarke', and was horrified to see the rest of the field now some 50 metres ahead. 'When I got going again, I don't know what I was thinking,' he later said.[13] But he kept running, smoothly accelerating into his trademark easy and efficient stride, and began reeling in the rest of the field.

Howard got ready to take the picture. Sure enough, Landy hit the front and crossed the line first. That was the traditional picture, but the real drama had been elsewhere on the track: Clarke, who had picked himself up, hurt, cut, and bruised, struggled on to finish fifth.

One of Australia's finest athletic coaches, Franz Stampfl, described Landy's actions as the 'most gallant thing I have seen in a lifetime of international athletics'.[14] The episode only heightened Howard's sense of anticipation for the Olympics.

*

In the seven years since the Rome triumph that gave Melbourne the Games, Sir Frank Beaurepaire had faced his share of difficulties as he navigated the realities of organising an Olympic Games. The first problem occurred within 12 months of Melbourne winning the bid, when Sir Frank lost the presidency of the Victorian Olympic Council to Wilfrid Kent Hughes. The newspapers were initially intrigued and then shocked that the man who had been central to the winning bid was being sidelined for a man who had had no role in Rome. Kent Hughes might have fancied himself as a defender of the amateur ethos, but his faith in the Olympics seemed questionable. At the height of the controversy about Japan's participation in the Games, Kent Hughes was quoted as saying: 'The Olympic Games are, in themselves, relatively unimportant ...'[15]

Sir Frank, though, had put a number of the Victorian Olympic Council offside and managed to generate remarkable hostility among some of his colleagues. '[He] has been a complete failure as a chairman,' one confessed. 'He has antagonised ... often by being very rude and he has not achieved our objectives ... I think Frank Beaurepaire's individualism and a certain circumlocutory approach to problems tripped him up.'[16] The most obvious issue was Sir Frank's support for the Melbourne Showgrounds as the site for the Games. Most of the VOC executive were opposed to the idea, dismissing the venue as being surrounded by some of the city's smelliest industries and being accessed by rail through a series of eyesores that would do the city's reputation no good.[17] Kent Hughes favoured the MCG, a venue that wasn't at all likely at that stage of deliberations.

Sir Frank didn't attend the meeting in June 1950 that sealed his fate, already aware that his claim on the job was a lost cause. The vote was a comprehensive win for Kent Hughes, 13 to 2, and a rejection of Sir Frank's robust commitment to the Showgrounds proposal. There was a sense that the energetic modernising influence that Sir Frank had brought to the bid was being marginalised, in favour of a return to the tweed suits and amateurism that was the hallmark of the VOC.

For the time being, Sir Frank remained chairman of the Olympic Games Organizing Committee, in addition to wrangling his business interests. Such a prominent position meant he was still caught up in the controversies, delays, political battles, and Olympic sparring that eddied around the Games. It all started to become too much for him. A heart specialist told him that he was risking his life to continue his high-pressure work on the Games, his business, and in politics. Something had to give.

Sir Frank's antipathy to physical frailty nagged at him, but he knew that resigning from the Organizing Committee could ease his physical and mental burden. For a time he tried to keep his ill health a secret, but eventually, in January 1951, he attached a doctor's certificate to his resignation letter from the chairmanship of the Organizing Committee, perhaps to remind everyone that he would still be in charge, if he were able.[18] Kent Hughes took that role too.

Despite these setbacks, Sir Frank refused to be idle, and as the Olympics grew closer, he increased his lobbying of his employees to make the most of the opportunities offered by the Games. Just after Christmas in 1955, Sir Frank wrote to his employees:

> I am sure it will have occurred to all representatives of companies in the Olympic group that each of us will need to be fully informed about many interesting aspects of the Games. With a name-association [sic] such as ours, it is a responsibility to become thoroughly acquainted with the whole subject.[19]

This was followed three weeks later by a memo from Sir Frank's advertising manager at Olympic Consolidated Industries, Graham Lomas, to all the business's executives:

> Occasionally one hears or reads incomplete or inaccurate accounts of the part played by our chairman [Sir Frank] … in getting the Games. To ensure that the members of this organisation are informed of the facts, press notes listing the major events are being distributed. Your personal copy is attached. These notes have been circulated to newspapers and periodicals throughout Australia. Any serious case of misstatement will be acted upon by this department, which would welcome our help in identifying such instances and being informed of them, if such are printed in local newspapers etc. If verbal misstatements are within your hearing, correction is needed only if the person is prominent in local affairs.[20]

Lomas was a loyal employee, and in no doubt about Sir Frank's claim to fame, but it seems clear that Sir Frank's firm hand was actually directing the memo's contents and intent. He could not be there personally, but no one was permitted to overlook or forget his role in bringing the Games to Melbourne.

Sir Frank also ensured that his company put out regular Olympic bulletins with Games-related content and images that newspapers could use for free. There was, of course, a rider attached to such largesse: an acknowledgement that Olympic Consolidated Industries was the source of the information. The bulletins contained a range of insights and materials, and covered diverse topics: such as the logistics of the radio coverage of the Games, trainees who were using radio equipment, and the progress of the building of the athletes' village in Heidelberg. Lomas diligently ensured that the materials were circulated within the company, and was keen for feedback from his sales reps, or from journalists who used the material.

There was little doubt among some members of the Olympic

organisations that Sir Frank deserved every plaudit; there was even talk of naming the new Olympic pool after him. And then, in what seemed a final endorsement of his role in getting the Olympics, Sir Frank managed to secure the lord mayoralty for the term that included the staging of the Games. It was a coup to hold such a prestigious position at the city's most important time. Whether Sir Frank was well enough to take on the honour did not appear to be a consideration. It was almost as if he had been biding his time for the final assault on the job, able to remain untouched by the controversies, missteps, miscalculations, and errors that had dogged the organisers between 1951 and 1955.

Sir Frank made no secret of his pleasure at his looming honour: 'I first thought of getting the Games for Melbourne in 1920. It took me a long time to get things moving, but thanks to those two great sportsmen, Sir Raymond Connolly [sic] and Sir James Disney — my dream came true and Melbourne won the 1956 Games.'[21] So it was Sir Frank's dream after all.

*

No one in Rome in 1949 had bothered to question Sir Frank and the bid team about just who was an Australian, or even what that meant. It was not a question that occurred to many Australians, so why would it be relevant to the International Olympic Committee? The whole idea of 'an Australian' was, on a superficial level, embodied in the 9.42 million white, largely English-speaking people who settled mostly on the nation's coastal fringes. But at a deeper level, it was a far more complex question of national identity, tied up with the White Australia policy and the deep racism that it signified.

If it was hard enough to define what 'Australian' meant, it was even more difficult to conceive of an 'Australian way of life', a term that took on greater currency during the early 1950s. A distinctive Australian way of life owed more to protecting what the nation had than to enlarging its view of itself. This was particularly true as the Cold War became more intense, and the priority from Menzies down was to defend the idea of Australia, whatever that idea looked like.[22]

Nothing appeared to be more relevant to the Australian immigrant than the nation's way of life: it was what migrants supposedly aspired to embrace, the incentive to become a member of their adopted nation, even if the welcome mat was discriminatory. If anything was known overseas about Australia, it was the White Australia policy. Six weeks before the bid deliberations, there were reports in some British newspapers about Labor immigration minister Arthur Calwell defending the White Australia policy from being undermined by the courts.[23] And then there was the controversy in the Filipino parliament, which pointedly criticised the policy's impact on Australia's Asian neighbours.

The White Australia policy came into being during the nation's first federal parliament in 1901 and was predicated on three important planks: that the native Aboriginal population would die out, most likely in the cooler areas of the country; that immigration from non-European nations was to be prevented; and that appropriate white colonists should be encouraged to settle in Australia.[24] It remained largely unquestioned through the first part of the century, and was emphatically endorsed by the high rates of migration from England and Ireland after World War I. But once England decided that its own birth rate was too parlous for it to continue its migration arrangements with Australia, the steady stream started to dry up.

Assisted migration from Britain was in steady decline in the lead-up to World War II: only 3,538 assisted migrants arrived in Australia in 1938–39.[25] In 1930 the federal government had decided to ban all European migrants, unless they already had relatives in Australia or could pay the extraordinarily high £500 'landing fee'. The other way migrants could get into Australia was by passing the notorious dictation test, which became infamous after the Czech linguist and socialist Egon Kisch was examined in Scottish Gaelic to guarantee his exclusion.

On the eve of World War II almost one in two migrants to Australia were British, a further 48 per cent were white non-British migrants, and only 4 per cent came from Asia.[26] It was on the back of this that Andor Mészáros left Budapest in 1939 to make his way to Australia. He had cobbled together £500, so there would be no dictation test for him.

Mészáros was a trained architect and sculptor. An aesthete, a man steeped in the rich artistic history of his homeland and the transmission of ideas and inspiration between like-minded souls, he was not the kind of migrant who would quickly fit in. Yet he had come to Australia because the rumble of another European war had convinced him and his family that disaster was imminent. In the first war Mészáros had been a Hussar in the Hungarian Army, a dashing young cavalry officer, who towards the end of the conflict found himself heading to the Ukraine to defend one of the last outposts of the crumbling Austro-Hungarian empire. Twenty years later, Mészáros' wife, Elizabeth, reminded her husband that his officer status in the Great War was likely to see him called up again. It was time for them to get out, to find a new home far from what was about to come.

Mészáros had previously spent two years in Paris, where he'd met Pablo Picasso, discussed ideas, refined his thinking, and developed his skills, before returning to Hungary. This time, he was reluctant to leave his homeland, to give up his nationality and deprive his children of their cultural inheritance — the poets, artists, and writers of Hungary. '[B]ut the adventurous spirit overwhelmed me and I went to the British Embassy,' Mészáros said.[27]

Mészáros had already spoken to the Canadian embassy, where he'd been shown an image of what he thought were 'bearded, illiterate Rumanian peasants'. Canada wanted pioneers, brave men with adventure in their hearts and the skills to tame the wilderness, not artists or architects. Thirteen days after he visited the British embassy, Mészáros received a 'landing permit' to go to Australia. Elizabeth and their young son, Daniel, would remain in Hungary until Mészáros was settled.

Mészáros' journey was one that thousands would later make, but his route to a new life took him first to Vienna, and then to Germany. 'History got hold of all of us; nations are turned upside-down, human rubbish governed Europe and I sat enclosed in the dark that brought me to the origin of all evil, to Germany,' Mészáros wrote of his arrival there.[28] It was mid-April 1939, and the threat of war hung heavy across Europe. In the middle of May, with £5 in his pocket, Mészáros left Tilbury dock in London, bound for Australia. His first stop was Perth, and with this initial glimpse Mészáros started to think that he would stay only for a little while before returning home when Europe had settled down. By the time Mészáros arrived in Melbourne, he was, like many other new migrants, struggling with the choice he had made. 'A feeling of dryness, futility, loneliness pervaded us all,' he wrote, 'the future was never more blurred, a kind of barrier between us and the world of Australia, a strange, hostile world, where as future proved, we were the underdogs — the bloody aliens, second-class citizens.'[29] It was not an auspicious first impression.

Mészáros got off the ship in Port Melbourne and tried in vain to find the 'city'. He found himself near Flinders Street Station, and had to ask a passer-by where the city was. It was a Sunday and Melbourne was as quiet as a church, largely because that was the only activity that occurred on the day.

Things didn't improve. There were the nagging difficulties of being a migrant, the creeping ignorance, the barely disguised intolerance and often the rudeness: one woman derided Mészáros' choice of cheese at the Myer food section as 'foreign muck'; doors were closed on him regularly as he searched for a place to live. Mészáros tried two or three jobs. His European qualifications weren't recognised and his artistic sensibilities seemed alien in this new country. 'It's a cultural desert,' he grumbled.

In one office where Mészáros found work, the boss told him he was going to cut his salary in half because his English wasn't good enough on the telephone. Mészáros resigned on the spot and went home to tell his family he would make his living as a sculptor. His predicament was common to many migrants, who found that even if they were granted equal pay with their Australian colleagues, they would never share in the employment security, access the better jobs, or participate in the camaraderie that were available to locals.

Mészáros' career choice would be precarious, but at least he was doing what he loved. Elizabeth Mészáros was multilingual and found work as a translator for the ABC to ensure a regular income.[30] Andor decided to pursue a niche area — portrait sculpture — that no one else in Australia was doing. He cultivated professional men — academics, lawyers, doctors — and offered to do small portraits of them for nothing. If the sitter didn't like the work, they didn't pay. Only two people among the dozens of whom he created portraits failed to honour the deal, and the quality of Mészáros' work was soon well-known.

In 1941 he held his first exhibition of medallions, small bronze portraits of men he knew, delicately created, with memorable likenesses. The exhibition was well attended but he sold only one medallion. The outcome provided him with a rare insight into his new country: 'I did not know then that an Australian does not honor a live fellow Aussie — a dead one is a different matter.'[31]

A decade later, Mészáros won the highest international award for medallion artists, the SIDEM, and international commissions followed, as well as three large sculptures on the grounds of Sydney's King George V Hospital. Mészáros was now an internationally recognised artist working in a distinctive form. Not surprisingly, he caught the attention of Kenneth Luke.

Luke was a self-made millionaire, the owner of a silverware and trophy manufacturing business, a successful farmer, racehorse owner, philanthropist, and vice president of the Victorian Football League. He was also a member of the Olympic Games construction committee. He contacted Mészáros with an offer: would he design the Olympic medallion that would be given to everyone associated with the Games, from athletes to torch relay runners?

In the conversation that followed, Mészáros realised that he was the only artist Luke had approached, and the lucrative £500 contract was his if he wanted it. Mészáros started work on the design in the middle of 1954. The plan was to send the medal dies to London and strike the first 300 medals there. The rest of the 12,500 medals would be made in Australia. It was, by any measure, a massive undertaking. But it would also be an extraordinary souvenir.

*

The national economy groaned through the first few years of the decade. Inflation reached 20 per cent in 1951–52, driven by the Korean War, the rising wool prices, international inflation, a rise in industrial action, and increased domestic demand fuelled by an expansive immigration policy. Two credit squeezes helped reduce the inflationary impact, but by 1956 the strike bogey was back. Waterside workers went on strike and then the shearers, who stayed out for four months. Affluence was elusive. Home comforts were far from universal. A quarter of homes in Melbourne, Sydney, and Brisbane still had no refrigerator in 1956. Two-thirds of homes in those three cities had no hot running water in the bathroom, and three-quarters of them had no hot water in the laundry.[32]

The Menzies government's economic problems at the start of the year were significant, and directly related to Australia's hunger for overseas goods. The affluence that had started to become noticeable across middle Australia was built on its growing demand for imports. Menzies' trade minister, John 'Black Jack' McEwen, alerted the country to the balance-of-payments problem that was, in large part, being driven by booming consumer demand and investment spending. Inflation had become a bogey that had to be reined in, and McEwen wanted to boost exports to redress the balance, without endangering the nation's prosperity.

Menzies' view was that if Australia was to be prosperous, there had to be sacrifices. After convening a panel of economic experts, which included departmental secretaries, bankers, a retailer, and a National Farmers Union representative, Menzies delivered a mini-budget on 14 March that increased the tax levied on the imported goods that had been central to the increased consumer demand — cars, jewellery, gramophone records, cosmetics — and raised company tax. Menzies explained his government's motivations: 'What we are trying to do is to prevent some elements in our prosperity from aggravating an inflation, which could, if left alone, undermine our prosperity.'[33] He told parliament: 'In the short term, the most effective immediate way to relieve the pressure is to reduce the volume of purchasing power, which creates it.'[34]

In practice, this meant cigarettes would go up 3d for a packet of 20, jewellery sales tax would increase from 16.23 per cent to 25 per cent, and petrol would rise by 3d a gallon. But the biggest slug was kept for cars, which were hit with a sales tax of 30 per cent, almost double the old rate.

Menzies tried to head off the grumbles. He stressed that cars were 'one of the great and growing industries', and only some 'temporary restraint' was needed. When it came to the fashionable practice of hire purchase, cars were the dominant category. In just two years, new car registrations in Australia had increased by almost 90,000, to 245,271 registrations in 1954–55. But where it all made an impact was when it came to imports: in the previous financial year, cars and all their spare parts made up almost a fifth of the nation's total import bill.[35]

This was a tough call for Menzies to make, but he knew that while Australians' love affair with their vehicles wouldn't stop with a bigger sales tax, it might slow things down a little.

The broader balance-of-payments issue pointed to a rapidly growing Australian embrace of what the rest of the world had to offer. It confirmed that some of the old notions of what Australia was and what drove its prosperity were changing: the sheep's back now had four wheels and drop earrings. McEwen had been agitating for almost three years that it was time Australia ended its discriminatory trade arrangement with Japan, and he finally received cabinet approval to pursue a trade deal that would secure Australian exports of wool, wheat, barley, and sugar to Japan. McEwen's determination was far-sighted and recognised that Great Britain, Australia's major trading partner, was not likely to remain in that prime position as the world changed. Japan was a non-communist buttress in the region, but memories of the war were still strong and there was resistance in parliament and the community to the final deal, which would eventually be signed in 1957.

Comfortable with the new budget measures that were in place, Menzies prepared to head overseas for the regular Commonwealth Prime Ministers' Conference in London. He left just one issue ticking in Victoria: what would happen with beer to rise by 2d on a ten-ounce glass in the midst of a referendum on the state's drinking hours?

*

The early forecasts of the number of American tourists who would come to Melbourne for the Olympic Games were not promising. 'They couldn't have picked a worse place to hold the Games,' one New York travel agent complained. 'The way conditions in Melbourne stand today I would be very surprised if more than 500 people from the United States make the trip.' One of these 'conditions' was that it was impossible to get a drink in Melbourne after 6 pm, unless you ordered food. A tongue-in-cheek piece of US reporting summed up the problem: 'Gin rummy, charades, spin the bottle (empty naturally) … All this is legal in the cool of the evening in Melbourne. But one for the road? No sir.' The American journalist went on: 'The primitive liquor laws won't bother the Olympic athletes, but for the travelling man, it's a privation he's just not buying …'[36]

Everyone associated with organising the Olympics in Melbourne knew it was an issue. What compounded it was the deadly dull weekends that went with it. The city was practically closed on Saturday afternoons, save for football in the winter. And Sundays were a write-off — if you weren't going to church, there was nothing to do: no shopping, no cinemas, no Sunday newspapers. The city might have been charming, with its impressive array of Victorian architecture and the elegance of Collins Street, with its nod to the fashion capital of Paris. The city's first coffee lounge had opened in St Kilda in 1954, but apart from that there simply wasn't much else.

The six o'clock swill was so well-known that artist John Brack's 1954 painting 'The Bar' captured workers' grim determination to guzzle as many beers as possible in the hour after they clocked off for the day. Queues of men clamoured for one, two, three, or more beers before the pub's doors slammed shut for the night. For some drinkers, it was the quickest way to get drunk. For others, it wasn't worth the battle to get to the bar. The early closing was initially introduced as a temporary measure during World War I but was made permanent in 1919. Other states had already abandoned it, but Victoria had held firm.

What would overseas visitors make of it — those who came from cosmopolitan European cities or energetic American capitals? Some local MPs couldn't care less. One Liberal man thought the Olympic Games was 'an international plot to alter the Licensing Act'.[37] Other conservatives, including country MP John Hipworth, wanted to change the law 'to avoid the State becoming the laughing stock of the world when the Olympic Games were held'.[38] With the Olympics looming, Victorian Liberal premier Henry Bolte decided to find out what the public thought about the six o'clock swill, and ordered a referendum to be held on Saturday 24 March 1956.

If anyone thought it was going to be a low-key affair, they were sadly mistaken. The United Licensed Victuallers Association, which represented the hotel industry, claimed that the Victorian population saw the sense of extending hotel trading hours from 6 pm to 10 pm, so it wouldn't be worth spending a great deal of money on its campaign. Its opponents, running on the slogan 'Stick to Six', refused to believe the result was a foregone conclusion. The temperance movement was still alive and kicking — and donating. 'In 1930 we spent more than 50,000 pounds [on a similar campaign],' the Reverend Robertson McCue said. 'Donations are pouring in and one gift alone of 1000 pounds of printing means one million leaflets will be distributed this month.'[39]

Reverend McCue was an experienced campaigner who understood that by mobilising the churches, he was engaging the resistance. Across the burgeoning suburbs, churches were finding congregations that were built on young families who were keen to be part of a church community.[40] They were receptive to the message that men didn't need any more encouragement to drink. Children would be neglected if their parents went out drinking, one woman told *The Argus*. A man said there was already enough money spent on alcohol and there didn't need to be any more.

The Argus conducted a straw poll on the eve of the referendum, testing the opinion of 200 people in Bourke Street: 73 supported the status quo, including 52 women. But 67 men and 41 women favoured 10 pm closing.[41] On that evidence the six o'clock swill was sunk.

What the straw poll inevitably couldn't survey were the thousands living in Melbourne's suburbs, including the women who dutifully waited for their husbands to come home from the pub to have dinner with their family. Many publicans refused to support the campaign for a new closing time, reckoning that they were doing good business from the swill. On referendum eve ULVA president Mr J. Kellaway found his voice and attacked the 'heretics, Quislings, saboteurs and disloyalists' among the publicans who had done nothing to push for change.[42]

When the vote was done, only six of Victoria's 66 state electorates returned a majority 'yes' result, and all were city seats. The Six O'Clockers' argument won by 300,000 votes. It was a thumping endorsement of the status quo. After Kellaway had attached some of the blame for the result on Menzies' budget increase to the beer price, he made a more withering observation that Victorians had delivered a 'no confidence vote in themselves'.[43]

The head of the Olympic Civics Committee, Maurice Nathan, tried to twist Premier Bolte's arm to allow some flexibility for hotels during the Games, but Bolte was having none of it. 'The people have determined the liquor issue by their vote and I will respect their wishes even during the Games,' Bolte replied.[44]

It might have been canny politics, but what would it say about Melbourne when the international visitors started to arrive later in the year? Bolte was prepared to wear the opprobrium. He would spend the next ten years working behind the scenes to liberalise the law once and for all.

Autumn
1956

Chapter Three
The Enemy Within

Every Australian athlete was fixated on the Olympic Games in Melbourne. It was the nation's first home games. This was the place to shine, in front of local crowds at the international showpiece of sport. Every previous Australian Olympian had travelled halfway around the world, competed, and maybe, if they'd won a medal, managed to get some newspaper coverage back home. This time they would hear Australian accents in the crowds and know that the cheers were for them.

There had been promising signs at the 1952 Helsinki Olympics that Australian athletes could hope for even better performances on their home turf: the team took home six gold medals in all, with sprinter Marjorie Jackson winning two gold, hurdler Shirley Strickland one, cyclist Russell Mockridge two (one with Lionel Cox), and swimmer John Davies one. There had been something about the Australian women sprinters, in particular, that caught the eye. They seemed faster, stronger, and more competitive than their rivals. And now it seemed that there was an assembly line of talent behind Jackson and Strickland, poised to make their own mark in Melbourne.

Marlene Mathews knew that her time was coming. There had been speculation that she would go to the Olympics four years earlier, but Mathews had known she wasn't ready. She was barely 18 then, a promising sprinter but still short of her best. No one was in any doubt that the girl who had first shown her talent at the Fort Street Girls School in Sydney had the speed to win Olympic gold. In 1949 Mathews had recorded the national best time in the 80 metres hurdles, and then the fastest time in New South Wales over the same distance. In March 1949 she won the junior 75-yard national championship in a record 8.4 seconds. By the time Mathews turned 15, she was training four days a week and relaxing with some tennis.[1]

Although Mathews had taken part in the usual sports day competitions at her South Strathfield Primary School, it was at the Fort Street Girls School that she reached another level. The school offered a rare opportunity for Mathews to observe some of the older girls who were already making a name for themselves on the track. No school in Australia had such a bounty of teenage talent. June Maston and Betty McKinnon, who had both been part of the women's silver medal 4 x 100 metres relay team at the 1948 London Olympics, and Judy Canty, who competed in the long jump at the same Games, were powerful role models for Mathews. They were older but were happy to guide Mathews, and on their urging she joined them at the Western Suburbs Athletic Club.

Sport was organised and competitive, and, most importantly for Mathews, she could see that athletics had a pathway that enabled her to commit to it. In the year Canty became the senior athletic champion at Fort Street, Mathews took out the junior title. In 1950 Fort Street proudly described Mathews as 'the runner of whom we are most proud', a big rap for a school that already boasted three Olympians. She ran a scintillating 11.3 seconds for the 100 yards during the school's Annual Field Day, and then, in what was to be a curse throughout her career, pulled a leg muscle and had to withdraw from the rest of the program.[2]

The blooming of Mathews' sprint talent coincided with the start of her senior school years. Fort Street tried to support her, and Mathews dropped one of her Year 11 subjects — geography — so that she could spend more time studying her other subjects. Mathews was cradling a desire to be a physical education teacher, but her running was occupying most of her time. She still managed to be one of nine girls to receive a bursary for 1950 on the strength of her academic results. It was a situation that puzzled Fort Street principal Nelly Cohen. In front of a crowded assembly Ms Cohen read out the names of the girls who had won a bursary. Before she got to Mathews' name, Ms Cohen stopped. 'I really don't know how this person was successful because she only seems to think about how fast she can run.'[3] Speed became Mathews' preoccupation, and it led her to consider taking the unusual step of leaving school to start an athletic career.

These were not easy decisions for a teenage girl in 1950. Some of her parents' friends encouraged them to let their daughter leave school. Let her have the experience, let her travel and see the world, they told the Mathews. She could always go back to school later, if she chose. Mathews herself was stuck on the idea of being a teacher, and was concerned what pursuing an athletic career at the expense of her schooling would mean when she wanted to get her teaching qualification.

It was a rare dilemma for a family that was typical of the time. Mathews' father was an electrical engineer with the NSW railways. Her mother had always done home duties, raising Marlene and her three younger sisters. The family lived in Strathfield, in Sydney's inner-western suburbs, and Mathews would catch a bus to Burwood to do her training. Her mother kept her dinner warm, on top of the stove, until she returned. There was nothing out of the ordinary about the family — except that their eldest daughter was one of the quickest runners in the country.

Inevitably, much of the family's activity focused on Marlene's athletics. The approach was rudimentary and unscientific but routine and predictable. On competition days Mathews would have a small piece of fillet steak with a poached egg on it. She would have nothing to drink from Friday lunchtime until after she finished competing on Saturday because liquids, so the theory went, made you heavy. Her father would then stop in at a pub near the track and buy her a shandy. It would be the girl's first fluid in 30 hours.

By the start of 1956, Mathews was in excellent form. She headed to Brisbane for the national women's athletics championship in April, primed to do well. She arrived in Brisbane only to find that the city had been caught in the aftermath of the cyclones that had battered Far North Queensland; the Gabba oval was a bog.

Everything seemed to be upside down. Olympic gold medallist Shirley Strickland was disqualified for breaking in her pet event, the 80 metres hurdles; the 220-yard event (as it was then) finished on a bend, not a straight, causing some agonised discussions between athletes and officials; and a 17-year-old called Betty Cuthbert, in her first nationals, beat Mathews in the 220 yards. Mathews witnessed the women's shot-put take place in farcical circumstances when the heaved shot became stuck in the mud. Even the official starter was 'timed out' by the crowd and replaced on the second day of competition.

Strickland, a straight talker, explained her breaking by blaming some spectators for banging the picket fence and making a sound like the starter's pistol. But she accepted the result. She was less accepting of the championships overall. 'It was shocking,' she said. 'The track was dangerous. We were up to our ankles in mud. The judging was better today: there were no tight finishes as on Saturday when the judges panicked and gave the wrong decisions.' Strickland shared with Jackson national pre-eminence as Australia's best female athlete, but Strickland thought these titles were hopelessly compromised by the conditions. 'These championships can't be taken seriously as Olympic Games' tests,' she said. 'The lightest girl in the best track won every race — the heavier girls, who normally would get wonderful drive from the cinder track were left floundering in the mud.'[4]

Strickland's critique was a sharp reminder of what was expected at Olympic level and how far Australia seemed from that standard. Not for the first time, athletes who had Olympic experience wondered if Australia could get it right in Melbourne.

The claggy surface was the worst kind of track for Mathews,

who derived her speed from a powerful leg action. Cuthbert, who had a lighter frame, seemed to run on top of the ground. When the provisional women's team was named for the Games, Strickland, Cuthbert, and Mathews were all included. There would be another competition in Melbourne, closer to the Games, to finalise the team. No one was sure how many sprint places there would be in the final team. But the Melbourne trials would at least take place on a cinder track, and provide a fairer picture of who should run for Australia. The Olympics were still eight months away, and Mathews knew that all roads led to Melbourne.

*

It was, said the legendary British actress Dame Sybil Thorndike, a piece of drama that could 'only come from the soil of the country'. She was talking about *Summer of the Seventeenth Doll*. It was unmistakably Australian in subject and idiom, written by Ray Lawler, a young man from the western suburbs of Melbourne, and featuring a couple of Queensland canecutters. Within weeks of its opening on 28 November 1955, London theatre agents were circling: suddenly, something artistic that looked and sounded Australian could be exported for overseas entertainment. There was no knowing how this could have happened.

In 1950 the writer and critic Arthur Phillips wrote a provocative short essay in the literary quarterly *Meanjin*, identifying what he called the nation's 'cultural cringe':

> Above our writers — and other artists — looms the intimidating mass of Anglo-Saxon achievement. Such a situation almost inevitably produces the characteristic Australian Cultural Cringe — appearing either as the Cringe Direct, or as the Cringe Inverted, in the attitude of Blatant Blatherskite, the God's-own-country-and-I'm-a-better-man-than-you-are Australian bore.

Perhaps *The Doll*'s success made better sense when it was viewed in the context of how it came to be performed — and that was, in a roundabout way, to do with the nation's enduring connection with the British crown. In 1954 Australia hosted a visit from the young Queen Elizabeth II, a trip that injected some glamour into the monarchy and had Australians in a kind of royal rapture. About 100,000 people waited to see the Queen at the Melbourne Cricket Ground. Thousands lined the street wherever she went. Newspapers talked about the arrival of a 'new Elizabethan era'. Across the country, there was a sense of excitement and a desire to celebrate how far the nation had come in what one newspaper calculated to be '166 years'.

The royal tour made a particular impression on Herbert 'Nugget' Coombs, an economist and brilliant public servant, who had been privately agitating the federal government for a decade to invest in the arts. Coombs was an incisive and strategic thinker, with a grizzled countenance and a fine line in patience. He had led Chifley's post-war reconstruction and became governor of the Commonwealth Bank, and he knew how both ends of town worked. After the Queen's visit, Coombs noted in discussions with businessmen how enthusiastically Australians had responded to the tour's colour and pageantry. He observed:

> Not that there were doubts about the fundamental loyalty of the Australian people, but rather that Australians who had a reputation for being hard-boiled and unemotional had responded vigorously [to the tour]. We said 'Surely, there is something in this which should be kept alive. When the Queen leaves Australia we should not just drop back and forget the pleasure that her visit has given us.'[5]

The result of Coombs' efforts, the Australian Elizabethan Theatre Trust, was an updated version of a proposal for a national theatre that he had presented to the Chifley government. Chifley was all set to implement it when he lost office. The big difference with the new model was that there would be less government and more private investment and engagement. Coombs held dinners in Melbourne and Sydney with executives from major businesses to enlist their financial support. Only when that was locked in did he go to Menzies, knowing that the government would not have to be the organisation's financial lifeline.

Coombs also wanted to inject some business acumen into the arts industry, so that there was a quality of administration and management attached to running it. Perhaps most importantly, he wanted the new trust to go beyond the local amateur theatre organisations and foster a national outlook for the arts that embraced theatre, opera, and ballet. Part of that approach meant enlisting experts including John Sumner, a former merchant seaman who was the director of the University of Melbourne's Union Theatre. And it was Sumner, an Englishman, who brought Ray Lawler's *Doll* to the stage.

The play had shared the 1955 Commonwealth Playwrights Advisory Board prize with Oriel Gray's *The Torrents*, another drama that captured the Australian experience. That recognition did little to ease the anxiety that there was only a small audience for local stories. Lawler was worried that his play was so unmistakably Australian that it would fail to be popular with audiences used to seeing overseas drama and international actors. The view of the prime minister's own wife, Dame Pattie Menzies, summed it up: 'We have no good theatre in Australia. There still aren't enough people in one town to make it worthwhile for a good company to open one. But we do get all the good films from Hollywood.'[6]

Theatre in post-war Australia was dominated by J.C. Williamson and overseas touring companies. Audiences came out in force to see Laurence Olivier and Vivien Leigh when their Old Vic company toured Australia in 1948. The stars arrived in Australia to be treated like some kind of exotic bird that had woken up miles from its gilded cage. 'We know practically nothing about Australia,' Olivier confessed at the start of the four-month tour. 'We want to see the country. We want to see every kind of animal or bird there is.'[7] Seven years later, expat Robert Helpmann and American Katharine Hepburn arrived in Australia with the Old Vic to tour Shakespeare's *The Taming of the Shrew*, *The Merchant of Venice*, and *Measure for Measure*.

The tour was well patronised and collected some breathless reviews, but the local actors' union made a formal note about the need for everyone who toured with such a company to be of 'world calibre'. '[O]therwise we shall refuse to agree to the importation of what often amounts to a touring company being publicised as a world theatre company,' the union stated. 'The Old Vic Company must understand that the Old Vic Company is always welcome but we should not be treated as provincials.'[8] 'Provincials' was a word dripping with a range of meanings, none of them good, for cultural purists, even if the actors' union was only trying to stress that local actors should not miss out on work.

The early days of Sumner's new job suggested that nothing much had changed. The opening night of his new Elizabethan Theatre, in Sydney's Newtown, in July 1955 starred two pillars of the British acting fraternity, Dame Sybil Thorndike and Sir Ralph Richardson, in two plays by their compatriot, Terence Rattigan. Not only was it odd that the new Australian cultural initiative premiered with overseas plays performed by overseas actors, but the point was reinforced at the opening night reception. The gala event was attended by Prime Minister Robert Menzies, Governor-General Sir William Slim, a list of Sydney society's finest and the overseas cast members. The Australian cast members didn't even score an invite.[9] It was self-evident that the best way for locals to find a vehicle for their talent was to create their own drama. *The Doll* arrived at the right time.

Ray Lawler was unmistakably a local product. He was born in Footscray, a tough part of Melbourne, the second-eldest of eight children. Lawler's father was a labourer, and the family, like so many, struggled through the Depression. Lawler left school at 13 to work in a factory that made farm equipment. For him there would be no high school or university, but he had passion and a determination to find a way into the theatre world.

Lawler believed British films were of 'superior quality', and the best way he could see them was at the Athenaeum Theatre, in Collins Street. It became his regular haunt: he'd visit the art gallery on the third floor, and eventually joined the Athenaeum Library on the second floor.[10] He found his way to the Union Theatre and started working on *Summer of the Seventeenth Doll* in 1954, drawing on his vivid recollections of seeing Queensland canecutters — confident, with an easy physicality — wooing chorus girls at the Brisbane theatre where he had once worked. Lawler's story featured two canecutters who travel to Melbourne in the off-season each year to visit two women living in a Carlton terrace. Each time, they bring a kewpie doll with them. While Lawler was touring *Twelfth Night* with Barry Humphries, Zoe Caldwell, and the company, Lawler would hole up in a hotel room, working and reworking *The Doll*.

Lawler had a long discussion with Sumner about an early draft of the play, and then presented him with the rewritten work, in a brown paper parcel, on the eve of Sumner's departure to Sydney to join the Australian Elizabethan Theatre Trust. Sumner got on with his new job and Lawler became the manager of the University Theatre. Later the following year, the trust put £500 towards a staging of the play, honouring its commitment to present original Australian drama. But both Sumner and Lawler knew it still needed work.

One of the elements that had to be worked through was its Australianness, which proved a challenge for the local actors, who had spent years playing parts that were far removed from the way their countrymen and women spoke and behaved. No one sounded Australian on stage. '[T]here is scarcely a glimmer of an Australian accent in the idiom of our concert halls and playhouses,' *The Sydney Morning Herald*'s theatre critic Lindsay Brown observed in 1954.[11] The Australian accent had been derided for years. Winston Churchill called Australia's version of English 'the most brutal maltreatment that has ever been inflicted on the mother-tongue of the great English-speaking nations'. Australians adopted an English version of their accent, a 'received pronunciation', that was designed to cover up any drawl or twang. Most of the nation's cultural institutions subscribed to this way of speaking; it wasn't until 1952 that the ABC allowed distinctively Australian accents on air.[12]

The nation's theatres took a little longer. Sumner got to work on *The Doll* and paid particular attention to the accents. According to Lawler:

> At first we all started on the same level with ordinary Australian accents but gradually Sumner graded the 'Australianness' of the speech. He pointed out that men from the outback would speak with rougher voices and would be less articulate than city women working in a hotel bar. Incidentally, the cast found the Australian rhythm of speech much more natural to them than the usual English or American rhythm they have to use.[13]

It wasn't surprising that Australian actors' own accent came more naturally, only that it had taken so long for them to find a vehicle for it. For a country about to embrace the world, it was important that it actually heard the sounds and characteristics of its own people too.

For Sumner, the challenge also went to the play's turn of phrase. 'We were in strange territory: until then little Australian drama had been able to catch the colloquial ear,' he said.[14] On opening night, 28 November 1955, in Melbourne, the audience hooted with laughter at the opening-act phrases they recognised — 'Goodo sport, be with you in a minute' ... 'steak and oysters' ... 'Young and Jacksons'. Niall Brennan, the theatre manager, knew instantly that the audience had found a connection with the play:

> [I]t was the best dressed and most sympathetic first-night audience I had ever seen at the Union. They came rolling in, in furs and starched shirts, and I remember saying to one of the usherettes ... 'I think this play is going to be a great success.' None of us could understand it ... They clapped every actor who came on and the roars which greeted Ray's own entrance

were tremendous. When the curtain came down at the end, the theatre almost shook …'[15]

The laughter no doubt dried up as the drama became more compelling, but Sumner and Lawler believed they were onto something. They discussed it with the trust's inaugural director, Hugh Hunt, at midnight after the first performance, and agreed the play should be transferred to the trust's theatre in Sydney. *The Doll* opened at the Elizabethan Theatre on 10 January 1956.

The Sydney season was a triumph. Within days of it going on tour in early 1956, the play became a sellout through regional Australia. The roads as the tour embarked were flooded from torrential rains, but the bleak weather did nothing to deter locals who wanted to see a play that sounded like them. Theatre critic and arts publisher Katharine Brisbane noticed something was stirring in the nation's cultural landscape. 'Self-assertion was in the air,' she said, 'uncertainly expressed in a yearning to mix on terms of equality with those older civilisations thousands of servicemen had glimpsed during the war and from which a daily increasing number of new Australians had come.'[16]

If only the nation's politics showed such self-awareness.

*

By 1956 Les Coleman was hanging on tenaciously to the last of his political preferments — chairman of the Olympic Games' construction committee — and to his place on the Melbourne City Council. He had been appointed to the Olympic role in 1953 by Premier John Cain, and helped the committee to get its financial house in order at a time when planning for the Games was at a low point. In the intervening two and a half years, Coleman had gone from being Cain's trusted cabinet colleague to a Labor Party pariah. He had turned his back on the party that he had supported — and that had nourished him — for almost 40 years, to effectively become the first leader of what would become the Democratic Labor Party. Coleman's political odyssey took place against the backdrop of Olympic controversies, but in the end it was the bitter Labor split that ended his political career. He was one of many who were consumed by Labor's internal fires.

There was little evidence to suggest that Coleman's career would take this path. He was a quiet and serious man, a skilful footballer and debater who became an accountant and also ran some hotels. Coleman had joined the ALP as a young man, but just what he believed in remained something of a mystery, even to his close friends.[17] His political philosophy was more altruism than ambition. 'I believe everybody should make some contribution by way of public service to the general welfare of the people,' he said. 'This applies particularly to those who have had someone success in life because they should give something back.'[18]

The one constant in Coleman's life was Catholicism, the faith he was raised in. It was also a source of fraternal support at a time of sectarianism and discrimination against Catholics. Coleman would do what he could to advance fellow Catholics, and his social circle in and around the heavily Catholic Port Melbourne, where he spent much of his time, included James O'Collins, who would become bishop of Ballarat and an important figure in the Labor split.

Coleman worked his way through the Labor branches, was a delegate to the Victorian Labor conference, and was then elected to the Melbourne City Council. In 1943 he won a seat in the upper house of the Victorian parliament, and when Cain became premier two years later he was given the job as assistant treasurer. It was Cain's first gesture of confidence in Coleman, and it would not be the last.

Coleman was voted Labor's leader in the Legislative Council in 1952, and Premier Cain gave him the transport portfolio to bring the railways' £9 million deficit to heel. Coleman's performance across his portfolios — and in the Olympic cause — suggested to some of his parliamentary colleagues that he was a potential successor to

Cain as premier. But there was no natural affinity between Cain and Coleman that might enable a smooth succession plan.

Coleman joined Bill Barry in a group of four Labor MPs, a tight constellation of Catholics that became the most enduring of his political associations. It was not a true factional base, which meant that Coleman had no safety net in troubled times. He was in Cain's favour because of the quality of his work, but if his performance became somehow compromised, there didn't appear to be any way of averting a fall from grace. And with the deep fissures that were about to open within the Labor Party, Coleman was vulnerable.

Cain's biggest problem in 1953 was trying to resolve the ongoing saga of the location of Melbourne's Olympic stadium. For months the IOC had been agitating Melbourne for a resolution: would it be the Showgrounds, Princes Park in Carlton, or the Melbourne Cricket Ground?

The debate dated back to before the 1949 bid, when the premier of the time, Tom Hollway, had counselled silence about where the main stadium would be until after the IOC made its decision.[19] It might have been smart short-term politics but it created a huge long-term headache. At one stage even the University of Melbourne's sports oval, Albert Park, and the St Kilda Cricket Ground were considered. The MCG was an outstanding sporting facility, close to the city and to public transport. The problem was that it had several significant stakeholders — the Melbourne Cricket Club, the MCG Trustees, the Victorian Cricket Association, and the Victorian Football League — and each of them had different priorities. The MCG would also need to be renovated, to add more seating and a cinder track. Some of the traditionalists in the MCC's Long Room no doubt reached for a large drink at the mention of such heresy.

By the time the IOC convened in Helsinki, the message from Melbourne was that Princes Park would be the venue. Back home, though, it was anything but clear, especially when it was estimated that it would cost £2 million to create an Olympic-class venue at the location.

Premier Cain was an MCG Trustee, and knew the history of the extensive and ultimately futile negotiations about securing the MCG as the Olympic venue that had been held in 1949, and again in 1951. He now decided that the best way of sorting out the issue was to ask a simple question: what could Victoria afford? Cain's tactics would be pure brinkmanship, linking the continued financial cost of the Games with a solution to the stadium mess, but he knew there had to be an end to the impasse.

The premier convened a meeting in Melbourne in February 1953 with Prime Minister Menzies, the MCG Trustees, Australia's IOC delegate, Hugh Weir, MCC representatives, federal opposition deputy leader Arthur Calwell, and the Melbourne City Council. Menzies had taken a similar line to Cain, and was cautious about committing more money to the Games. Cain's two confederates on the city council were Les Coleman and Bill Barry, but they both supported the Carlton plan. So too did the prime minister. Weir believed that shifting the venue from Carlton to the MCG would spell the end of Melbourne's Olympic bid, because the IOC would not tolerate Melbourne making another change so late in the day. Also, he didn't believe there was a way to turn the MCG into a suitable venue. Even Menzies was sceptical, pointing out that the MCC hadn't even put forward any details of what the stadium could look like. Cain was unfussed. 'It's the MCG or you get no money from us,' he told the Olympic officials.[20]

Coleman's value to Cain was that he delivered independent, occasionally uncomfortable advice, but that didn't mean Cain had to listen to him. Now Coleman warned Cain that some MCC members would get together to challenge the right of the Olympic Games to use the ground. Cain didn't care about that either, and reminded Coleman who he worked for. 'If there is any trouble in that direction I will bring in legislation at the top of Bourke St to prevent it, and you will help me,' he told Coleman during the meeting.[21]

Cain's strategy carried the day, and it was agreed that the MCG would be the main stadium. Weir left the meeting consumed by gloom: he was certain the venue change spelt the end of the Melbourne Olympics.

Nine days later, Cain appointed Coleman to a subcommittee to liaise with the MCG Trustees about the terms of the agreement for the Olympics occupancy and the necessary preparations that had to be made to the MCG. By the end of May 1953, Coleman was in charge of the Olympic Organising Control Committee (later to become the construction committee) after Arthur Coles — a member of the supermarket family — resigned in frustration. Coles had famously declared when he took on the job, 'I don't get ulcers, I give them.' But the constant battles within the committee and the mixed messages that were going to the IOC exhausted even his patience.[22]

Coleman was swiftly on the offensive, telling *The Age*:

There should no place in this organisation for the individualist or one with a chip on his shoulder. All must work together if we are to achieve success because there is less than three years in which the job must be done. Time is fast running against us and when you appreciate the fact that only one site has been chosen, and that neither a sod has been turned or a nail driven, it will be appreciated how difficult the task is going to be.[23]

It was a pointed reference to end the infighting and a reminder of the need for an urgent resolution to the problem. Coleman wasn't by nature a panicker, but he understood that the Melbourne Olympics was at a perilous moment. His membership of the government and the city council gave him a powerful presence on the two most important non-Olympic organisations. He was the right man for the job, calm, meticulous, sensible, and focused.

Cain again turned to Coleman to resolve an Olympic matter in 1954, when he made his party ally chairman of the new Olympic Park Trust. It didn't appear to be a contentious appointment, but it wasn't long before the trust's old stagers started to mutter that Cain's intervention was really about marginalising amateur sport. Cain's move again highlighted the divergent interests that were involved in the implementation of Melbourne's Olympic dream.

Cain was one of those in Melbourne — along with Sir Frank Beaurepaire, Sir Raymond Connelly, and a few other modernisers — who understood that the purity of amateurism was all very well, but it probably wouldn't get the job of organising the Olympic Games done. That needed the practical application of some sound business skills. Cain's appointment of Coleman was part of a broader restructure of the Olympic Park Trust that left the new board of management with just two representatives from amateur athletics.

This wasn't acceptable to Edgar Tanner, secretary of the Olympic Organising Committee and something of a Beaurepaire bête noire. 'This is definitely a State political move and indicates that the State government thinks the amateur body is not capable of controlling Olympic Park,' Tanner grumbled.[24]

He was right — Cain didn't think the amateurs could do it, but he kept his own counsel. Coleman took the reins without further ado. But Cain and Coleman were soon about to be caught up in something much worse.

*

In the aftermath of Labor's narrow loss in the 1954 federal election, leader H.V. 'Doc' Evatt denounced the activities of the right-wing anti-communist agitators within the party, known as the Groupers. The 'industrial groups' worked within labour unions against Communist Party candidates, or even those who were comparatively less radical but still left-wing. The Petrov Affair only emboldened the Groupers, who fed off the growing anxiety across Australia about the communist menace.

Initial support for the Groupers came from B.A. Santamaria's Catholic Social Studies Movement (known as the Movement), which began to take on what some on Labor's left believed was a sinister and covert role agitating within the ALP. Under Santamaria's charismatic leadership, the Movement became a political force, and managed to effectively control the Groupers — and therefore key elements of the Labor Party.

Those in the Movement believed they had God on their side. Pope Pius XII had, after all, decreed in 1949 that any Catholic who collaborated with communists in any form would be excommunicated.[25] In Victoria, where the battle was at its most intense, Archbishop Daniel Mannix became the Movement's patron and Santamaria its strategic director.[26] When Evatt prevailed against the Groupers in a battle at the Labor Party's national conference in March 1955, the Groupers opted to set up their own Australian Labor Party (Anti-Communist) in Victoria. The fallout was significant — Labor Party members resigned and trade unions disaffiliated. The Victorian ALP's sectarianism, which had largely been kept away from public scrutiny, emerged to divide the party.

Coleman found himself in one of the key battlegrounds: transport, where left-wing unions had strong representation. Coleman had reduced costs across the railways, helping set up the platform for Cain to extend and fund his social reforms in other portfolios. Coleman's ultimate success was to ensure the railways' revenue grew ahead of inflation. This was the triumph at the core of Coleman's fiscal discipline. But his political instincts could not match his feel for a balance sheet, and Coleman's problem crystallised around the so-called One-Man Bus dispute.

It seemed a simple enough issue: the Tramways Board maintained that the new 41-seat buses needed only a driver, not a conductor, during off-peak times. Under this initiative, the driver would collect the fares. The union's response reflected concern among bus crews that drivers needed conductors, and it told its members not to man the buses. Coleman fired back a rejoinder that played into the loaded language of the day: 'I appeal to the union members to reject what appears to be an instruction from the Kremlin and not be misled by those leaders who have done little to improve working conditions in the industry.'[27] In the febrile and paranoid political environment, even legitimate disputes took on greater significance.

It was soon clear that the One-Man Bus dispute was going to be a political stoush between some formidable ideological opponents. Typical of the time, it was a dispute made up of a mosaic of ideologies and personal vendettas, subterranean alliances, and deep animosity. Former communist-turned-Grouper Denis 'Dinny' Lovegrove was the ALP's state secretary, and suspected the Tramways Union's strong communist base was preparing for a major confrontation with Cain. Lovegrove urged Coleman to stand firm.[28]

The union was led by the communist Clarrie O'Shea, who was prepared to settle in for the long haul, knowing that he had the support of Trades Hall secretary Vic Stout. O'Shea's dealings from the first day with Coleman fostered in him a long-standing, almost visceral, dislike of the minister. The feeling was mutual. Coleman detested communists and quite simply wanted to get rid of O'Shea, but it was a battle he was never going to win.[29] There were personal issues, too, between Stout and Coleman: the trade unionist was a non-smoker and a temperance advocate, so it was no surprise that he looked askance at Coleman's interest in pubs and judged the transport minister accordingly.

Coleman's propensity for acting unilaterally in the dispute, taking initiatives that he only later reported to the ALP caucus, accelerated his declining support within the party.[30] The longer the dispute went on, the greater the political cost to the Cain government. Despite the growth in car ownership, more than 60 per cent of Melbourne's workers still used public transport to get to their jobs and back home again.[31] That was a big constituency to be affected by any kind of industrial discord, and Cain could not afford the stand-off to run for too long.

Even so, the One-Man Bus dispute ground on for almost a year before an independent arbiter ruled on 7 January 1955 in favour of the unions. By then the Cain government had lost significant skin, and Coleman's star was fading.

Two months after the dispute was resolved, the divisions came to a head at the ALP's national conference when two Victorian 'executives' — one led by Groupers and the other by Trades Hall secretary Vic Stout — presented themselves to be confirmed. In tumultuous proceedings and a subsequent picket, Stout's ticket was endorsed, leaving the Groupers to retreat to Melbourne, where they held a meeting of their own. Stout warned those who planned to take part that they would be expelled from the party. Coleman defied the directive and went ahead and joined the meeting of 25 state and federal Victorian MPs. Perhaps Coleman's decision was motivated by a bruised and vengeful mood after the One-Man Bus dispute; more likely it was his Catholicism and anti-communism that motivated him to attend the meeting that would ultimately end his time in the ALP. There were personal elements to his decision too: while there was scant evidence of Coleman having anything but a cursory relationship with Santamaria, and he knew Mannix only through their paths often crossing at official functions, he certainly disliked Stout's militancy.

When the 17 state MPs were subsequently suspended from the Labor Party, Cain demanded that the four cabinet ministers among them, including Coleman, resign. All four tried to stare Cain down, but the premier went to see the governor, who issued Cain with a new commission to form government. Cain selected a new cabinet and tried to go on as before. But the world had changed irrevocably. Coleman, who remained on the Melbourne City Council with fellow expelled cabinet minister and Catholic Bill Barry, formed an alternative group, called the Coleman-Barry Party, which became a forerunner of the Democratic Labor Party.

It was Barry, with his tub-thumping rhetoric about Doc Evatt being 'the most dangerous man in Australia', who garnered most of the headlines. And it was Barry whom Cain would later publicly demonise for his treachery, linking him with state opposition leader Henry Bolte in the no-confidence motion that tipped Cain out of government on 20 April 1955. Cain did, however, go public with a criticism of Coleman's intransigence on the One-Man Bus dispute, blaming his former transport minister for bringing the wrath of the community down on the government's head.[32]

Barry was a bluff soul who was more comfortable in the lime-light than Coleman, who, although he had cultivated the press while in government, eschewed building a profile in the aftermath of the split. The Movement had a view about who should lead the new Labor offshoot, and neither Barry nor Coleman suited their goals. Barry was already in parliament but was considered to be rough around the edges — and he was associated with an old conniver and fixer of Victorian politics, John Wren. Coleman was a smoother, more measured character for the job but lacked popular appeal.[33] The end result was a compromise leadership, a double act, which immediately made the new grouping — the Anti-Communist ALP — look like a party run by committee. In reality, Coleman and Barry had no real issue on which to contest an election, other than what they opposed among their former colleagues. For many voters the new grouping was inevitably linked to the Catholic Church, and to a group of faceless men engaged in subterranean activities that seemed to have little to do with governing. Such conditions could only lead to one outcome.

Cain was forced to fight the 1955 state election on two fronts — the enemy within and the enemy without. He was a second-genera-tion Irish-Catholic, but Cain's attitude to Catholicism shifted from tolerance to distance as the sectarianism within the Labor Party pulled it apart.[34] When Cain delivered his election launch at Northcote Town Hall on 9 May 1955, he felt he had to repudiate the Barry-Coleman group before he even addressed his plan for re-election:

> There is no room for those who would do the work of Labor's enemies; no room for those who refuse to carry out the decision of its governing bodies or the policies that have been hammered out at conferences and have made the party great. The attempt to link the Labor government with Communism is fraudulent

and false and those responsible for such statement know that they are false. Let me make it perfectly plain that we are opposed to Communism in every shape and form.[35]

It did no good. The election was bitter and discordant, full of vitriol and recrimination. The new grouping failed to make an impression on the electorate, and Barry lost his seat in the lower house. Labor's primary vote plummeted, prompting Calwell to call the result an unmitigated disaster.[36]

The Legislative Council elections were held in June, and Coleman, as the other half of the leadership group, and a councillor, took up the cudgel. His pitch to voters was entirely in keeping with the tenor of his public life, and a stark contrast to Barry's gruff electioneering. 'The lesson of the Legislative Assembly election was that Labor cannot have electoral success until it faces the people united,' Coleman said during a radio address. And governing would only occur when the unions were 'in sound and sensible Labor hands'.[37]

That approach didn't work either: Coleman and ten other candidates on his ticket were defeated. Coleman himself only received 40 per cent of the vote that the Cain Labor candidate achieved in his Melbourne West province. But if there was one foretaste of what was to come for Labor in the years ahead, it was that the Coleman-Barry Party overall garnered 16.53 per cent of the council vote, compared to Cain Labor's 39.42 per cent.[38] Henry Bolte became premier on the back of the Coleman-Barry discord, with an almost 13 per cent swing. It was a model of how Labor would be shut out of power for almost two decades.

Through all of this, Coleman somehow managed to maintain his hold on his Olympics roles. It spoke volumes for Cain's cool appraisal of Coleman's work. Cain also understood that it was wise to keep his former cabinet colleague working on the Olympics because it would help mollify the IOC. Avery Brundage was coming to Melbourne for a final inspection of venues and facilities, and it would be disastrous to remove the man in charge of the stadiums.

Coleman himself put his head down and kept doing the job. By the early months of 1956, as the Games accelerated into view, there was no time for political point-scoring and personal agendas. At the start of the year Coleman expressed doubt that the boxing venue in West Melbourne would be finished in time. Two months later, he announced that the gates at Olympic Park would commemorate the late Sir Raymond Connelly, because no one would forget the work the former lord mayor had done to secure the Games for Melbourne.[39] It seemed to be a mundane and uncontroversial statement compared to the brutality of the politics in the previous 18 months.

Chapter Four
The Bomb in the Outback

The first British nuclear tests in Australia took place on the Montebello Islands, 70 kilometres off the Pilbara coast in Western Australia. Nobody lived there until scientists, engineers, politicians, and sailors turned up, creating a temporary village that would monitor, test, and record the fallout. It was 1952, in the middle of the Korean War, where Australian troops were defending South Korea from Soviet- and Chinese-backed communist forces to the north. No one in the Australian government — or, indeed, the general public — showed any great concern about the British tests. If anything, there was a scent of national pride that the United Kingdom had chosen Australia for the 'honour' of testing its bombs. The prevailing view was that these explosions were miles away from where most Australians lived, and they were probably harmless.

On 16 May 1956 the first of a new set of tests — called Mosaic — started in the Montebello Islands. It was the fourth British test, after the first in 1952 and a pair of Totem tests at South Australia's Emu Field a year later. Australian radio journalist Norman Banks was on HMAS *Fremantle*, about 12 miles from the blast site, and described the explosion 'as the most exciting thing I've seen in my life'. 'This is a purely defensive weapon,' he stressed. 'The potential enemy, the Reds, have been engaged in a cold war and it's up to us to make certain they don't get away from us. We must keep abreast with their atomic development ... it is part of the price of preserving the democratic way of life.'

Banks described a clear day with wispy cloud and a strong wind. Everyone aboard was told to close their eyes at the moment of explosion, and Banks described feeling heat on the back of his neck. Then he saw the massive mushroom cloud that travelled from 10,000 to almost 15,000 feet, changing shape to become more like a toadstool, thick at the top, and then more conical in the minutes that followed. The crew of the Australian aircraft that flew into the radioactive cloud to take scientific measurements were quarantined once they landed. No one was to touch the plane's fuselage, and the air crew had a special exit plan to ensure they made no contact with the outside of the plane. As far as Banks was concerned, he had witnessed something memorable and vitally important.[1]

There was an official clamouring to declare the test a success. A monitoring station in Canberra did not record any radioactivity from the blast, and the minister responsible for supervising the tests, Howard Beale, gave it his stamp of approval. He declared that there had been no risk to anyone on the Australian mainland, to ships at sea, or to the aircraft used in the tests. And he promised there would be another test in several weeks.

Beale's confidence was misplaced. Within days, there were reports of increased radioactivity in places as far apart as Cloncurry, in Queensland, and Sydney. A fortnight after the test, a laboratory in New Zealand picked up radioactive particles that were undoubtedly from the Montebello explosion.

A second test was held at the Montebello Islands on 19 June, and this time, after the radioactivity reports from the earlier test, an effort was made to convince Australians that there was no danger. With Menzies overseas, Sir Arthur Fadden was acting prime minister and had the job of reassuring the nation. 'Both the United Kingdom and Australian governments insist that in all weapons tests the emphasis must be on safety, and the Australian people may therefore be fully assured on this point, not only in relation to past tests, but to any others which may take place,' he said.[2]

Unofficially, Fadden had been far less sanguine. 'What the bloody hell is going on, the cloud is drifting over the mainland?' he cabled London.[3] One other important fact wasn't revealed at the time: the second bomb was at least 60 kilotons, four times the size of the first, and the biggest atomic device ever exploded in Australia.[4] The cloud was seen on the mainland, at mining town Port Hedland, 320 kilometres away, as it rose to 46,000 feet, well above the predicted level of 36,000 feet. The spread of the cloud above the mainland made the government's reassurances look hollow, especially after rumours started circulating that a miner in the Pilbara, in Western Australia, had picked up high radioactivity readings on his Geiger counter.

Beale was in Maralinga, in central South Australia, to announce a new set of tests, and had to scramble to quell the rumour, which was becoming a story that visiting journalists were keen to report. The official line was that most of the radioactive material had fallen harmlessly into the sea, and the rest was drifting at such a high altitude that it posed no threat. The lessons for the government and the scientists about providing a basic level of assurance to Australians about the size of the tests and their cloud's likely path were never heeded. Beale and his atomic-minded friends had already moved on. Beale was already lauding the efforts of those who had built a scientific village at Maralinga to accommodate the experts and equipment that would be required to monitor the tests on the proving ground later in 1956. He added that although there was a railhead only 50 miles from the range itself, the place was still so remote that there would be no risk to 'life and property'. Nothing living would be exposed to the effects of radiation, Beale promised.[5] There was no mention of the Indigenous Australian communities in the area. As far as Beale and the government were concerned, they were not part of the plan and not even part of the area.

West Australian author Tom Hungerford offered his own reassurance after a visit to the Maralinga camp, claiming the bombs would harm no one because no one lived there. '[T]he aborigines

… have long since departed either to a happier hunting ground or to more congenial regions nearer to the sea coast,' he wrote. 'As a further precaution, a close contact is kept with missionaries so that no natives on "walk-about" will penetrate the dangerous areas.'[6] A camp official or one of Beale's staff had apparently briefed Hungerford on this misapprehension. The reality was radically different.

What no one was mentioning was what had happened three years earlier, during the first atomic test on the Australian mainland, at Emu Field, about 200 kilometres north of Maralinga, in the western area of South Australia. At Wallatinna, a remote cattle station homestead where many of the Yankunytjatjara community camped, the real story of Indigenous exposure to the atomic explosions could be heard.

Yami Lester was only 11 when he heard a deep and profound rumble through the depths of the ground. Perhaps it was three or four explosions. No one sitting around the morning campfire could be certain. The next day, Yami Lester saw a black cloud low over the horizon, appearing like a mist but moving without wind. It moved slowly, blocking out the sun, blanketing the bush and the ground in an eerie silence. Yami Lester and the family around him were frightened. They had seen nothing like it. Some dug holes to hide in, and Yami Lester jumped in one before the mist rolled over them, rich with the smell of metal and burning, leaving a black oily coating on the bushes.

Several days later, some of the community became violently ill. Yami Lester was sick, and his eyes were sore. It wasn't certain how many of the community died following the black mist because they kept moving on, as was their way. Yami Lester lost the sight in his right eye. Some time later, his left eye went too. At other places, other communities were exposed. Some became ill. Others later gave birth to children who had significant physical problems. No one seemed to notice.

Prime Minister Menzies told parliament:

If the experiments are not to be conducted in Australia with all our natural advantages for this purpose we are contracting out of the common defence of the free world. No risk is involved in the matter. The greatest risk is that we may become inferior in potential military strength to the potential of the enemy.[7]

Three years later after the Emu Field test, fewer people were prepared to accept such thin reassurances. Hedley Marston, a celebrated biochemist based in Adelaide, was determined to highlight the risks associated with the tests. Cantankerous, egotistical, fractious, but often right, Marston wrote to his friend Mark Oliphant, one of the physicists who had pioneered nuclear fusion, after the Montebello tests: 'I am more worried than I can convey about the expensive, quasi-scientific pantomime that is being enacted at Maralinga under the cloak of security: and even more so about the evasive lying that is being indulged [by the] public authorities about the hazard of fall-out ...'[8]

The trade union movement — and some of its more militant members, through the columns of the newspaper *Tribune* — had become increasingly agitated by the tests. The ACTU's policy was to oppose nuclear explosions anywhere in the world. The Labor Party's deputy leader, Arthur Calwell, pledged that the party in government would not allocate any money for nuclear tests.

For those who had followed the federal parliamentary debates about Indigenous Australians, none of this would have been surprising. Paul Hasluck, initially as a Liberal backbencher and then as minister for territories, drew on his experience as a journalist travelling extensively through Western Australia to attempt a different approach to Indigenous issues. He not only focused on their plight but also offered an alternative perspective. 'When we enter into international discussions, and raise our voice, as we should raise it, our very words are mocked by the thousands of degraded and depressed people who crouch on rubbish heaps throughout the whole of the continent,' he said six years before the Maralinga tests.[9] Finding solutions to this problem was to be debated at a 'native welfare conference' in September 1951. Giving Indigenous Australians the vote was one proposal that never got up. Hasluck told parliament later that the contact between whites and Indigenous Australians was so far advanced that 'two thirds of the Aborigines were de-tribalised', so segregation was not an option. Instead, the philosophy would be assimilation, which would, in time, mean that all those of mixed or Indigenous Australian blood 'would live like white Australians'.[10] The premise was that Indigenous Australians would come to share in the country's prosperity and overcome disadvantage and discrimination.

It might have been somewhat of a change from the paternalism of the past, but it did little for human rights and didn't eliminate the notion of 'protection', which would remain for years as part of the system of administering the affairs of Indigenous Australians. Central to 'protection' was that each state (and the missions) retained responsibility for administering their local Indigenous Australian communities, which included Aboriginal protection boards. Inevitably, assimilation, let alone Indigenous rights, became a lower-order priority among the states.

Just a year after Hasluck's announcement, the Australian Council for Civil Liberties released a confronting pamphlet that documented the health and housing challenges faced by Indigenous Australians in the outback. These were not idle issues that could be solved with a handout: leprosy, tuberculosis, and venereal disease were rife. Housing conditions and nutrition were so poor that diseases that had been common in the nineteenth century, such as scurvy and beri-beri, were prevalent.[11] The evidence was real, but the discussion was muted. Other than a vigorous exchange of letters in the West Australian press, the pamphlet received little coverage.

Although the federal government decided in 1953 to fund the missions so they could take responsibility for improving Indigenous health and education, there was still no measurable improvement in their quality of life. And when the United Kingdom came calling on Prime Minister Menzies to host the nuclear tests, there was no equivocation — even when the tests were to be held on Indigenous Australians' reserves. No one asked those communities if they wanted a nuclear bomb exploded on their homelands.

The vast, apparently uninhabited areas of the outback were considered safe and appropriate for such tests. Britain was so keen on Maralinga that it asked Menzies in 1954 to make it the permanent testing site, and Menzies agreed. Maralinga was considered a place far beyond the boundaries of any kind of settlement. It seemed to be days away from anywhere, a hot, dry, inhospitable place that was unable to sustain a settled population. In short, it was an ideal atomic testing ground. Or it was if you believed that the movements of radioactive clouds were predictable and no one lived anywhere nearby.

Maralinga was 1,000 kilometres north of Adelaide, a long drive on some difficult tracks but not completely isolated. And as some scientists soon started to work out, the winds that blew through the area could move the atomic cloud a lot closer to where people lived than they had originally thought. What no one really considered was the way Indigenous Australians moved through the area, crisscrossing the region in search of food and shelter, as they had always done. The Indigenous Australians were the only people most likely to be directly affected by any atomic fallout. No one — not the British scientists, not the politicians, and no one on the ground — had any idea how many communities were out there in that flat, red place where the bombs were going to go off.

There was one man at the start of the tests who had the job of keeping an eye on the Indigenous Australian communities. He was Walter MacDougall, a former missionary from Melbourne, and he had been given the role of patrol officer in the region. MacDougall had been educated at Scotch College in Launceston and then its equivalent in Melbourne, but he was anything but a privileged young man. He worked on a mission in the Kimberley in Western Australia, where he honed his outdoor skills and began to develop an affinity with the local Indigenous communities.

MacDougall could be crotchety and combative, but he was also shrewd and resourceful. He started to pick up some language in 1940 when he moved to the Ernabella mission, in the north-west corner of South Australia, where he was dealing with the Pitjantjatjara people. MacDougall was keen to enlist for World War II but was ruled out by a rifle accident that badly damaged his right hand. He went back to Melbourne and worked with army transport, driving trucks between Alice Springs and Darwin. After the war and a stint back at Ernabella, MacDougall was employed by the Weapons Research Establishment at Woomera, South Australia, where guided missile testing was being conducted, with the brief of controlling any impact the testing had on the 'habits of Aborigines and any areas of special interest to them'.[12]

MacDougall was also given the grand and patrician title of Protector of South Australian Aborigines, which meant he had two bosses: the Aborigines Protection Board and the Woomera superintendent. The implied scale of his job title was only exceeded by the distance he had to travel to do it. Yet MacDougall had to wait three years before he was given a vehicle to cover his patch. Frustrated, he told his bosses that a camel might be the only solution.

His lack of mobility failed to dampen MacDougall's willingness to work with local communities and to try to understand how and where they lived. One particular site, at Ooldea, illustrated just how hard it was to know how many Indigenous Australians there were and where they were. In 1919 Daisy Bates had begun working with local groups there, but in 1933 the United Aboriginal Missions set up a mission that provided rations for visiting communities. It also offered dormitories where local children were unsuccessfully encouraged to abandon their language and culture.[13] The location was important: Ooldea was on the edge of the Nullarbor Plain and the Great Victoria Desert. Ooldea's fresh water made it an important place both for Indigenous Australians — it was a meeting place, lying at the intersection of a number of communities, including the Pila Nguru people to the north and north-west — and for whites, who established a station nearby for the Trans-Australian Railway that ran from Port Augusta to Perth.

The railway and the missions, including Ooldea, changed the patterns of Indigenous Australians' migration. Populations shifted and moved. Old migration paths were altered. By 1952, when the mission closed, the Indigenous Australians had dispersed. Some went 140 kilometres south, to Yalata station, closer to the coast, but it was impossible to know if the lands that were left — and which became the nuclear testing grounds — were in fact 'uninhabited wastelands'.[14] This was now ostensibly MacDougall's job: to find out just how many Indigenous Australians might be in the vicinity of the Woomera rocket range and, later, the test sites.

After undertaking a patrol in 1952 that covered 3,485 kilometres and took him into an area in the southern part of the Central Reserve that was a vast 155,399 square kilometres, MacDougall admitted he was mystified about how many Indigenous Australians were in the huge area. 'Owing to the gradual drift South, which I believe has been going on for hundreds of years almost imperceptibly, but has accelerated when white contacts occur, it *is* difficult to determine the boundaries of tribal country,' he wrote in his official report.[15] By any measure, it was an impossible task. His job inevitably became something more practical: trying to keep Indigenous Australians safe, however many there were and wherever they were.

MacDougall had no doubt that the nuclear tests were making an important contribution to world security. And he saw the best way of achieving his task of keeping the Indigenous Australians safe from the tests as threefold: reconnaissance, census, and vigilance. His approach was to try to find out where the Indigenous Australians were, and — if they were in potential danger — to find incentives to lure them away from risks. If that didn't work, MacDougall would intervene directly — by withholding rations, manipulating Indigenous Australians' beliefs, and directly intercepting their movements.[16]

The rations were a strong incentive for Indigenous Australians to turn up at some central locations, such as Ooldea, where food was part of the mission's regular offering. Finding ways to end rationing would remove an incentive for the communities to move in and around danger zones, MacDougall believed. He thought some local communities had given him a special place in their community, a nominal membership that afforded him some special insights in to their thinking and culture. MacDougall wanted to use those insights to help move the Indigenous Australians out of danger. He described it as using 'their own beliefs and fears of invisible spirits and invisible avengers … [to] convince them that the area is no safe place for them'.[17] The power of this approach grew once the stories started to circulate about the first tests at Emu Field in 1953, and what would become known among the locals as the 'poison'.

The final element of MacDougall's strategy was to prevent the former Ooldean community from reconnecting with their former lands. He had tried to recover the old spiritual elements from the site and create some new elements at Yalata, but members of the community drifted back there, risking exposure to any bomb. MacDougall decided to establish a series of ration points around Yalata, which enabled the communities to continue their migratory existence and have access to some rations, while remaining connected to the land.[18] This didn't happen until 1955, however, when the first of the Maralinga bombs was not that far away. And MacDougall was just one man.

A.P. Elkin was an Anglican minister and the first chair of anthropology at the University of Sydney. He studied in London and did extensive fieldwork among the Kimberley communities in Western Australia. Elkin considered himself a campaigner for Indigenous Australians' social justice, and shared Hasluck's faith in assimilation. But his views, by modern standards, were painfully short-sighted. In 1939 he had advised the then interior minister, Jack McEwen, about Indigenous issues, and was well connected to the Canberra mandarins. When *The Sydney Morning Herald* was searching for someone to write a long article on the history of Indigenous Australians for its royal tour souvenir in 1954, it chose Elkin. Australia, he wrote, had moved on from:

... protesting against this atrocity or that injustice, or against some outrageous treatment of aborigines ... about assimilation and citizenship and about the best methods of attaining these and other objectives ... Indeed, today, as far as legislation goes, there is not much to be done: the problem is mainly one of personal relations and adjustment. This includes a two-way process between the aborigines and ourselves.

When discussions started about someone to help MacDougall, Elkin was approached and nominated one of his former Sydney University students, Robert Macaulay. While the appointment was recognition that MacDougall could not do the job alone, it looked suspiciously like window-dressing. It seemed implausible that one other man could make a significant difference to either determining Indigenous Australians' numbers or keeping them safe. That suspicion only grew when Macaulay's inexperience was revealed.

Macaulay was only 23. He had gone to the University of Sydney on a Commonwealth scholarship, and had studied two years of ancient history before switching to anthropology. The anthropology course was still in its early phase — third-year undergraduates could study a term of what was called 'Aboriginal language structure', but it was of little practical use for those working in the field. And Macaulay hadn't enrolled in that subject. In fact, Macaulay wasn't even certain what he would do with his degree.

Elkin's intervention changed all that. Macaulay would be employed by the Department of Supply, which had overall government control of the tests. He understood that part of his brief was 'to take measures as you deem practicable and necessary to prevent any natives suffering physical harm from scientific tests'.[19] Macaulay would leave his fiancée, Jean, behind in Sydney. He had a driver's licence but had never owned a car. Macaulay was uncertain if the official policy for dealing with Indigenous Australians was 'assimilation' or 'integration' — both words were bandied about, yet they appeared to mean different things to different people.

Macaulay was interested in Indigenous Australians' extended kinship systems, their mythology, and their ability to survive in the desert.[20] But he had had no previous contact with traditional communities, and he was about to work with a man he had never met, thrown into an inhospitable tract of 1 million square kilometres to try to protect communities of people whose language he couldn't speak.

Macaulay was appointed as a native patrol officer and given the same salary at MacDougall. He arrived at the Giles Weather Station on 31 August 1956, ten days before the first scheduled blast at Maralinga. Whatever MacDougall knew about the looming nuclear tests was not communicated to his new colleague. And Macaulay's employment contract contained no mention of the Maralinga tests.

*

Frank Beaurepaire's regular barber was at the stately Windsor Hotel, in Spring Street, Melbourne. He walked there around lunchtime on Tuesday 29 May 1956, for his usual trim. Sir Frank had invited a long-time friend, Sir George Holland, who was president of the Returned Sailors' Soldiers' and Airmen's Imperial League of Australia, to have lunch with him at the Windsor.

Sir Frank's star was in the ascendant — again. In August he was set to return to the lord mayoralty he had held 14 years earlier, and to become the first former Olympian to be the host city mayor of the Games. There couldn't have been a finer way for Sir Frank to cap off his stellar career as a sportsman, as a businessman, and as an agitator for change in the city he called home. The two other men who had been part of that winning bid in Rome seven years earlier — Raymond Connelly and James Disney (both of them knighted and former lord mayors) — had both passed away. Sir Frank had also seen off some of his rivals, men who had taken a conventional, even staid approach to Melbourne's evolution. They hadn't shared Sir Frank's vision for an energetic, modern city, nor for his grand obsession with Melbourne hosting the Games. This had been, in many ways, his purpose in life. One report enthusiastically described Sir Frank as a 'friendly little man who shuns the limelight [and] sidesteps publicity', which was only partly true — he was indeed a friendly little man.[21]

Sir Frank settled into the chair and started joking with the barber. It was just another appointment — and then something went wrong. Sir Frank slumped forward in the chair. The barber tried to help, a passing doctor excused himself because he was a surgeon and claimed he couldn't be of any use, and then an ambulance was called. But it was all too late. Moments later Sir George Holland walked through the barber's door and saw his old friend stricken by a cardiac arrest. Sir Frank Beaurepaire was dead, aged 65.

Sir Frank, whose health had steadily deteriorated in the previous few years, had one final gesture in store: a donation of £15,000 to build change rooms and showers at Albert Park, as part of a memorial to athletes who had died in World War II and the Korean War. Work had already started on the building, and Sir Frank was due to lay the foundation stone on 10 June.[22] He had also pledged £200,000 to improve the University of Melbourne's sporting facilities, the biggest donation in the institution's history. The largesse was impressive, but it put a significant strain on his family's finances and forced his son Ian to sell a big parcel of shares in Olympic Tyre & Rubber.[23]

The responses to Sir Frank's death came from across the political spectrum, and expressed widespread admiration for his achievements. Acting prime minister Sir Arthur Fadden crystallised the sense of loss at such an important time. 'The tragedy is that the culmination of his dreams of seeing Australia as host to the Olympics will not be realised,' Fadden said.[24] For a city about to host the Games to lose its greatest champion was a sombre moment indeed.

*

In 1956 the standard dinner for most Australian families was meat and vegetables. Cutlets, chops, sausages, and stews were the proteins on the plate. It was all very well for Melbourne to think of itself as a 'cosmopolitan' city, but the reality, when it came to food, fell some way short. How would the Olympic host families cater for their international visitors when their tastes were expected to be so different? Should hostesses offer something uniquely Australian? One cooking expert suggested damper, another creamed crayfish with mushrooms, another a traditional but improved roast lamb, and another a meringue shell filled with homemade ice cream, passionfruit, and cream.[25] These offerings used some distinctive local ingredients, to be sure, but what if visitors really didn't like them?

This crisis of kitchen confidence was addressed on the day after Sir Frank's death, when the principal of Melbourne's prestigious culinary training college, the William Angliss Food Trades School, spoke to the Travel League of Victoria. Mr H.E. West wanted to reassure his audience that Australia had such a bounty of produce that no one, neither hostess nor continental visitor, should have any fear about what to put on the table. European immigrants had already made a significant contribution to the range of vegetables and the variety of herbs on the national dinner plate. This great food was complemented by a natural bounty of fruit, fish, cheese, and meat. 'Truly we have a land which is running over with milk and honey,' Mr West gushed. 'Just as important, at no time in the recorded history of man has the ordinary fellow on the street or the land had more of the means of exchange to partake of this abundance of nutritional wealth.' He urged families who were hosting Olympic visitors to 'not be ashamed of your Australian garnered processed foods'.

There were traps to be avoided: Mr West suggested Olympic hosts avoid cooking vegetables in the morning to be served hot at the evening meal, or expect 'browned up boiled meat' to taste like a roast. William Angliss would also help potential hosts with a series of demonstrations in September of dishes that were popular in Europe and the 'Near East'. 'The purpose is to help prepare for the visitor who because of language difficulties may become a little homesick,' Mr West explained.[26]

When the time came, 90 'hostesses' — including three men — turned up to the first class to find out what they should offer their guests. The courses were run by an accredited chef over several weeks, and showed the hostesses how to prepare, cook, and serve the kind of exotic fare that was far removed from what they were used to. There were instructions on how to plan a buffet to take the strain out of hostessing, how to prepare and decorate a turkey and ham, and then a menu that included a consommé with marrow dumplings, the 'king of savouries', oyster cream, followed by Queensland barramundi with a piquant sauce ravigote and then a Viennese puff pastry.[27] This was continental fare with flair, and superior to what was on offer in many Melbourne restaurants. It sounded more appetising than what the Olympic athletes were going to get.

The Olympic Organising Committee had its own catering committee, which was supposed to finding international cooks for the athletes' village — and ideally who would then take jobs in Melbourne restaurants. The committee convened in August 1954, just a little more than two years before the Games. As it turned out, this wasn't enough time to get the knives, forks, chopsticks, and spoons in order.

There was a flurry of anxiety in the committee's first few meetings about how it was going to find cooks with the required skills. Early attempts at solving the problem involved a complicated process whereby the Department of Immigration vetted potential cooks in their country of origin. The strategy failed to deliver: nine months out from the Games, the committee admitted that the cooks who had arrived from overseas were 'not satisfactory'.[28]

The scale of the problem wasn't just about the shortage of cooks — the cuisine they cooked was also an issue. The plan for the athletes' village dining was based on 11 distinct dietary groups across 18,000 daily meals. That translated into a range of offerings, from prawn fritters, to curry, to kangaroo tail soup. The actual daily amounts were calculated to the nearest ounce — 9 pounds and 5 ounces, to be precise, of food (and apparently drink) for every athlete, every day. And although no one in Victoria could get an alcoholic drink without a meal after 6 pm, athletes in the village would get a beer or wine, as long as it was part of their national diet.[29]

This highly detailed analysis of athletes' dietary needs was an understated attempt at fairness after the Americans had sent 15,000 chocolate bars to their athletes and flew fresh bread daily to London for the 1948 Olympics.[30] London had been subject to post-war rationing, but, even so, this was not an example Melbourne wanted to emulate.

As organised as the menus were, they still needed someone to cook them. After the initial strategy failed, the committee decided to send Melbourne hotelier Tom Carlyon to interview cooks in England, Italy, Germany, Switzerland, Holland, Denmark, Sweden, Austria, France, and Greece. The department of immigration's role was to help smooth over any hurdles. Carlyon left Melbourne with a shopping list of 110 cooks.

The early reports were promising. Carlyon's trip cost a whopping £1,866, but he did find some decent recruits. The committee did the maths, dividing the cost of the trip by Carlyon's number of cooks, and found that the recruitment of each cook cost £15. This was 'less than the cost of the return fare of a cook from Brisbane to Melbourne but th[e] quality of the cooks is infinitely greater than could have been gained elsewhere in Australia', the committee was told.[31]

The arithmetic might have been correct, but it represented only a partial solution, because there were still significant shortfalls. There were plenty of European cooks, but what about everyone else? The Games were expected to have the highest percentage of Asian athletes of any Olympics to date, and no one had yet been hired to cook Asian food. There was a palpable sense of what was either overconfidence or the catering equivalent of whistling in the dark.

Plans to engage overseas visitors were progressing with more certainty, even when the initiative came from the community rather than an Olympic bureaucrat. A local schoolteacher and his wife had gone on holiday to Denmark in 1955 and seen a tourist program called 'Meet the Danes'. It became the inspiration for Melbourne's 'Meet the Australian', which aimed to serve any tourist who was interested in meeting a local family, or visiting a local business, or spending time in a nearby tourist destinations. Farmers, students, artists, and professional men and women were all matched with a local volunteer who could help them. Some 8,000 posters with 'Meet the Australian' across a background of two hands clasped together circulated across the city, and 5,000 car stickers were handed out. There were another 5,000 'courtesy badges' that carried the word 'visitor' to alert locals to the strangers in their midst, to whom they could offer help.[32] It was a reminder that it might be Melbourne's Olympics, but the nation's hospitality was on display too.

Winter
1956

Chapter Five
It's a Men's Game

Robert Menzies reached London in June 1956, two days before the Lord's Test match of the Ashes series. Menzies assumed a seat on the Australian team's balcony at the fabled home of cricket for the first day's play after Australian captain Ian Johnson won the toss and opted to bat. It was a pleasant day to be an Australian: England skipper Peter May dropped three catches, and, after an interlude for bad light, Australia reached stumps in reasonable order at 3–180.

England held the Ashes after a 3–1 trouncing of Australia at home in 1954–55, and the tourists had not started the 1956 tour in great form, failing to defeat a county in the lead-up to the Tests, and recording their first loss to an English county side since 1912. The First Test, at Nottingham, had ended in a draw, so the teams went to Lord's for the Second Test with the series well and truly alive.

On the Saturday evening of the Test Menzies hosted a reception for the Australians at the Savoy. Earlier that day he had sat with Indian prime minister Jawaharlal Nehru and Sir Donald Bradman, and watched Australia struggle in its second innings, after going in again with a lead of 114 runs over England.

Reports emerged that the British authorities, mindful of Menzies' love of cricket, had installed a television in the Daimler that was his vehicle while in London. It turned out that, despite his wariness about television, Menzies paid £70 to have the TV put in the car.

He left the ground early on Saturday and turned on the television, expecting to watch some cricket. Instead, Menzies saw *Robin Hood*. It was the children's hour.[1]

Menzies' official business in London was the Commonwealth Prime Ministers' Conference, an event that brought together the leaders of Britain, Australia, New Zealand, Canada, India, South Africa, Pakistan, Ceylon, and the Rhodesian Federation. Such was Menzies' reputation in Britain, fresh reports emerged that he was contemplating retiring from politics in Australia and assuming a position in the British House of Lords.

Menzies usually timed his trips to England to coincide with the cricket. The game offered a particular form of relaxation that he could not find anywhere else. 'It is occasionally left to people like me to carry with them through life a love and growing understanding of the great game — a feeling in the heart and mind and the eye which neither time nor chance can utterly destroy,' he wrote.[2] The game not only engaged him but provided him with a store of pleasant memories. 'It is one of the glories of cricket that, when one looks back at it, one remembers the hours, not as something static but as something alive, and vivid, and full of action,' he said in retirement.[3] Cricket was also, of course, a fundamentally English game that underlined Menzies' belief in the supremacy of the Empire and its civilising effect on the rest of the world.

But his enthusiasm for sport extended beyond cricket, to tennis, golf, and Australian Rules football — in particular, the Carlton Football Club. A special platform was made in Menzies' later years at Carlton's home ground, Princes Park, on which Menzies' driver could park his Bentley so the former PM could watch the Blues play. Menzies moved among sportsmen with an ease but found particular comfort among cricketers, despite his inability to play the game with any skill. He established the Prime Minister's XI match in 1951, a contest between an international touring team and a local side he helped to pick. The innovation enabled Menzies to get even closer to the men he admired. The presidency of the Australian Olympic

Federation might have come a close second to his own cricket match, but the honour ensured Menzies had an extra level of connection to the approaching Games.

Menzies' interest in sport meant that he shared something fundamental with many Australians. The nation's international sporting success gave the prime minister a cachet, especially among his Commonwealth brethren. He could revel in some of the reflected sporting glory. Australia's sporting triumphs, so often beyond what a small, remote nation should realistically have achieved, were an ideal way for him to promote the nation. The suggestion was that a land with an emphasis on the vast outdoors, with endless sunshine, and with a happy bounty of fresh fruit and quality meat, was the sort of nation where athletes could thrive. Arthur Hodson, the secretary of the Amateur Athletic Union of Australia, had no doubt about how sport carried the nation's image to the world, saying in 1950:

> Sport has become Australia's biggest and best medium of world publicity. I doubt if there is a worthwhile newspaper or radio anywhere in the world that has not had to pay some tribute to Australia during the past 12 months. Now no one can deny that our successes this year have been worth a thousand times more than the Government spends yearly on publicity through the Department of Information.[4]

Others saw Australians' preoccupation with sport not so much as a flippant activity but as an indicator of national maturity. 'Australians are sometimes twitted [sic] by overseas visitors for spending too much time on sport to the neglect of other pursuits which might fill their leisure more profitably,' G.V. Portus, the University of Adelaide's former professor of political science and history, observed.

> The gibe is not new … It derives from the grim outlook of the earlier stages of the industrial revolution, when God-fearing

puritans worked little children for 14 hours a day in cotton mills. Moreover, as a gibe, it might (and in fact is) directed against many other countries besides ours. For a growing preoccupation with sport is characteristic of this stage of modern civilisation.[5]

Sporting success only increased Australians' interest, not just in watching it but in taking part. And in the pre-television era, watching sport meant going along, either buying a ticket or watching park sport for free. A 1954 Melbourne survey found that 40 per cent of people spent their leisure time watching sport, but twice that number were actually playing it.[6] It was evidence of a nation that wore its sporting commitment lightly, and whose anticipation of success rarely waned. This was particularly true in the Australian winter of 1956, when the nation's cricketers, tennis players, and golfers were in Britain, still considered by many back home as the ultimate proving ground for Australian sports men and women.

Not only was it an Ashes year, but Australian tennis players were also expected to do well at Wimbledon's All England Club. Lew Hoad, Ken Rosewall, and Ken McGregor were part of the boom in Australian tennis. They were at home on grass courts, masters of the serve and volley, tireless and usually impregnable. And on the links courses that were the home of golf, Peter Thomson had few rivals. Another British Open title — his third in a row — beckoned.

There was an unspoken belief in Australia that the country had an assembly line of talent that the rest of the world envied. Emerging talents came from the suburban blocks or the paddocks, rough, ready, steely-eyed, without a hint of wavering in their commitment to being the best. They might be unsophisticated, raw even, but they were world-beaters in the making. Look at that kid over there, the story went, he's been playing cricket since the sun came up and he'll be playing until it goes down again. He'll be a champion. Every success story had its tale of precocious industry — a young Don Bradman practising with a golf ball and a cricket stump against a corrugated-iron tank at Bowral; Ken Rosewall playing tennis as a three-year-old, naturally left-handed but drilled by his father to become a right-hander; Peter Thomson becoming a club champion at 16.

The sporting system might have appeared haphazard to the casual observer, but there was method and organisation behind spotting and training talent. When tennis coaching legend Harry Hopman cast his eye over Queensland's best tennis teenagers in 1954, he picked out two boys: Frank Gorman, 14, and Rod Laver, 15. Both had left school to pursue tennis and landed jobs in sports shops, like others had before them. Hopman could clearly spot talent – Laver became one of the finest male players of all time. Hopman's confidence that potential could be translated into something permanent was based on the Queensland system that provided incentive and opportunity for young tennis players.[7] There was a structure that provided the support, coaching, and competition that underpinned success. There was one other element, common across all the sports that Australians were playing internationally at the time: all of them — Hoad, Rosewall, Thompson, the cricketers — were amateurs. But that wouldn't last. The era of professional sport was coming.

A new level of Australian success beckoned in July 1956. Athletes including John Landy, Dave Stephens, and Jim Bailey, had set new records; the swimmers, including Lorraine Crapp, Murray Rose, and David Theile, were setting new marks in the pool; the Australians went on to win the Second Test; Hoad defeated Rosewall to win the men's singles at Wimbledon, and then teamed with him to win the men's doubles. On the same Wimbledon Sunday Thomson won his third straight British Open.

The celebrations underlined just how much sport meant to reinforcing Australia's sense of itself. 'How proud we are of our unofficial ambassadors of cinder-track, centre court, oval, pool and fairway! These clean-limbed stout-hearted young people have made Australia known around the globe as a land of champions. They've given us — at the best possible time — a pre-Olympics boost impossible to evaluate in terms of cash,' *The Argus* shouted.[8]

This rejoicing, maybe even triumphalism, pointed to a significant emotional investment in how Australian athletes would perform in Melbourne. The expectations were high, especially as success was popularly linked to Australia's international kudos. It didn't matter what else Australia did or was known for around the world, the path to international recognition seemed to be through the nation's sporting achievements.

*

Television's infancy meant that communicating and sharing that success was in the hands of the newspapers and radio. Precious few would be able to see what was going on if they weren't at the MCG or the pool. Yet some nursed concerns that televising sport may actually have a negative impact on sport itself.

The arrival of televised sport in the US in 1948 triggered divergent views about its impact on gate takings and spectator numbers. Some sporting organisations blamed television for a drop in patronage, while others were thankful for the sponsorship or advertising dollars that came with being televised. Sports fans were in no doubt: 'Sport is the best thing TV does,' one Los Angeles correspondent claimed.[9] It gave you the best seat in the house, with several cameras for different angles, and usually you didn't miss a moment.

The man who would find himself televising some of the Games, Colin Bednall, was equally enthusiastic:

Spectator sports, like tennis, boxing, wrestling and football are nothing short of sensational [on television]. Sitting back comfortably at home, the television viewer sees incidents and even facial expressions that are denied to the crowd around the arena. Even people who would never think of joining a sports crowd are mesmerised by sport on television.[10]

Bednall had gone from the royal commission on television to the leadership of one of what Wilfrid Kent Hughes referred to as 'infant TV stations'. At any other time such a swift two-step would have been considered unseemly, perhaps even a conflict of interest, but if the commission had revealed anything, it was Bednall's clear agenda. Bednall believed in the need for commercial television, not a government-run monopoly; no one was under any illusions about that. One of his fellow commissioners, chairman of the Australian Broadcasting Control Board, Robert Osborne, found it all wearisome and aggravating. 'We continue to be embarrassed by Bednall, who not only cross-examines crossly as before, and discloses a patent bias by continual argument with witnesses,' Osborne wrote to commission chair George Paton, who was overseas at that time.[11]

Osborne outlined Bednall's latest transgression, which involved Bednall complaining about remarks the postmaster general (and therefore the minister responsible for television), Larry Anthony, made at a private dinner party given by the broadcasters. Bednall had taken issue with Anthony's remark that the commission had been established to tell the government what it already knew. Bednall was unnecessarily sensitive about the commission being no more than a rubber stamp, as the framework for the Australian TV system was already well underway.

Legislation for the introduction of television was brought to the federal parliament on 18 February 1953, three weeks before the commission sat for the first time, and a year before its final report was released. It overturned the Chifley Labor government's bill to establish a government-controlled television station in each state, which would have prevented any commercial player from entering the field. Not only that, but in September 1953 — after the commission had finished its public hearings but before it had reported — federal cabinet affirmed that it would go ahead with a dual system, comprising commercial and public stations.[12]

Bednall claimed to the acting prime minister, Sir Arthur Fadden, that Anthony's remarks put him and the commission in an invidious position. Osborne pooh-poohed the idea. He had been at the dinner and assured Paton that the minister's remarks were 'facetious, as well as private'.[13] Osborne was not particularly interested in the mechanics of broadcasting, and was particularly keen not to offend his political masters. He had a distaste for Bednall's front-on approach to the issues thrown up at the commission's hearings. Nor did Osborne care for breaches of protocol, such as making public reference to private speeches.

Bednall, on the other hand, had spent a career tilting at governments. He didn't like the sound of the minister's statement because it suggested the commission didn't have a role to play. It most certainly did, but it didn't have much to do with making the case for introducing television to Australia: that was already decided. Instead, it was trying to identify a system that enabled competition between the commercial networks (a hard task with a disparate regional and rural population and the high cost of television), as well as advise the government on how best to regulate the commercial networks.[14] The broader consideration behind these challenges was how to make best use of television broadcasting in the public interest. Commercial operators could not just be on the new airwaves, pushing out material without regard for content and audience. The most pithy solution to this problem came from Noel Nixon, the president of the Australian Association of Advertising Agencies, who told the commission: 'We believe that self-regulation takes care of morals and competition is going to take care of quality.'[15]

Bednall's views about such things were what might be expected of someone who had written for and edited mass-market newspapers:

What is beyond doubt is that most people would react adversely to earmarking huge sums of public money to establish and maintain a service which was out of touch with popular taste. One wonders for instance the reaction of the Australian public to a TV service which presented *Mourning Becomes Electra* over two nights in the main listening hours. Yet this was regarded as one of the really big achievements in the BBC television service.[16]

Bednall had no time for elitism or high-end aesthetics when it came to engaging the public. The BBC could do it, because it was the government's broadcasting authority. If people were going to pay to own a television, they would expect to be entertained. A government-funded television station would take care of the high culture so that Bednall and his commercial network didn't have to.

Of course, Bednall did not come to the table with clean hands: he was working for Murdoch in Brisbane when he was appointed a commissioner. Sir Keith had been an aggressive defender of his own print business interests when ABC's radio service was established in 1932, and the newspaper — and radio — tools he had at his disposal to prosecute his case in the looming battle for television licences were formidable. Bednall might have thought he was being the noble patron of a multifaceted commercial television industry, but it didn't take much imagination to suspect he might actually be helping the newspaper industry.

Bednall did not think the ABC should have a monopoly, nor get a head start on its commercial competitors.[17] His questioning of ABC general manager Charles Moses and ABC chairman Richard Boyer in the commission was pointed and argumentative. The commission's final report was more nuanced than Bednall's point of view, and recommended the gradual introduction of television across Australia. This would supposedly help ensure some level of sustainability and quality programming. Osborne's Australian Broadcasting Control Board would be the regulator of quality. Moses' ABC would be the national broadcaster that would be funded by viewers' licence fees. Two commercial stations would be established in Melbourne and Sydney, with similar ownership constraints that applied to radio. Other stations in other cities would follow. These recommendations were delivered in 1954, with the intention of the nation being ready for the new medium in time for the Olympics.

*

On 25 June 1956 a handwritten letter arrived at the Customs and Excise offices of the Commonwealth government in Melbourne. Its tone was urgent, even demanding. 'Dear Sir, I am writing to request you to forward a novel which you extracted from a parcel of books, posted to me by a friend in the USA,' the letter began. The letter-writer, believed to be a young man from regional Victoria, was inquiring about his missing copy of *The Catcher in the Rye*, which Customs had confiscated some months earlier. Not that the book was named. It was not even clear that the writer knew which book was missing. He had some correspondence from Customs, he wrote, which explained the book had been kept to be reviewed, but the office had had it for five months now, so perhaps the review was over and he could have his book back? 'I contacted my friend [in the USA] and he stated that no book in the parcel was objectionable and all could be purchased anywhere in the US. He was astounded that one had been taken.'[18]

It didn't really matter what the gentleman's friend in the USA said — those Americans were part of the problem, with their louche behaviour that encouraged people to write about such things with such unchecked candour. The office hadn't finished with the book. Not by a long way. In fact, it had been sent to the Comptroller-General of Customs, Sir Francis Meere, in Canberra, who would make an adjudication on whether the book would be allowed into the country.

All of this was done in secret. No one beyond those who had seen the book at Customs and the young man in regional Victoria had any knowledge of what was happening. That was the way the process worked. It kept Australia free from the problem of fraying morals that was, it seemed, besetting many nations and their artistes. By association, it was the faceless bureaucrats who knew what was good for the rest of the country, and especially for one young man who wasn't even sure what he was missing out on. He wouldn't get his copy of *The Catcher in the Rye* any time in 1956.

It was perhaps just as well no one knew that one of the United States' more successful novels was about to be banned in Australia. There was an enormous effort being mounted to get Australia — and Melbourne, in particular — on the world tourism map. Having an international debate about censorship six months out from an Olympics might well have been unwelcome publicity. The Olympic Games Organizing Committee had a subcommittee which focused on promoting Australia as a destination, with Melbourne and the Games as the centrepiece. At its first meeting, held at the Melbourne Town Hall on the propitious date of 26 January 1954, the committee resolved that its goal was to 'convince people abroad that we were going to stage the Games properly and to work up enthusiasm for the Games in Australia itself'.[19]

Central to these goals was a perception within the Melbourne Olympic organisation that the world didn't think the city (or the nation) could pull off the Games. There was a lingering lack of confidence among some Melbournians, who felt that the danger of falling short of delivering an eye-catching Olympics would, in some ways, confirm the view that Melbourne was a backwater in every sense — cultural, economic, political, and sporting.

Local journalists who had covered previous Olympics made it clear exactly what was at stake for Melbourne. 'The Melbourne festival … will be the most international sporting series staged in this country,' Melbourne journalist Peter Banfield wrote in *The Argus*. 'That is important, but more important still is the immense amount of publicity it will gain us overseas in countries in which Olympics are almost a religion.' Banfield had been in Helsinki and had a good idea of the impact a successful Games could have on a host city and nation:

We will be host city to large numbers of visitors and we must do our best to impress them with our hospitality, our willingness to aid them, and with the manner in which we produce the Games. To them, their reception by Melbourne people will be as important as the size of our stadium and the success of our team.

They will judge us on a short stay and their countries will judge us on their reports and letters home.[20]

Every statement like Banfield's only increased the heat on the locals.

The benefit of having seven years to prepare for the Games was that, if you were shrewd, you could build interest and a potential audience over time. Promotional material about Melbourne was distributed at the 1954 Empire Games in Vancouver, the 1955 Pan American Games, and the Mediterranean Games of the same year. There was a map of Melbourne with the Olympic locations marked, a world map with routes converging on Melbourne, pictures of venues, and action sporting photographs, accompanied by text that gave some historical background on the Games, and information about Melbourne and accommodation options for visitors. It was printed in English, French, and Spanish but not in any Asian or other language.[21]

Radio Australia started a monthly broadcast on the Games in April 1954, which eventually went to Singapore, Sarawak, North Borneo, the Philippines, Hong Kong, Burma (Myanmar), Ceylon (Sir Lanka), and Pakistan. The Australian National Travel Association printed 165,000 copies of a travel booklet featuring the Games and the nation, and sent them to 'all leading travel agencies in the world'. It was also distributed through Australian government offices, consulates, and embassies around the world.

An Australian News and Information Bureau film about the opening of the Olympic box office in Melbourne was screened in 3,000 US cinemas. A Qantas Olympic Information Bureau opened in New York's Rockefeller Center, with 5,000 promotional booklets and 5,000 folders on Australia and the Games. Even the International Scout Jamboree in Ontario was sent 10,000 promotional folders. A thousand ham radio operators around Australia sent out special monthly postcards that included Olympic material.

The sense of activity was impressive, driven, it seemed, by a naive faith that it was just a matter of telling the world Melbourne (and Australia) was here, and people would turn up. But it didn't go anywhere nearly as well as hoped. By December 1955, just 11 months out from the Games, there were crisis talks within the publicity committee to deal with (among other things) problems around the overseas exposure the Games were getting.

There were complaints from some British travel agents that they couldn't get adequate promotional material in London. Other observers judged the publicity coverage 'inadequate', the committee heard, and 'most press stories featured unfavourable angles'.[22] Some visiting US journalists had little good to say about Melbourne, in particular, and the six o'clock swill.

There had been plenty of grim post-mortems in Finland after the 1952 Helsinki Games, where expectations of a big international contingent of 50,000 visitors were rudely deflated to estimates as low as 13,000. Criticisms from some US journalists of the shortage of entertainment in Helsinki created a degree of anxiety in Melbourne about how the city would be seen. US journalist Tom Van Dycke wrote in *Variety* magazine after the Helsinki Games that the only night-time entertainment in the city was the midnight sun. There were no licensed cafes, and alcohol, only available from government-controlled outlets, was rationed. A worried Australian Olympic official admitted: 'We are isolated from the world and handicapped by incredible drinking and entertainment laws.'[23] The spectre of Melbourne getting a version of Van Dycke's corrosive judgement on its nightlife loomed large.

The city's isolation was an important consideration. The Melbourne bid's forecast in 1949 that air travel would be quicker and more efficient by the time the Games rolled around was correct, but only up to a point. The introduction of Lockheed Super Constellation aircraft in 1954 made a difference to travel times, but the price of flying between London and Australia was almost the equivalent of buying a car, and it still took around three days to complete the journey, often in uncomfortable proximity to storms and turbulence. The inescapable conclusion was that if you wanted to come to Melbourne in 1956, you had to be reasonably wealthy, have time on your hands, and be resilient. Or live a little closer to Australia.

Sir Frank Beaurepaire had tried to dampen expectations about the number of overseas visitors, pointing out that Victoria's country men and women were the most likely Olympic patrons. 'Australia is off the beaten track and less than 20,000 people, including New Zealanders, will get out here,' he forecast in 1955. 'Melbourne will have to rely on Australians for good attendances ...'[24] Sir Frank knew Australia was still too far away and too much of a curio to engage the rest of the world. Australian National Travel Association managing director Charles Holmes spelt out another important consideration:

[I]t is well to remember that Australia is an outpost country on the travel map and that the majority of people with the time and money to travel half the world around are matured folk: they want comfort and are not much concerning with sporting events, even the most important international ones.[25]

Maybe there wouldn't be that many people to impress after all.

Qantas Empire Airways, as it was then known, launched its inaugural Super Constellation flight to Japan in May 1955. The route was Tokyo–Manila–Darwin–Sydney, and it took 27 hours. Among the first passengers were five Japanese journalists and four Filipino journalists en route to Melbourne to tour the Olympic venues. The tour was an important reminder of the bid dynamics of 1949, given the issues then surrounding the Philippines and Japan.

The 1955 visit was the first time Japanese journalists had ventured to Australia since the war. Inevitably, one of them was asked directly about Japanese brutality. 'I can see why Australians are strongly antagonistic to the Japanese. It is one of those things you can't brush off,' George Somekawa acknowledged.

Could it happen again, the Sydney journalist asked.

'I hope not. I pray not. We want to meet Australians so that international barriers can be removed. We are both trying to fight Communism,' Somekawa said.[26]

The communist threat might have turned previous combatants into allies, but there was no sense that this new-found détente was widespread in Australia.

*

Another visitor provoked more column inches and anxiety than the Japanese journalists: Avery Brundage, who by now had ascended to become president of the IOC. The chairman of the Melbourne Olympic Games organising committee, Wilfrid Kent Hughes, spent a great deal of time trying to find a way to placate the man he called 'Mr Sonavovitch'. It was no consolation that his difficulties with Brundage were pretty standard fare. The legendary US sports journalist Red Smith watched Brundage up close for many years and observed that he was 'the official target of abuse in every Olympic year since the invention of the discus'.

Brundage had competed in the 1912 Olympics for the United States as a decathlete and pentathlete, and was a Freemason, a Chicago hotelier, and developer. If he had a faith, it was in amateurism. It framed his world view, coloured his judgement, skewed his common sense, and, on occasions, put the Olympic movement under profound pressure.

That was only part of Brundage's problem. In 1934, as president of the American Olympic Association, Brundage went to Berlin to check out the status of Jewish athletes in the Third Reich. There was growing support for an American boycott of the 1936 Games because of Hitler's rise to power and increasing fears for the safety of the Jews across Germany. The US team's participation in the Games would send a powerful message to many Western democracies which were starting to feel squeamish about what was going on in Berlin. Equally, the US withdrawal from the Games would show resolve in the face of Hitler's bullying, wheedling, and aggression.

Brundage spent six days in Berlin, inspected some Olympic facilities, visited a museum, and seemed to run out of time for a deeper look at just what was happening to Jewish athletes in the capital or anywhere else. When some Jewish athletes told Brundage that they were barred from joining German sports clubs, the AOA president replied: 'In my club in Chicago Jews are not permitted either.' He returned home and told his Olympic committee that the German Jews were happy enough with their situation, and that the AOA should accept Germany's invitation to take part in the 1936 Olympics.[27]

A more outward-looking Melbourne Olympic organisation might well have devised ways to treat Brundage differently, but the organisation instead opted to defer to Brundage's belligerence and became hostage to his explosive missives, public-relations strategy, and toe-curling visits, almost all of which were larded with threats about taking the Games away from Melbourne. To be fair, he had some basis for frustration. The constant to-ing and fro-ing over where the main stadium would be, issues around the cost of the Games, the quarantine restrictions that eventually necessitated the Olympic equestrian competition being moved to Stockholm, and the trade union disputes on building Olympic facilities were a source of almost endless annoyance to the American. But these were even more frustrating for Kent Hughes and his committee, who struggled for several years to find their way through the haphazard and seemingly endless delays, obfuscations, and changes.

The clash between Brundage and Kent Hughes, in particular, was a battle between Brundage's bustling can-do urgency that characterised his business approach and Kent Hughes' more reactive strategy. For Kent Hughes, the role of leading Melbourne's Olympic bid demanded a capacity to balance competing interests, seeking some form of consensus while trying to rein in a natural urge to speak his mind. It was a public role that he saw in old-fashioned terms of public duty. Brundage was belligerent by instinct, and couldn't have cared less about treading on toes: he wanted the job done, quick smart, and for the greater good of amateurism and the Olympic movement. The two men might have shared a commitment to the amateur ideal and, consequently, to the Olympic goals, but that was about their only common ground. They were never going to become firm friends.

Brundage's espousal of amateurism's virtues was often married with an American zest for personal liberty and faith in free enterprise. He seemed to believe that the Olympics were above the exercise of base politics, but in practically all his dealings with the Melbourne organising committee Brundage displayed a refined sense of how to bully, belittle, and abuse those who were committed to the same Olympic cause.

When it became clear that Australian quarantine rules would prevent overseas horses being brought into Australia in time for the Games, Brundage wrote to Kent Hughes: 'Some [IOC members] have already stated that they would prefer to have the Games cancelled than to violate the Olympic rules that all events must be held in the same city.'[28] Kent Hughes reasonably replied: '[B]ut any serious suggestion to change the venue of the Games at this stage would wreck the whole of the confidence in the Olympic organisation.'[29] Brundage kept on about it, just in case Kent Hughes was unaware of the gravity of what Australia was asking of the international Olympic movement:

> There are many who are not very happy about this situation and when they are added to the number who felt the Games should not have been given to Melbourne in the first place because of the time, the distance and the expense involved, it makes a very considerable group that harbour unfavourable views. I trust you and the Organising Committee will always bear this in mind and that you will endeavour to make the Games even more of a success, in order to off-set this condition of affairs. In this I promise you my co-operation.[30]

Brundage's 'cooperation' might have represented a highly important ally for Melbourne among the enemies he had referred to within the IOC, but there was no mistaking his intent: Melbourne was going to be held to a higher standard than other Games because of the difficulties that had littered its path, in the years from the bid presentation to the opening ceremony.

Brundage decided to see for himself how things were working out. He arrived in Melbourne on Tuesday 5 April 1955, and stayed for six days. The city's major newspapers reported that Brundage seemed cautiously pleased with the progress of the facilities and Melbourne's general preparedness. Then, on Easter Monday, Brundage gave a press conference that caused a massive fright among the city's Olympic executives. He also made public the sentiment he had expressed to Kent Hughes about the possibility that the IOC had erred in giving Melbourne the Games. It was an old-fashioned backhander to a recalcitrant child, without giving the kid any chance to explain himself.

'The Olympic Games were given to Melbourne in 1949. That is a long time ago,' Brundage told the assembled reporters.

A group of leading citizens of Melbourne came to our meeting in Rome. They had the idea it would be a wonderful thing to get the Olympic Games here in Australia. They were pretty smart. I don't know how they did it ... Did we make a mistake? ... Those other [bid] cities, willing to spend more than $20 million on them, thought they were the greatest international event of any kind. Those citizens of Melbourne thought they were doing a service to Melbourne and Australia to bring back this great prize, but many people thought that the IOC had made a serious mistake. They thought Australia was not ready for the Games; that it was too far away.

Brundage then returned to his analysis of the problems that had beset Melbourne:

For six years we have heard nothing but squabbling, a change of management, bickering. I can tell you that today more than ever, people all over the world think we did make a mistake. I think somebody let you down and let us down too.

… I spent a week looking over the preparations and venues. How do I know [Melbourne will be ready]? You ask me to tell the world. Is that my responsibility? I don't know whether they realise here yet what the Olympic Games are. This is a movement which has swept the world. Over 80 countries are interested now.

The country that stages the Games has to spend a lot of money to stage them and it gets the benefits. It is not the only place that has to spend money. It is going to cost the United States Olympic Committee almost a million dollars to send a full team of approximately 400. Every one of the other 80 countries that comes is going to have to spend money here. The aggregate will be far more than is spent in Australia. The gate receipts, and the benefits which should last a generation or more, come to Australia and to Melbourne if the job is done properly. But will it be done properly? Frankly I don't know.

Brundage was not someone you could accuse of being subtle. In case anyone missed the message, he went back to the well:

If it [the Games] is not a success Melbourne and Australia will be a laughing stock. You have an opportunity here you should not fumble. It will be a long time before you live it down and it is going to hurt us, too.

The eyes and the ears of the world are on Melbourne and will be until these Games are over. There is only one way to redeem the honour of this community, and that is to make a smashing success of these Games.[31]

The press conference was a tour de force. Brundage knew exactly what he was doing by pinching the Melbourne Olympic committee's vulnerability. It is difficult to know just how real his threats were to take the Games off Melbourne. There had been suggestions that Detroit and Rome (which had been chosen to host the 1960 Games) were being lined up if Melbourne fell over. And Brundage theatrically referred to a cable in his pocket from a city offering itself as the saviour to Melbourne's supposed ramshackle preparation.

It is problematic to try to assess just how devastating to Melbourne and Australia's international reputation a poorly organised Olympic Games would have been. In the mid-1950s the capacity for international incidents, stuff-ups, and disasters to be communicated around the world relied on the limited electronic media coverage, newspapers, and perhaps word of mouth. Brundage was bullying the Melbourne bid team to get its act together with the threat of international criticism. Kent Hughes craved an opportunity to respond to Brundage's critique but held his tongue, knowing that a 'public controversy' with Brundage would have been 'a mistake'. There was, however, no mistaking his mood. 'I hope no country or individual will in future be treated in similar manner by IOC leaders,' Kent Hughes wrote.[32]

Don Chipp, a gifted runner, tennis player, and budding politician who was secretary of the Games civics committee, saw it all up close, and his view accorded with Brundage's assessment, especially of the first few years after the bid. 'We were slack on the job,' Chipp said some years later.[33] Kent Hughes took one positive away from Brundage's press conference: 'Brundage did one good thing in that he frightened the life out of the Treasury. In all other words, he is a B ...'[34] Kent Hughes couldn't even bring himself to spell out the full word.

Brundage headed to Canberra to talk to Menzies after dropping his Melbourne bombshell. The prime minister assured Brundage that Melbourne would deliver a successful Games, but there were no details about what that meant for the Games' budget or anything else. Exactly 12 months later, the Melbourne Olympic Games' press and publicity committee decided that it would end its overseas publicity campaign in June 1956. The rationale was that five months out from the Games would be the very latest anyone could plan and organise a flight to Melbourne. From now on, the committee would focus on what Australians thought about the Games. The rest of the world could look after itself.

Chapter Six
One-Armed Bandits

The seeds of a political disaster that would propel Menzies into an invidious role on the world stage started with an act of retribution. On 26 July 1956 Egypt's President Gamal Abdel Nasser nationalised the Suez Canal after US president Dwight D. Eisenhower cancelled a $56 million grant promised to Egypt to build the Aswan Dam. Nasser planned to use the revenue generated from nationalising the canal to compensate for the loss of the US money.

Of course, there was much more at stake than the future of the Aswan Dam. Egypt had formally recognised communist China, and Nasser was also encouraging Soviet investment in the dam. Both were provocative acts in the Cold War. Britain had been in Egypt in one form or another since 1882, and nearly two-thirds of Britain's oil came through the canal. The canal had been built (and designed) by the French, and the company that ran it was still based in Paris; the British had acquired a major interest in the company years earlier.

Conservative British prime minister Anthony Eden had been careful not to push Egypt into a Soviet embrace after it had started receiving tanks and aircraft from the Soviet bloc in 1955. But as soon as Eden heard the news about Suez — during a dinner at his Downing Street residence — he reached the view that Nasser had to be removed, probably by military action. The initial rhetoric set an appropriate diplomatic tone, but behind the scenes 20,000 British reservists were called up. Eden secretly assembled an 'inner cabinet' of five men, who would coordinate a detailed military operation. Eden had to determine if Britain could act alone when it deployed force, or whether it would have to join with the United States in a military incursion to drive Nasser from power.

Eden condemned the nationalisation of the canal in parliament, and all Egyptian funds in Britain were blocked. He worked on building support for Britain's response at home, and his view was echoed in the newspapers' condemnation of President Nasser's actions. The early days of the crisis were Eden's best, but it didn't take long for support for his position to fragment. The Labour opposition leader, Hugh Gaitskell, initially agreed with Eden but soon became critical and advocated for the United Nations to intervene. Eden contacted Menzies, who was in the United States, between Chicago and Washington, and on his way home. The plan now was to hold a conference in London of the main maritime powers, to discuss ways of managing the canal. Nasser was invited but unsurprisingly declined.

The conference was convened for foreign secretaries rather than prime ministers, but Menzies consulted his cabinet, which urged him to attend; ultimately he was one of two prime ministers there. His external affairs minister, Richard Casey, who was regarded as an expert on the Middle East, went as well. Casey was wary of Britain pushing for any military solution and argued that Australia had limited involvement in the conflict. The canal was important to Australia's interests, but no Australian oil imports went through Suez, so the nation's stake in the crisis was significantly less than Britain's. Casey tried several times to offer Menzies counsel on the issue but found no support for his argument. The two men had a history of difficulties, initially as rivals to succeed Joseph Lyons as prime minister in 1937. Casey was sceptical about Britain's impatience and unwillingness to negotiate with Nasser. Putting British troops in Suez would look like an act of aggression, Casey told Menzies, but the prime minister did not engage with the point. There was little rapport between the two, and all Casey's advice on the canal would be ignored.

There were no such problems between Eden and Menzies. The pair were, in Menzies' words, 'old and intimate' friends. The British prime minister was grateful to Menzies for lending his gravitas to the crisis, especially given the regard in which Menzies was held in Britain; *The Times* had described him as the most well-known Australian in the country after Donald Bradman, an observation that no doubt pleased Menzies greatly.

Menzies was a Commonwealth man who was observing how the old order was changing and how the Empire was shifting. The 'new' Commonwealth required a different approach. 'To put it another way, the future of the British Commonwealth is no longer a matter to be decided by formulates or by generalised expressions,' Menzies wrote in *The Times* in 1956. 'Everything will turn upon our means and spirit of contact and consultation.'[1] Now was the time for 'contact and consultation', but there would be no pandering to extremists or dictators, and no obeisance paid to the United Nations.[2]

As he confronted what was looming as a serious Cold War conflict, Eden believed he needed a Menzies, not a Casey.

*

On 31 July 1956 the NSW Labor cabinet agreed to legalise poker machines. It made New South Wales the first state in Australia to do so, and one of the few jurisdictions in the world to make money-paying pokies legal. Southern Maryland in the United States was arguably the first, in 1947, but New South Wales jumped on board quickly, confirming for many temperance and church opponents that there was a devil in the machine. 'We believe that gambling is a social evil and also that the legislation of lotteries, poker machine and other forms of gambling is not only a step toward moral degradation but will have the effect of perverting the true spirit of adventure in

Australia,' the nation's Council of Churches claimed two weeks after the cabinet decision.[3]

Compromising the spirit of adventure was a novel reason for opposing poker machines, but it was also calculated that poker machine gamblers could lose their average weekly pay packet of £16 in only 27 minutes.[4] The Bishop of North Queensland, Ian Shevill, was not fazed by the mathematics. For him, the gambling spirit was embedded in the Australian character. 'The founding fathers gambled their future and the lives of their families,' he argued.[5] Bishop Shevill might have been onto something: gambling had come to Australia with the First Fleet, most prominently in the form of card games. Over time, gambling on two-up, lotteries, horses, dogs, and pretty much everything in between became part of what many Australians did for leisure and entertainment. And it was widely known that some of the more regular punters wore clerical collars.

When in 1956 the US sports journalist Red Smith visited Flemington, the home of the Melbourne Cup, he was amazed at just how far afield racegoers spread their punting pounds. 'There are … 261 bookmakers under green parasols, some of them booking races in Sydney, Adelaide and Tasmania. The 66-page booklet that is your race program lists entries for other tracks and you can play a horse a thousand miles away and hear his race broadcast in the betting ring,' Smith told his US readers.[6] There was no doubt: gambling was integral to the Australians' recreation.

The goal for some NSW politicians, though, was that by legalising pokies they would end the years of conflict between pubs and clubs about the role poker machines played in pubs' declining business. They were wrong. Some of an even more naive mindset might have expected that the sinister personalities who had risen to the surface in the previous few years during the legislation debate would skulk back into the shadows now that everything was legal. They too were wrong. In fact, the whole poker machine industry was about to take off; bizarrely, it would have a strange and compelling presence at the Olympic Games.

Poker machines had a rich and complicated history in New South Wales. They had been operating illegally since the 1880s but openly tolerated, because authorities understood that they were situated in clubs that provided some kind of social benefit to their members. Clubs were seen fundamentally as not-for-profits, and were originally subsidised by members' fees. As the 1932 royal commission into greyhound racing and fruit machines said: '[S]uccessive [government] Ministers took the view that club members using these machines were in reality, contributing to the support of their own clubs, and that there was no element of private profit for the occupier or owner of the premises.'[7]

That effectively meant the police didn't care about gambling machines in clubs but made sure they were outlawed in pubs. But with the influx of money from the machines, clubs became more affluent. Many of them were connected to ex-servicemen (the RSLs), and as a result occupied a special place in their communities. In comparison, many pubs were run-down and hamstrung by the restrictive trading hours that followed World War I. By contrast, you could get a beer at a club at any time. The growth of the clubs was remarkable: from 85 in 1905 to 793 in 1955.[8] As far as the government was concerned, the new legislation would give it control over the proliferation of machines. Incredibly, perhaps cynically, it did not publicly admit to any forecast big increase in gambling.[9]

There was also something entirely in keeping with the kind of place Sydney appeared to be and the arrival of the poker machine. 'It is a gay, pagan, boisterous, raffish city, full of oysters and beer and pretty girls in summer frocks and white sails on the harbour, but full also of hard-faced businessmen and angry policemen shouting at street corners and traffic jammed in narrow streets,' one Scottish migrant wrote of his adopted city.[10] Sydney sounded just the place for what would become 'one-armed bandits'.

There were occasional outbreaks of concern about trying to control the prevalence of gaming machines. The clubs offered to pay a tax on each machine, and the hotels responded with what became

TOP, LEFT: Former Melbourne mayor and Olympic bid champion Sir Harold Luxton.

TOP, RIGHT: The man who led the Melbourne bid in Rome, James Disney.

ABOVE: Sir Frank Beaurepaire, Olympic swimmer, philanthropist, lord mayor, and force of nature.

ABOVE, RIGHT: A young Barry Humphries, supervised by a Moonee Ponds housewife called Edna.

RIGHT: An early cast of *The Summer of the Seventeenth Doll* — featuring Madge Ryan (seated), June Jago, and Ray Lawler, who also wrote the play. (Courtesy Black Swan Theatre)

J. D. SALINGER

THE
Catcher in the Rye

A BOOK-OF-THE-MONTH CLUB SELECTION

This unusual book may shock you, will make you laugh, and may break your heart— but you will never forget it

A SIGNET BOOK
Complete and Unabridged

ABOVE: Bruce Howard, from his Olympic press pass.

LEFT: *The Catcher in the Rye* — banned in Australia in 1956. This is the 1953 edition, published by Signet Books. (NAA C3059, *The Catcher in the Rye*)

BELOW, TOP LEFT: Colin Bednall, journalist and TV executive.

BELOW, BOTTOM LEFT: Les Coleman, one of Victorian Labor's favoured sons, who made the journey to the DLP. (Courtesy of Les Coleman)

BELOW, RIGHT: Sculptor Andor Mészáros and his youngest son, Michael. (Courtesy of the Mészáros family)

LEFT: Wilfrid Kent Hughes, soldier, Olympic sprinter, politician, and much put-upon Melbourne Olympic chief, visiting Japan before the Games. (The Herald and Weekly Times)

MIDDLE, LEFT: An explosion at Maralinga. MIDDLE, RIGHT: The denuded landscape after the first Maralinga explosion. ABOVE: Peter Finch (front row, second from left) at the premiere of *A Town Like Alice* in Alice Springs. (McCaffery Collection, Central Australian Historical Images, courtesy of the Alice Springs Public Library)

ABOVE: Nina Paranyuk.

LEFT: Ron Clarke lights the cauldron. (Newspix)

ABOVE: Canecutter Ray Kahl. (Courtesy of the Kahl family)

RIGHT: The first Indigenous man to carry the Olympic torch, Anthony Mark, in Cairns. (Newspix)

ABOVE: The Olympic torch arrives in Collins Street on its last leg towards the MCG. (Newspix)

LEFT: Prime Minister Menzies flew to the US to meet President Eisenhower after the failed Suez summit with President Nasser. The Australian ambassador to the US, Sir Percy Spender, is to Eisenhower's left, and the US secretary of state, John Foster Dulles, is to Menzies' right. (Newspix)

ABOVE: Marcus Marsden, torch relay organiser. (Courtesy of the Marsden family)

RIGHT: The corner of Swanston Street and Flinders Street is illuminated with a special torch design, one of several city streets decorated for the Games. (Newspix)

BELOW: The kids are all right — excitement builds outside the Olympic village in Heidelberg. (The Herald and Weekly Times)

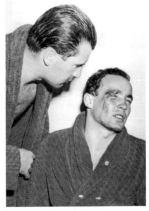

MIDDLE: Betty Cuthbert (right) has gold and Marlene Mathews the bronze after the women's 100 metres final. (Newspix) ABOVE, LEFT: The Australian gold medal–winning women's 4 x 100 metre relay team: Fleur Mellor, Norma Croker, Betty Cuthbert, and Shirley Strickland — but no Marlene. (Newspix) ABOVE, RIGHT: The aftermath of the 'Blood in the Water' water polo match between Hungary and Russia. Hungarian Ervin Zádor nurses his wounds after being hit by the Soviet Union's Valentin Prokopov. (Newspix)

ABOVE: The TV studio —
cameramen get ready for
television's debut. (State Library
of Victoria)

LEFT: The first group of
Hungarian refugees arrives
at Sydney airport, December
1956. (Courtesy of the National
Archives of Australia, NAA:
A12111, 1/1956/5/11)

a highly organised, if covert, operation to identify the number of machines and their revenue across NSW clubs. The state Labor government announced the machines would become legal in clubs as long as they paid a licence fee to the state's Hospital Fund. So far, so good. But what was happening on the ground revealed a far more disturbing picture.

The machines themselves had been imported at the start of the twentieth century, and were only made in Australia after World War II. A company started by Sidney Muddle and Roy Nutt became a manufacturer of machines under the eye-catching trading name of 'Nutt and Muddle and Sons'. Soon a young man called Len Ainsworth, the son of a dentist, wanted to find a way to make some extra money so he and a mate could build dentist chairs, where they thought the real money was going to be. They started making poker machines and the business took off. According to Ainsworth:

> The contact in the first place was for two machines a week, and within a week [our agent] was back saying 'could he have four a week' ... Then another week went past and it was eight a week ... and then it became 16 a week ... and then it was 32.

It all seemed to be too good to be true — and it was. Things started to get a little willing. Ainsworth answered a telephone call from the man who lived next door to the Ainsworth factory: the factory roof had been blown off with a bomb. Outside, there was mayhem: fire engines, ambulances, and a reporter, who asked Ainsworth if he had any enemies. 'You know, I'm beginning to wonder,' Ainsworth told him. The police eliminated any doubt. 'The police said to me "buy a shotgun and put chicken wire on your windows. You're in the big league now, son."'[11]

Another member of the big league was Raymond Smith, a man with a notorious criminal pedigree and a bad habit for living up to it. Smith's father — or part of him, at least — was famous for all the wrong reasons. In April 1935 a four-metre tiger shark was caught off Coogee Beach. After being kept alive for several days so it could be viewed at the Coogee Aquarium on Anzac Day, the shark disgorged a human forearm. Featuring a tattoo of a couple of boxers, the well-preserved limb had once been attached to Raymond Smith's father, James. No one was sure where the rest of James was, but it was clear he had met a premature end — not because of the shark but because of his criminal associations. James was a former boxer and SP bookie who was involved in a number of nefarious activities around Sydney. The police investigation turned up a couple of likely suspects for Smith's murder; one soon died in mysterious circumstances, and the other was acquitted. Who killed James Smith remained a mystery, to be forever known in Australian criminal history as the Shark Arm Murder.

Raymond Smith was a little luckier than his father in 1954, when he ran foul of some of his competitors in the poker machine distribution business. Smith's business employed six people and was sufficiently lucrative for him to live in a pleasant house in Drummoyne. On the night of 3 December 1954 — only a few weeks after the explosion at Ainsworth's factory — Smith was in Wollongong on business. While he was away, two men placed a homemade gelignite bomb in his car, which was parked outside his home. It blew off the roof and sent shrapnel and shards of glass 20 metres down the road. No one was hurt, but Smith was shaken up, perhaps even more so after he was questioned for four hours by police. He couldn't think of anyone who would do such a thing, he told them.

Later that day two men approached Smith, and one of them demanded £500. Smith refused to pay, but he was getting a little tired of all the unwanted attention. At 2 am on the next Saturday morning, just two days after the explosion, Smith and his family were disturbed by an intruder at their home. That was it for Smith — he announced he was going into hiding.[12]

Smith's predicament was the clearest indication that the stakes in the poker machine business had reached a new high. As one clear-eyed Sydney journalist explained:

It is probably the surest, most ruthless and lucrative money spinner ever invented. And the fact that it flourishes in an atmosphere of barely tolerated semi-legality is an added inducement to the underworld to hop in for its cut. Slot machines in Australia are almost in the same position as the world's oldest profession; they are tolerated, but not condoned, restricted but not protected, and their clients are generally assumed to be 'asking' for it.[13]

And the planned arrival of legalised machines had the Sydney's criminals' eyes spinning at the prospect of a big payout. Police were nervous that an underworld war could erupt. There were only seven recognised manufacturers, so there were clear targets for anyone seeking to exert some leverage.

Smith's fear for his safety led the police to take an unusual step: they assigned him a bodyguard. This was a police constable named Murray Riley, who was also known as an Australian rowing champion. Riley and fellow NSW policeman Merv Wood were aiming to win gold in Melbourne in the double sculls.

Wood was a 19-year-old Sydney police cadet when he went to the Berlin Olympics in 1936 as part of the police rowing eight. He had been rowing for six years by then, despite a childhood elbow injury that gave him recurring pain. Wood won gold in the single sculls at the London Games in 1948, and carried the Australian flag at Helsinki in 1952 at the age of 35. He went on to win a silver medal in the single sculls.

By this time Wood's police career had started to take off. He was a highly regarded fingerprint expert, in demand in court cases for his learned explanation of scientific evidence. The year before the 1950 Empire Games, to be held in New Zealand, a couple of unnamed scullers told Wood that he may well be Australia's representative in the single sculls, but they had the double sculls selection sewn up. 'I didn't like their tone,' Wood said. 'I set about looking for a partner.' Wood turned to the police club and identified a young policeman who he thought had promise — Riley. '[B]eing his senior in the police force I was in a position to nominate the terms,' Wood later said. 'And I virtually ordered him to row with me.'[14]

The pairing of Wood and Riley worked out so well that they not only qualified for Auckland but won gold in the double sculls. Then they repeated the success in Vancouver four years later. In 1956 the pair had medal hopes for Melbourne, even though by now Wood was 39.

Riley was an enigmatic figure: no one seemed quite sure what he thought about anything. He had joined the force in 1943, eventually reaching the rank of detective sergeant. The NSW CIB at the time was notorious for its methods, only some of which were legal. Its two biggest names were Ray 'Shotgun' Kelly and Fred Krahe, two coppers who were happy and willing to verbal witnesses. They pushed the law, stepped over it, cultivated a range of snouts, played hard, and had the loyalty of those young detectives who thought the Kelly and Krahe way was for them too. Riley was one of these acolytes. What soon emerged from Riley's work protecting Smith was that Smith had his own set of important connections — and one of those was with Len McPherson, one of Sydney's most notorious crooks.

The hotels had been fighting to keep up with the clubs for years, and attempts to provide entertainments, such as talent quests, caused an eruption of infighting about costs, timing, and, well, talent. But as the legalisation of poker machines loomed, the NSW hotel industry started to get serious and to get organised. At a ULVA meeting in January 1956 it was resolved to 'take all possible constitutional and legal steps to see that the use of mechanical gambling machines in Clubs is eliminated'. The hotels were desperate. This would be a bitter fight. 'Competition from clubs was continually increasing to the detriment of hotelkeepers, particularly those in Country Areas ... The use of gambling machines in Clubs gave them a decided advantage over hotels,' the minutes recorded.[15] The ULVA linked up with the Council of Churches so they could campaign together against the evil of poker machines.

The ULVA stepped up its campaign in the first half of 1956, lobbying members of Labor premier Joe Cahill's government and spending £3,000 of members' money to investigate and object to clubs' licence applications. It also hired private investigators to go into clubs across the state, at various times on different days, to record how many poker machines were active, how many people were playing them, how long they played for, and how much they won. The reports were detailed and revealed a picture of extensive poker machine use across the state. These were clearly illegal machines, but few MPs were bothered about it.

An exception was Cyril Cahill, the Labor MP for Tamworth and a staunch Catholic, who expressed his views in a letter to the Reverend Gordon Powell, of St Stephen's church in Macquarie Street:

> In some of the mushroom clubs, gambling is permitted all night and all day Sundays, and they provided certain officials with the opportunity of picking up big money. In many instances it is these officials who are spearheading the agitation for legislation of the Poker machines. They fear the loss of a highly lucrative racquet [sic].[16]

His observations were accurate, but the clubs were not about to surrender their advantage. They directed members to boycott those hotels that had objected to their licences being granted on the grounds they had poker machines. Club members who didn't observe the ban on patronising those hotels would be asked to restate their reasons for joining the club. Until the licence issue was resolved, the clubs said, 'we carry on as before'.[17]

The hotels were outflanked, and the clubs were in a prime position to make the most of the new legislation.

*

On Tuesday 24 July 1956 a plane wobbled down onto the tarmac at the Alice Springs aerodrome. A banner reading 'Welcome to a town like Alice' fluttered in the warm breeze. On board the plane were a number of out-of-towners, celebrities, including the actor Peter Finch and the writer Nevil Shute. They were in Alice Springs for the Australian launch of *A Town Like Alice*, the movie starring Finch in an adaptation of Shute's novel.

The film had already premiered overseas, and had been scheduled to debut amid the glitter and elegance of the Cannes Film Festival. But in what was an extraordinary gesture, the organisers withdrew the movie in case it offended Japanese festival-goers, who would have seen Finch's character being tortured by Japanese prison guards. The international sensitivities about the war, and Japan's role in it, remained. Yet somehow there was a secret screening in Cannes for a Japanese audience, who appeared to be neither offended nor uninterested in the movie.

By the time Finch and his planeload of celebrities arrived in Alice Springs, the locals were ready to show them some authentic Alice activities. A hockey match between local girls had been organised, along with an Australian Rules football game between Indigenous players and other locals. Later, the film would be screened outdoors under a big outback sky, by the River Todd, with the audience reclining in canvas chairs.

The film was set in Malaysia during World War II, and, unusually for its time, featured a predominantly female cast, led by Virginia McKenna, playing an Englishwoman (Jean Paget) who finds herself in charge of a group of women and children who are captured by the invading Japanese and forced on a brutal march through the jungle. Paget befriends an Australian POW, Joe Harman (Finch), and they fall in love, although both believe the other is married. Harman helps the women with supplies, against Japanese orders, and when his cooperation is revealed Harman is tortured and left for dead. Paget finds out much later that Harman has survived, and she decides to find him. When she's asked if she knows where

Harman came from, Paget replies: 'A town called Alice. He made it sound ... all right.' She sets off for Alice Springs and manages to track him down.

The irony was that the film itself, for all its supposed sense of Australia, was a strange hybrid that was unrepresentative of the Australian experience, let alone a rich portrayal of Alice Springs. The town features for only a few minutes towards the end of the movie, with wide shots of the streets, and Indigenous horsemen trotting across the screen. Most of the film was shot at Pinewood Studios, in England, including a scene purporting to be a conversation in Alice Springs' main street. Similarly, only a small film crew went to Malaya to shoot wide-angle jungle footage that could be used as a backdrop for the set-piece moments filmed at the studio. The Japanese sergeant was played by Kenji Takaki, who was not even an actor but a lampshade maker based in London. Perhaps the most Australian element of the movie (and the book) was that the title was appropriated by some wits in Melbourne, who described their city and its meagre nightlife as 'A Town Like Paralysis'; in the Olympic year, this was a little too close to the truth.

The book of the film was written by a London-born aeronautical engineer who was already a well-established novelist before he and his family migrated to Australia. Nevil Shute Norway (to give him his full name) arrived in Melbourne in 1950 and wrote *A Town Like Alice* in the same year. For Shute, Australia represented a kind of naive and decent alternative to his homeland, with all its post-war problems. It was a charming faith to have in his adopted country, but that element of Shute's novel never even made it to the cutting-room floor: the film omitted the portion of the book in which Jean Paget establishes a new life in Australia.

Finch was also born in London, migrated to Australia when he was ten, and returned to London in 1949 after Sir Laurence Olivier had seen him perform and offered him a leg-up in the industry. Perhaps it was Finch's role in *A Town Like Alice* that helped define the image of the Australian male for overseas audiences: the lean and laconic, resilient man, with no respect for authority and a capacity to endure the consequences. Finch's and McKenna's performances won them each a British Academy award, and the movie was a commercial success overseas. Unsurprisingly, though, it did little for Alice Springs.

Finch's reputation for charm and ease in female company preceded him. His guest for the launch in Alice Springs was an airline hostess, Beryl Oliver, who had been on Finch's flight up from Melbourne. Eyewitnesses recounted how Beryl had helped Finch put on a navy woollen coat for the screening, and the pair smoked cigarettes during the film. At the intermission some of the local Arrernte people attached to the Hermannsburg mission appeared wearing khaki riding pants and tartan shirts to sing 'Lest We Forget' and 'The Lord Has Ascended, The Lord Has Ascended on High' in their language.[18] It was a vivid, if somewhat incongruous image of how to launch a movie in the Top End.

For Shute, *A Town Like Alice*'s success was a pleasant prelude to the far less happy outcome of *On the Beach*, his bestselling novel published the following year, which became a more infamous piece of celluloid. Shute was not particularly worried about such things — he never saw himself as highbrow and happily admitted that he struggled to finish Patrick White.[19] But in 1956, there were some rather more high-minded types in Australia who agreed with him.

The overseas reaction to Patrick White's fourth novel, *The Tree of Man*, had begun with a breathtaking endorsement of the Sydney writer's skill in that benchmark of critical acumen, *The New York Times Review of Books*, which referred to it as 'a timeless work of art'. That enthusiasm was echoed in *The New York Post* and *The Herald Tribune*. The reviews helped shift 10,000 copies of the book in two weeks in the United States.

It was a giddy prelude to the novel's Australian publication in June 1956. White had started to give Australian literature some recognition in North America after US critic James Stern spoke of White's 1948 novel, *The Aunt's Story*, with deep enthusiasm:

I had never been to Australia, yet here was prose which, by its baroque richness, its plasticity and wealth of strange symbols, made an unknown landscape so real that I felt I could walk out in to it as into country I had been brought up in. I could see the black volcanic hills, the dead skeleton trees … I could all but touch the rock, scrub, bones, the sheep's carcass, the ox's skull, as they lay bleached in Australia's eternal greyness … under the immense blue of its skies.[20]

White was not only being recognised internationally for the quality of his writing, he was doing so through his rendition of the Australian landscape and way of life. The US reaction was more than flattering, but White knew that *The Tree of Man* — a novel that followed the domestic fortunes of the Parker family — was fundamentally an Australian book, and Australian reviews would 'really be the test'.[21]

The task of reviewing the book for *The Sydney Morning Herald* was given to the poet Alec Hope, who was professor of English Literature at University College, in Canberra. He would become one of Australia's finest poets and a venerable literary presence, but Hope's review of *The Tree of Man* affirmed the difficulty many Australian artists faced in the 1950s to find acknowledgement among their peers. Central to the judgement in this instance was the suspicion that White's book was perhaps that rare and desirable thing called the Great Australian Novel. Hope didn't think so.

In his most memorable assertion, Hope wrote: 'When so few Australian novelists can write prose at all, it is a great pity to see Mr White, who shows on every page some touch of the born writer, deliberately choose as his medium this pretentious and illiterate verbal sludge.'[22] Hope's beef with White's style was that it contained too much poetry, which is perhaps a strange observation for a poet to make.

White was appalled and wounded by the review. It wasn't the only critical review — *The Age* actually criticised the enthusiastic overseas reception to the book for being based on mistakenly believing White had accurately captured Australia. Not at all, the reviewer said. 'He has nothing much in common with other Australian novelists ...'[23] It didn't seem to occur to *The Age*'s reviewer that such a difference might be a good thing. Here again was an example of local reviewers churlishly dismissing international recognition of an artistic work that aspired to the highest standard.

The premise behind this form of criticism was that there was a common but unstated understanding of what it was to be Australian, and there was an agreed artistic form or style for expressing it, whatever it was. The approach raised some compelling questions. Just how well did we know our country and the people who lived in it? And what exactly was this essence of 'Australianness', which remained, silent and amorphous, at the heart of our national imagination? Either way, it appeared the Australian reviewers had got it wrong. Australian book buyers in 1956 were perhaps more interested in finding out why overseas critics thought so highly of an Australian novel: 8,000 copies of *The Tree of Man* were sold in Australia in the first three months after publication.

*

If White — or any contemporary Australian writer — was expecting some kind of affirmation and recognition in the Olympic cultural program that was scheduled to coincide with the 1956 Summer Games, they were to be sadly mistaken. The festival's literature component was actually an exhibition of published works, most of which were secreted away in the State Library of Victoria. Despite some agitating from the frequently agitated editor of the literary quarterly *Meanjin*, Clem Christesen, for a standalone literary festival, the literature element of the arts festival contained no novel more recent than Roy Connolly's *Southern Saga*, published in 1940. White never got a mention. Nor did Kylie Tennant, Alan Marshall, Dymphna Cusack, Ruth Park, Katharine Susannah Pritchard,

D'Arcy Niland, and Jon Cleary, all of whom had published significant novels in the previous decade.

Geoffrey Serle, later to become one of the nation's finest historians, wrote in the festival catalogue: '[O]nly in comparatively recent years has Australian literature developed in quality, quantity and distinctiveness.' The reason for this late flowering of local literature, Serle argued, was because Australia had inherited the English literary canon, stretching back to Chaucer. 'In a sense, literature had to start from scratch, had to be created entirely afresh. Similarly, literature would not flourish in Australia until the country's baffling strangeness had been overcome and it was seen through appreciative eyes as a fit and proper subject for the artist.'[24]

Whatever this 'baffling strangeness' was — presumably, different things to different writers — White and his contemporaries apparently did not qualify. But each of them, in their own way, and none more so than White, had deemed Australia to be 'a fit and proper subject'. At the moment when the world was supposedly turning its gaze on Australia, the nation's foremost contemporary novelists were nowhere to be seen.

In fact, it was lucky that any novelist, poet, or dramatist was there at all. In the early discussions, the University of Melbourne's professor of English, Ian Maxwell, proposed that literature should not be part of any proposed arts program during the Olympics. His position was sufficiently regarded for the Fine Arts Festival subcommittee, of which he was a member, to agree 'that Literature be eliminated from the Festival as it would be difficult to organize satisfactorily'.[25]

Professor Maxwell's deeper reasoning is not clear. He was also chairman of *Meanjin*'s Advisory Board, so was probably aware that his magazine's founder and editor disapproved of the eventual decision to stage a limited display of Australian literary works, plus a selection of the State Library's aged holdings. By the time a decision was made to hold the exhibition, the budget was set at only £200. The catalogue budget for the whole arts festival was £500.

The festival itself was another Brundage moment. Previous Olympics had actually run a cultural Olympiad, whereby local artists in the Olympic host city competed for medals. Brundage, bear-hugging amateurism close to paralysis, determined that 'professional' artists should not be part of what was an avowedly 'amateur' sporting festival. Brundage directed Melbourne, instead, to hold an arts festival. As it happened, Brundage fancied himself as a man with some artistic credibility: he had a 3,000-piece collection of Asian antiques and professed to a love of literature.

The initial reaction in Melbourne to the idea of a festival was positive. 'Most of our visitors will probably have very little idea about Australia's cultural achievements: they may not know we have any at all to show,' one arts critic wrote. 'To the world at large we are the nation which produces fine wool, Davis Cup players and John Landy. We have something else to show them ...'[26]

But the organisers were less than impressed. Don Chipp, who was the secretary of the committee that had oversight of the festival, said it was against the idea from the start. Organising the festival was 'a thankless task', he said later, in an implied recognition that no one was ever going to be happy with the outcome.[27]

Contrary to the staid literary selections, the festival curators showed much more dare and insight with their selections for the painting and sculptural exhibitions. Bernard Smith, the distinguished Australian art critic and historian, bemoaned that Australia was better known internationally for its athletic achievements than its artistic prowess, but he nonetheless identified an emerging sense of Australian art. 'There are many paintings in this exhibition in which the attempt to meet the claims of place and tradition have been met, and it is to that we must look for the emergence of an Australian artistic tradition,' he wrote.[28] The exhibition featured work from contemporary artists John Brack, Charles Blackman, Russell Drysdale, Arthur Boyd, and Sidney Nolan, as well as the 'old masters' Tom Roberts, Arthur Streeton, and Frederick McCubbin. The overall impression was of something new emerging from the gloomy artistic focus of the 1940s.

The English art critic John Berger had identified this three years earlier, when he reviewed a London exhibition entitled *Twelve Australian Artists*. 'One thing, however, I am certain about: very few mixed exhibitions in either London or Paris imply the underlying unity which this one did,' he wrote in *Meanjin*.[29] 'This unity had nothing to do with any common style but with something much subtler: the birth of a national tradition.' As evidence, Berger singled out Drysdale, Lloyd Rees, Nolan, and Boyd.

In sculpture, too, there was an attempt to capture 'the moment', rather than just the artefacts of previous generations. The approach meant the cast of exhibitors was broad and diverse. A batch of migrant sculptors, including Andor Mészáros, became part of the festival program. Mészáros had consolidated his reputation since his first exhibition 15 years earlier, and now the catalogue noted that he was a sculptor 'of note and a medallist of world renown. If the Commonwealth Government could be induced to commission this designer of the Olympic Medallion to design future coinage they would at least succeed in putting aesthetic value in to a highly inflated pound,' the catalogue noted waspishly.[30] Mészáros had three pieces in the festival, and helped to organise the sculpture exhibition at Wilson Hall, at the University of Melbourne.

Although Mészáros had won the first prize in the 1951 world exhibition of medallists, it was his Olympic medal that gave him an international profile beyond artistic circles. As the newspaper reports about his medal noted, with a distribution to Olympic representatives from more than 70 countries, the 'medallion will take Australia's art to every part of the world'.[31] Mészáros had effectively made it: he had been 'claimed' as an Australian artist by the nation he had adopted. Perhaps no less significant was the recognition of the medallion as art, affirming Mészáros' own ambition for the Olympic souvenir.[32]

The medal could have come spectacularly unstuck but for a last-minute intervention from an unlikely source. While Mészáros was working to finish the medal templates before they were sent to London, his ten-year-old son, Michael, noticed something about the wording on one side of the medal. Mészáros had been given free rein on the design of the medallion: on one side he had set the City of Melbourne's coat of arms amid the five Olympic rings. On the other side was a range of athletes bearing the Olympic flag, and around the medal's edge was the march of athletes. In the middle of the medal was the Olympic motto: 'Citius, Altius, Fortius' — faster, higher, stronger. Except, as Michael pointed out to his dad, the words weren't in the right order. Mészáros told his son he was wrong. Michael said he was right. They checked, and Michael was proved correct. Mészáros went back and fixed the die, and just in time. Otherwise 12,000 Olympic athletes and officials might have wondered.

*

On 1 August, with the Games less than four months away, the Olympic catering committee admitted it had employed no 'Asiatic' cooks to prepare food for teams from the region. The Melbourne organisers had searched across the nation but had been unable to find suitable Muslim or Hindu cooks anywhere. It was a bizarre problem to have so close to the Games — but then again, the Melbourne Olympic organisation had been characterised by a Western focus from the day it started canvassing for votes.

The shipping line P&O offered to return to Melbourne after the Games and transport any 'Asiatic' cooks home at the lowest tourist fare. Air India was about to start a regular service to Australia and might be able to send 18 Pakistani and Indian cooks to Melbourne. Yet neither option guaranteed a solution.

By the end of August, the situation was getting desperate. Air India announced it couldn't help, so negotiations were opened with the British Phosphate Company: could they spare any of the Indian cooks working on their ships, which traded between Australia and Nauru? Similar approaches were made to the Dutch Royal International Ocean Line, which offered to select suitable Indian and Malaysian cooks and bring them to Australia at nominal cost.[33]

If all of this seemed to be happening at the eleventh hour, it had nothing on the Olympic torch relay. This had been one of the innovations of the 1936 Games in Berlin, and was the perfect way for the host nation to engage a sizeable portion of its population in the excitement of the Games. On Wednesday 13 June 1956 an academic in the University of Melbourne's geology department, Marcus Marsden, was summoned to a meeting with the University Sports Union's secretary, Bill Tickner. Tickner had been told by Olympic technical boss Bill Holt: 'It's about time we did something about the relay.'

The university — the only one in Victoria — was being used as a venue for Olympic training and accommodation. It was also providing a good number of volunteers for important Olympic roles. Marsden had, until then, had no exposure to the Olympic movement or the organisation of the Melbourne Games. He was, in the most benign sense of the phrase, an Olympic novice.

Tickner asked Marsden to choose between two Olympic roles: to put his familiarity with the French language to use and become the liaison officer for the French Olympic team, or to take charge of the torch relay. On the face of it the liaison officer role would have been the less demanding job. The relay seemed like a task that could go spectacularly wrong at any moment. Marsden was a keen sportsman who played Australian Rules football and cricket, and he was also an administrator at his cricket and football clubs. His geology background also meant he was used to getting out and about, roughing it if need be. He later reckoned it was this combination of skills — sport and practical outdoor knowledge — that might have explained why he was being considered for the torch relay. Even so, it seemed a random choice — but ultimately it proved an inspired one. So what did Marsden think — would it be the French role or the relay? He'd do the relay, thanks very much.[34]

Marsden embarked on the task in his spare time and in the university holidays. He managed to captain the University Reds football team to the finals, and finished the season with the personal triumph of 101 goals, but sadly they didn't win the flag. Then it was on with the relay. It was going to be some journey.

All Marsden knew when he took on the job was that he was pretty much going to invent it as he went along. Marsden knew the Olympic flame would be flown from Athens (via Darwin) to Cairns, in Far North Queensland. After that, it was Marsden's role to get the flame from Cairns to Melbourne in time for the opening ceremony. That was a distance of 3,000 kilometres as the crow flew, but of course the relay route wouldn't always follow the main highways. By the time the final route down the east coast of Australia was measured, it was calculated that the torch would travel almost 3,900 kilometres.

Some preparation had been done in New South Wales and Queensland, and Cairns as the starting point had shown admirable enthusiasm to organise itself. But there was still plenty of work to be done, especially in Victoria. An early itinerary for the route was actually based on the petrol company Shell's road maps. On the evidence of the lack of early planning the relay was a poor cousin to the Olympics, in organisational terms, and therefore as a priority. In the circumstances, it was no surprise that the torch design for Melbourne was not new but a close replica of the torch used at the London Olympics, where Bill Holt had also been technical director.

There were several basic rules that Marsden had to follow. The first was that no relay runner was to be a professional athlete. That made sense, given the amateur nature of the Olympics. There was no mention of the relay participants being prominent local citizens or former Olympians. Each participant was expected to run a mile, and do it in seven and a half minutes. There would be official receptions at some towns along the way, where the torch would come to rest, but otherwise it would travel day and night for about 16 days. Each runner would receive a commemorative medal.[35] And there was one other rule: no women runners.

The torch relay gender restriction was just one example of the way in which the Olympic movement treated women. Six years before the Games, the Victorian Women's Amateur Sports Council lobbied to become part of the Olympic Games Organising Committee to ensure that women's sports were adequately represented. Their argument was that the men sitting around the table often forgot about female athletes, and therefore female sports had no say in the raising of funds for overseas competition. An attempt by women sports administrators to join the Olympic committee in 1949 was fobbed off with the line that women would be catered for; if necessary, a special subcommittee would be set up.[36] Similar approaches were rebuffed in 1950 and in 1953, when women tried to join the Victorian Olympic Council.

One journalist wondered why women would bother trying to join what was, in practice, a men's club. 'No self-respecting woman would step inside the meeting room door. The language at last Thursday night's meeting would have had the most seasoned bullocky running up the trunk of the nearest mulga tree from sheer fright,' he wrote.[37]

Two women were eventually given roles within the Melbourne Olympic organisation: Dorothy Carter, director of the Women's Royal Australian Air Force and a former Olympian, and Sybil Taggart, an architect, former hockey international, and president of the Victorian Women's Amateur Sports Council. Both were appointed to the Olympic Games Organizing Committee in what was thought to be the first time any woman was appointed to such a committee. When the announcement was made, the head of the AOF made it clear that the women would have nothing to do with the sport; they would, instead, help with the general organisation of the Games.[38] That turned out to mean advising on 'amenities for women athletes and catering arrangements'.[39]

*

Prime Minister Menzies flew to London for the Suez conference, arriving on 9 August. Casey arrived soon after. The conference, to be opened by the US secretary of state, John Foster Dulles, began at Lancaster House three days later.

Casey visited Menzies at the Savoy and urged him to dissuade Eden from any thoughts of using force. The minister for external affairs recorded in his diary:

> I pointed out the difficulties (from my own knowledge of the area) which this sort of thing would present — apart from the fact that it would put us completely in the wrong with public opinion in practically every part of the world. I recommended that he should seek to get an appreciation from the UK of the military side, of which we were entirely in the dark. I said I failed to see what could be achieved by action of this sort.[40]

The advice seemed to have no effect on Menzies. The conference finished with 18 nations, including Australia, backing a US proposal for the Suez Canal to be run by an international body associated with the United Nations. Five nations opposed the proposal: the USSR, India, Ceylon, Indonesia, and Spain. The agreement included a decision for a group of five representatives of those nations which had supported the US motion to travel to Egypt and discuss it with President Nasser. The toughest decision was to work out who would lead the mission.

Spring
1956

Chapter Seven
With Open Arms

To cope with the influx of Olympic visitors to Melbourne, the plan was to ask suburban families to throw open the doors of their homes to strangers. The psychology behind this gesture involved winning over Victorian women to the idea. As early as July 1954, Melbourne's lord mayor, Robert Solly, invited all the city's women's organisations to a special meeting at the Town Hall to discuss the idea. Representatives of the Country Women's Association, the National Council of Women, the Girl Guides Association, the Housewives Association, and the Young Women's Christian Association attended. Alongside them were representatives of business, union, and sporting organisations, united in the goal of finding ways to meet the accommodation shortfall. Premier Cain told the meeting that women would have the greatest responsibility for making visitors welcome and comfortable in their homes.[1] (It seemed that Melbourne's men were going to be too busy.) The result of the meeting was the establishment of the Olympic Civics Committee. Yet when the committee was convened under Maurice Nathan's leadership, it contained no women. So much for that, then.

The implication at every step of the Games was that women should be willing and available to volunteer some kind of housekeeping role across the city. As the athletes' village was nearing completion, organisers came up with another idea to involve women in what was billed as a 'Housewives Brigade' to help make beds and tidy the athletes' rooms. 'We will want them to come in for a few hours after Johnnie has gone off to school and breakfast dishes have been done at home,' one of the village officials explained. 'After earning money for Christmas shopping in the mornings they would be free to see the Games in the afternoons.' The Housewives Brigade was to make 6,000 beds a day, and would start its duties a week before the athletes and officials arrived in Melbourne.[2]

If it wasn't housekeeping, it was driving. More than 340 women from across the nation volunteered to become drivers for Olympic officials. Brundage had three drivers at his disposal, two of whom had driven in London and the United States. Car number 103 was Brundage's black limousine, used to ferry him to Olympic functions and the Games. An Olympic pennant fluttered from the bonnet and five Olympic rings garlanded the registration plate. The other drivers had access to a fleet of 123 donated cars, including Holdens, DeSotos, Pontiacs, and Dodges, which had free daily maintenance and a night-time tyre check from Sir Frank Beaurepaire's Olympic Tyre & Rubber Company. The drivers even had their own hunter-green uniform, topped off with a green beret.[3]

The household hospitality was a complex logistical task that fell to Nathan's civics committee. A team of inspectors was appointed to assess properties, and potential hosts were asked questions about which nationalities they would prefer, what their family arrangements were, and what hobbies they had. A team of women attached to the committee would then match up the Melbourne families with visitors. More than 6,000 households said they'd be happy to take an overseas visitor. After some preliminary inquiries, 5,600 homes were assessed and given a grading.

There was no policy to positively discriminate one nationality over another, but Nathan's committee was secretly delighted at the number of locals who 'took Asian and dark-skinned people'.[4] The importance of such community support was as much about saving money as it was about spreading the Games spirit. Essentially, the committee was seeking the donation of millions of pounds' worth of services across Melbourne. Implicit in that support was a growing sense that the Games were galvanising the community, uniting city and suburbs, friends and families, in a shared purpose, often drawing on some surprising sources of inspiration.

A Melbourne couple who had previously offered classes in how to prepare for meeting Queen Elizabeth II during her 1954 tour provided a 'finishing school' for those who were going to have contact with international guests. Two years earlier, the papers called the anxiety about meeting the new Queen 'tour terror'. The couple who were going to cure it were 'a pair of monocled New Australians who themselves do automatically what they teach their pupils'.[5] They were described as German aristocrats, who had emerged from the 'grim, grey castles of their childhood'.

This description, redolent of something from Grimm's fairytales, wasn't quite accurate: Hans and Alice Meyer's real incarceration had been in Australia, as they were both former internees, deprived of their liberty in Sydney when World War II started. They were not European aristocrats but Germans fleeing the Nazis. Hans was Jewish, on his mother's side; Alice, because of Hans, was also in peril.

They were dance instructors with their own school in East Prussia but were expelled from the German Chamber of Culture in 1935. The only way the dance school could reopen was if Alice divorced her husband. The couple had escaped to England, and then, through the sponsorship of the Quakers, migrated to Sydney in February 1938. They became something of an exotic addition to Sydney society, but their growing profile spelt trouble when war broke out. They were interned in September 1939, and released five months later on the condition they not return to Sydney — but, after moving to Wagga Wagga, Hans was re-interned in June 1940.[6]

The Meyers were considered intelligent, sophisticated, and worldly — and, according to the suspicions of the time, well qualified to work for the enemy. A deep distrust ran through the security assessments of foreigners, little of it justified. 'He made a very deep impression of unreliability and insincerity ... this person ... is a slippery and unreliable man,' a security service officer concluded after interviewing Hans Meyer in 1942.[7]

The Meyers had some high-profile supporters from their time in Sydney, and the wife of Australia's wartime governor-general, Lord Gowrie, was instrumental in helping to get them released in February 1944. Residual suspicions about Hans continued to dog him, though, and the security services successfully delayed his application for refugee alien status.[8] Buoyed by Lady Gowrie's encouragement, the Meyers set up a dance and deportment school in Melbourne, where, by 1953, they were ready to deal with all those Australians who were terrified of doing the wrong thing in front of Her Majesty.

In an inspired move, the Meyers decided to offer Australians guidance on how to deal with 'continentals' and all those other foreign tourists who were on their way to Australia for the Games. The offering covered elements of international etiquette, some geography, and some foreign languages too. The pupils were made up of Olympic officials, local councillors, the wives of diplomats, and families who were planning to host visitors. 'It's an important part of hospitality to receive other nationalities without showing surprise or confusion at their customs and mannerisms,' Hans explained.[9]

There were some intriguing tips: a Portuguese visitor pulling their right ear and winking their right eye was a sign of approval at the meal they had just eaten; a Tibetan poking out his tongue was a polite form of greeting; 'continental' gentlemen would not kiss the hands of single girls because it was considered too forward, although married women could expect a hand kiss. Mrs Meyer was quite clear about the appropriate topic of conversation with a Frenchman:

[N]ever ask a Frenchman personal questions, such as where they were yesterday or what is their occupation. However, they don't consider their opinions personal property — you can go ahead asking their opinions on anything at all. On the other hand, an

Italian will take as a mark of friendship if you encourage him to discuss his family affairs with you.[10]

For Japanese visitors, the advice ran, always carry personal greeting cards with your details that could be exchanged. When dining with Chinese guests, expect to eat ten-year-old eggs, and anywhere between 40 and 50 courses, but never touch the final bowl of rice lest your Chinese hosts think your appetite has not been properly sated. And then, of course, there were local customs, of which many Australians were arguably unaware:

Never leave a room facing out of it, but gracefully back out. And many of us forget that it is one of the rules of etiquette to remove gloves before smoking. [And] that an Australian would not handle a male visitor's coat or hat but let him put it down himself and that it is the woman's place to first acknowledge the presence of the man.[11]

People from 76 nations were due to arrive in Melbourne in 1956.[12] There had been no event in the nation's modern history which had exposed it to so many countries at once. The pressure to deal with those different demands and expectations was starting to build.

What should have been simple often became complicated. The Australian Olympic uniform was an ideal opportunity for a local manufacturer to show off their designs, but that too became unexpectedly problematic. The uniforms were an important part of each national team: their colour scheme, fabric, and design were supposed to resonate with the nation's sense of style. In Melbourne, Olympic organisers approached a Victorian-based manufacturer which had begun in Warrnambool and by the end of World War II was supplying 123 retailers in four states.

David Fletcher Jones' clothing business was built on the federal government contract it won in 1941 to make trousers for the Australian Army. It gave the company a regular revenue stream, a creditable client, and a profile to match. Fletcher Jones' trousers, in a hard-wearing 'coverdine' material, became a staple of the rural man. Queues formed for several city blocks when Fletcher Jones opened his first city shop, in Queen Street, Melbourne, in 1946. Fletcher Jones was an astute marketer before the term was invented, and he promoted his clothes with a sign: 'Fletcher Jones of Warrnambool — nothing but trousers. 72 scientific sizes. No man is hard to fit.'[13]

Fletcher Jones only made men's trousers: they were durable, practical, and reliable. That was their business — and it meant a problem for the Olympics, because they didn't make womenswear. Fletcher Jones was reluctant to supply an Olympic team of men and women, when his company's slogan — and its business — was all about men. The man himself stonewalled the Olympic committee, telling them he was too busy and that he was worried about how he would make a feminine pleat for the women's skirts.[14] The Games' organisers persisted, and finally Fletcher Jones relented. For his business, a bonus was that the Olympic skirts became the forerunner of a new product line.

*

Menzies' initial thinking was that US secretary of state John Foster Dulles would lead the expedition to present Nasser with the London conference's resolution. No one from Britain could go because their nation was in direct dispute with Nasser. Menzies expected someone from the Commonwealth would accompany Dulles, but he didn't believe it should be him. Once the conference was over, he went back to the Savoy to contemplate his long-awaited return to Australia.

At 2 am on 22 August Menzies was woken at the Savoy by a telephone call from the US ambassador to Britain, Winthrop Aldrich. The ambassador was meeting with Eden and Dulles about Nasser and they wanted to talk to Menzies immediately. Menzies was reluctant, but Aldrich insisted, promising a car would be sent to take Menzies to the ambassador's residence in Regent's Park. Menzies got dressed and set off in the middle of the night.

When he arrived, Eden told him that they wanted him to be part of the Egypt delegation. Dulles was more pointed. 'No, Anthony, not a member, Chairman. We want him as our chief spokesman, because he knows how to put a case.'[15]

Menzies resisted and offered alternative names. But for Eden and Dulles, it was Menzies or the whole committee would have to be reconsidered.

Their insistence seemed to fly in the face of what was already known about Menzies' lack of suitability for such a task. During World War II, British prime minister Winston Churchill asked Eden, who was then foreign minister, to help him identify an appropriate candidate to be minister of state in Cairo. The position was strategically important because of the war in North Africa, but the candidate did not have to be British. Menzies by this time had lost the prime ministership to John Curtin and was therefore able to be considered. But Casey got the job instead. Eden admitted later that Menzies had been rejected because 'he probably would not get on with the people in the Middle East, being a somewhat difficult person'.[16] Now Eden was about to send Menzies on a far more difficult assignment.

Eden's original observation was perhaps borne out several years later when Menzies was in Cairo on a different mission. 'These Gyppos are a dangerous lot of backward adolescents, full of self-importance and basic ignorance,' Menzies wrote in his diary.[17] The attitude, not uncommon at the time, extended beyond the Egyptians. A former Australian high commissioner to India, Indonesia, Italy, and Kenya, Sir Walter Crocker, noted in 1955: 'Menzies is anti-Asian; particularly anti-Indian ... he just can't help it.'[18]

While race proved challenging for Menzies, perhaps the more confronting charge was his apparent lack of curiosity about other nations, his unshakeable faith in English superiority, and his lack of engagement with European languages. One of his contemporaries, Alick Downer, was mystified by it: 'I fail to understand how he could have deprived himself of these fountains of our civilisation.'[19]

Casey counselled Menzies to 'make every effort to try to get into personal and private discussion with Nasser alone — little as he [Menzies] might relish doing so'. Casey's experience of the Middle East had taught him the importance of personal contact and the need for Menzies to gauge how committed Nasser was to his course of action. Casey's advice was fulsome: 'I explained the extreme fanaticism of the Egyptians, which I thought was far beyond that of any race I knew. The issues at stake were very great.'[20]

Indeed they were, but Menzies didn't pack Casey's advice with him. Menzies cabled Sir Arthur Fadden in Australia, outlining the pressure he had been put under to lead the mission and explaining that Eden and Dulles would send the reasons they wanted Menzies to go so that Australians could know that it was not a role 'of my own seeking'. Dulles' message was brief and grand. After some preliminary remarks, he told Fadden: 'I trust you and your colleagues will acquiesce in your Prime Minister thus serving in this work which is so vital to the peace and well-being of so much of the world.'[21]

Fadden and the cabinet agreed that Menzies needed to go. 'My colleagues were, as I now know, delighted. They regarded the appointment as a compliment to Australia, though they (and I) fully understood the immense risks, perhaps the certainty of failure,' Menzies reflected.[22] His position on Suez was in lock step with that of Eden and Dulles. He had appeared on BBC television to outline the dimensions of the crisis:

> Colonel Nasser's action in respect of the Suez Canal has created a crisis more grave than any since the ending of the Second World War. The leading trading nations of the world are vitally concerned. You in Great Britain are concerned, for a threat to the Suez Canal will, if not resisted, encourage further acts of lawlessness and so reduce the economic strength of your country, that the whole standard of living may be drastically reduced.[23]

Menzies believed that a strong response might be required to get Nasser to appreciate Britain's point of view. Menzies was, in the public eye, the 'Commonwealth man'. He had walked that stage, found a spot of obeisance near the Crown, and felt like a valued elder statesman within the Commonwealth club of nations. But this mission to Egypt propelled him into a new kind of universe, where the old verities no longer applied. He was about to embark on a delicate international mission of diplomacy, trying to negotiate with a new leader who was driven by forces Menzies could not fully comprehend, in a region about which he had little knowledge, or indeed interest. And whether he knew it or not, he was about to do it with one hand tied behind his back.

A few weeks after his television broadcast, Menzies was on his way to talk to Nasser, to convince him to accept the US proposal to put the canal's operation under an international board. He arrived in Cairo at dusk on 2 September. Menzies stepped into a sea of cameras, bobbing around the stairs leading from the plane to the tarmac. In the gathering gloom, Menzies, accompanied only by his personal secretary and press secretary, struggled to find his way to the waiting car and the Australian minister to Egypt, Roden Cutler.

Menzies had worked assiduously in London to get command of the brief for his mission. He and four advisers had held nine meetings exploring the finances of the canal, and had spoken to the canal's directors and even an engineer who was expert in the area.[24] Yet there were no discussions about the social and personal elements he needed to understand: why the Suez Canal was so important to Egyptians, and why Nasser felt that now was the time to express his independence of thought and action.

The consequences of this short-sightedness became clear early on during Menzies' meetings with Nasser. Menzies conducted the discussions like the barrister he once was, laying out the evidence, interrogating opinions, prosecuting a case, just as Secretary Dulles had expected him to do. Nasser, Menzies confided to his staff, was naive and uncertain. Menzies believed he could influence him.[25] Menzies' base view was far less hospitable. He told Eden that Nasser was 'in some ways a likeable fellow but so far from being charming, he is rather gauche ... I would say that he was a man of considerable but immature intelligence'. Menzies had more generalisations to make: '[L]ike many of these people in the Middle East (or even in India) whom I have met, his logic doesn't travel very far; that is to say, he will produce a perfectly adequate minor premise, but his deduction will be astonishing.'[26] Nasser had his own description of Menzies — he was 'a mule'.

Menzies couldn't understand why his carefully presented argument — that the proposed canal board would run the canal, keep the waterway open, maintain sound financial discipline, be apolitical, but be a tenant of Egypt — wasn't persuasive. Nasser had dismissed the idea as 'collective colonialism'. Menzies tried to clarify the point that tenancy did not diminish or compromise Egypt's ownership of the canal. For Nasser, the reality was that international control was still on the table, and that meant Egyptian sovereignty was compromised.

Menzies struggled to see Nasser's point. He believed that the proposal he brought to Cairo actually maintained Egypt's sovereign rights. Nasser had an answer for that too: 'The small nations are more touchy about sovereignty than great ones. Great Britain may find it not inconsistent with her sovereignty to have American bases established in Great Britain but that is only because Great Britain is a great nation and is not sensitive about sovereignty.'[27]

Perhaps it was just as well that, back in the United States, President Eisenhower stated that he would never support the use of force against Egypt in resolving the conflict, and if the talks broke down, other peaceful options would have to be considered. Eisenhower had eliminated the one sanction left to Britain and Menzies by taking force off the table. The talks broke down. It was 5 September 1956.

*

The Olympic Village in Heidelberg was ready for its first inspection. The Victorian government had originally earmarked the site for a housing commission development but offered it to the Games for the athletes' village. On the first weekend of September journalists were invited there to have a look around.

One was Harry Gordon, a seasoned reporter on *The Sun*, a morning tabloid. Gordon had been only 24 when *The Sun* sent him to cover the Korean War. It was a bitterly cold winter and a challenging assignment, with every word he wrote supposed to go through the US censors. Gordon, though, was resourceful and dedicated. He wasn't interested in sending home bland bulletins that came from some American censor's pencil. Instead, he found a way to get his own copy back to Australia, via Japan, so that readers could find out what was really happening to the Diggers.

Gordon's next big assignment was the Helsinki Olympics, a radically different reporting task that started his life-long affection for the Olympic movement. By the time the Olympics arrived in Gordon's home town, he was ready and willing to immerse himself in everything related to the Games.

The tour around the athletes' village was a pleasant diversion for most journalists, even if it didn't produce a news story. Yet Gordon saw something no one else saw — something that disturbed him. He took to explaining his misgivings in *The Sun*:

> Someone has made a very bad blunder in the naming of the streets at Melbourne's Olympic Village ... Most of the streets have been named after famous World War II battles in which Australia took part. In any other part of Melbourne, they would be thoroughly suitable — in fact, desirable. But the Olympic Village — the place where the finest athletes in the world live together in what all of us hope will be an atmosphere of sheer goodwill — they are completely out of character.[28]

Gordon's point was a simple one: Olympic officials needed to be aware of international sensitivities. The German athletes, for example, would have to walk to their meals down Alamein Street, named after a World War II battle that had ended in a German defeat. The Japanese were not spared either — they would be reminded of their crushing losses in the first stage of the New Guinea campaign every time they walked down Buna Street.

Gordon's column created a last-minute panic to fix the faux pas. It had originated, it turned out, when the street names were chosen for the housing commission development. Even so, no one had spotted the problem in the months leading up to the Games. What was this blindness to the rest of the world? Were there other issues lurking in the Olympic preparation that hadn't been spotted yet? With red faces, the organisers acted quickly, and within two days the street names had been changed.

*

On 11 September 1956, some 12,000 miles away from the supposedly sedate Melbourne, the film *Rock Around the Clock* premiered at the London Trocadero. It soon became more than a film premiere: young filmgoers started to get excited, even agitated. Some newspapers said it was a 'riot'. The police were called. The general public knew exactly what was to blame for this eruption of anti-social behaviour. 'The hypnotic rhythm and the wild gestures have a maddening effect on a rhythm loving age group and the result of its impact is the relaxing of all self-control,' a letter-writer to *The Times* said, demonstrating a superior understanding of the frailties of the youthful mind and body.[29] One of London's Harley Street psychiatrists was moved to observe: 'This kind of music is excessively stimulating only to the maladjusted or to people of a primitive type.'[30] *Rock Around the Clock* was soon banned in several cities in England.

When the film hit Australia, 'wild dancing' erupted in Sydney's George Street, near the cinema, and then outside police headquarters. The gyrations were sufficiently lewd for the teenagers to be charged with offensive and indecent behaviour.[31] There was a similar reaction in Brisbane, and in Perth, where teenagers emerged 'jiving and singing' after the movie and then blocked traffic. Eight youths and a young woman were charged with disorderly conduct.[32] In Melbourne the reaction was only marginally more restrained. The film broke local box-office records after only six weeks, but only a firm hand from the theatre manager ensured the young rock'n'rollers in the audience were kept under control.[33]

The movie seemed innocent enough: the story centred on a small-time dance band manager who discovers a rock'n'roll band and decides that they are going to be the hottest new thing. It was the film that proved to be hot, making eight times its production costs at the box office. The film's prelude was Bill Haley and the Comets' single '(We're Gonna) Rock Around the Clock', which had been released in 1954 and had sold 2 million copies worldwide. In Australia Festival Records had to run a special night shift to keep up with demand for the record. By September 1956 the record had sold 150,000 copies across the country, and was declared the fastest-earning song in Australian history.[34]

The record — and then the film — tapped into something that was emerging among teenagers, a post-war generation who had experienced a range of influences and experiences their parents had never known growing up. The motion picture industry, which had for years told the same stories, was starting to target a new audience, young people who had the money to pay for and the inclination to watch stories about themselves. In 1955 *Blackboard Jungle* was released, with its story of interracial tensions in the classroom and its rock'n'roll soundtrack (including 'Rock Around the Clock'). Marlon Brando, in *The Wild One*, came next, wearing a white T-shirt, riding a motorbike, and exuding an air of brooding menace and rebellion. The movie was banned in the United Kingdom until 1967 because it presented a 'spectacle of unbridled hooliganism', but Australia, the country that had banned *Catcher in the Rye*, was, inexplicably, more tolerant of *The Wild One*. Brando and *Blackboard Jungle* struck an instant, jangling chord.

Then there was that young and dangerous American singer called Elvis Presley, and his hit 'Heartbreak Hotel', which entered the charts in 1956. Australian DJ Bob Rogers was so appalled that he refused to play it. Presley didn't have 34-year-old Bill Haley's cute curl on his forehead. He was 21, with loads of something that no one in polite society mentioned — sex appeal — and his hips swayed in ways that were, depending on your age, either completely intoxicating or utterly lascivious.

Australia was still trying to catch up with the rest of the world, particularly the United States, when it came to popular music. Johnnie Ray had a hit in 1951 with 'Cry', but his star had largely fallen by the time he made his first tour to Australia three years later. When he returned in 1955, there were near-riots in Brisbane and at Sydney airport. Ray was not so much a rock'n'roller as a singer whose body became part of the performance, a physical expression of emotion. It was uninhibited, wild, and new. Teenagers loved it. Others referred to him derisively as a 'sob singer'.

Ray was an unlikely star — he wore a hearing aid as a result of a childhood accident, and physically resembled one side of a tuning fork. He was also a closeted gay man, which brought with it a degree of sadness that seemed intrinsic to his career. But he made a connection with his young audiences in ways that older Australians found mystifying and amusing. 'Although his voice is pleasant enough to listen to, he packs such a wallop with his display of super-charged emotion, that the entire audience is swept away on a wave of hysteria,' an older female reporter in Brisbane wrote. 'I heard him last night at one of his sessions in the stadium and found it completely ridiculous to hear women in the audience screaming with delight.'[35] Sydney DJ Alan Toohey didn't much care for Ray's music either, and broke 'Cry' over his microphone in protest.

When Ray returned to Australia for the third time, in March 1956, the result was even more harrowing. He was met by 4,000 screaming fans at Sydney Airport, and despite police warnings he waded into the crowd, with terrible results. Ray's Shantung suit was ripped, his watch was taken from his wrist, and he was crushed against a wall and then dragged headlong into the crowd. A Sydney airport official called it 'the most disgusting and hysterical exhibition we have ever seen here'. Six policemen picked Ray up and carried him to safety at the nearby terminal, before he composed himself and was driven to his hotel. Ray, in what perhaps was the first time such an endorsement was made, claimed that the loyalty of his Australian fans was 'unequalled anywhere in the world'.[36]

The teenage rebellion that occurred across Australia in the 1950s became best known for a minority of colourful, sometimes criminal, but often harmless gangs known as bodgies and widgies. Young boys (bodgies) and girls (widgies), many of whom came from working-class families in inner-city suburbs, were the sharp end of a problem collectively referred to by their elders as 'juvenile delin-quency'. They were routinely demonised in the press, partly because there was something decidedly 'un-Australian' about the way the bodgies and widgies dressed and behaved, and the language they used. At one point, a magazine defined *bodgie* as 'anyone pretending to be American'.[37]

The United States was indeed the cultural touchstone for so many teenagers — in part because of the lingering influence of the US troops in Australia during the war, who left behind elements of what they wore, how they spoke, and how they swaggered. Other teenagers embraced the new milieu because they could afford to be part of it, and access the imported consumer goods, including record players and records. The conflict between the establishment and the delinquents was sharp and, on occasion, violent. In February 1956 reports emerged in Brisbane of national servicemen assaulting anyone they suspected of being a bodgie.[38]

In Melbourne the 'gangs' were just one more problem that the city wanted to solve before the Olympics. Victoria Police established its own Bodgie Squad, a group of young coppers, fresh out of the academy, with the licence to dish out a bit of physical psychology on any errant teenager they found lurking in the city streets. The copper who set up the squad, Senior Sergeant Fred Galliver, saw its role as getting back control of the city. 'There were numerous bashings and gang fights in the CBD,' he said. 'People were waylaid and accosted walking to Flinders St station and other places to use public transport. Theft of motor cars was prevalent and "shop stealing" ... was out of control.' In three and a half years the squad made 1,700 arrests; Galliver boasted that it pushed the bodgies and widgies out of the city and into the suburbs, where they lingered a little longer.[39] Some bodgies gave the coppers a special name — the Purple People Beaters, because purple was Elvis's favourite colour.[40]

Many of the kids congregated on the Flinders Street steps, where a primitive hierarchy was at work, denoting influence and importance. 'It all depended how highly ranked you were in the mob — where you stood, where you were allowed to stand on the steps,' said Pauline, a widgie. 'Nobody from other mobs could go through that area — that was their turf ... [but] they wouldn't notice anybody else in the city ... I mean they'd walk through the city like there was nobody else there. They just lived in their own world.'[41]

They identified with their tribe by the colourful and styled clothes they wore, a vivid contrast to the drabness of the uniforms of city workers — grey and white suits and skirts, hats, coats, and sensible shoes. While they borrowed some American slang, they found ways to adapt it to their circumstances. The popular stereotype was the widgies were 'loose'; the evidence was one woman dubbed the Melbourne Queen of the Widgies, who had numerous consorting charges and a de facto husband.

The bodgies were thought of as tough, threatening, and sexually voracious. Yet many of them congregated around that pillar of suburban innocence, the milk bar. Some milk bars had jukeboxes, which meant there would always be music; the milk bar owners who wanted to avoid 'trouble' often got rid of the jukebox.

There were few attempts from the broader community to engage with the bodgies and widgies. Newspaper reports helped foster the idea that many of the teenagers were nascent criminals and threats to social stability. After spending three nights among the 'juvenile delinquents', two Melbourne reporters — one aged 25, the other 21 — concluded:

> 99 per cent of them mean no harm. But there is a vicious 1 per cent, a core of tough, Americanised milk bar Brando's. A 'core' that could take over the milk bar 'movement' and make *The Blackboard Jungle* a Sunday school picnic. This core could turn the present happy, harmless, idle milk bar 'cowboys' into gangs of irresponsible young thugs.[42]

But the other part of the message — that teenagers were actually better behaved than at any time since World War II — was often lost amid the dramatic reporting. What was notable, though, was the curiosity about how different these teenagers were: they were a tribe apart, observed in the wild like a social science experiment. '[C]onversations we had with teenagers ... [with] crew cut "cats" and "sharpies" who speak a weird "lingo" taken from American films ... oddly-dressed, strangely-spoken lads sipping soda and replaying the current "craze" record Rock Around The Clock.'[43]

The Victorian government took the problem seriously enough to commission a special inquiry by Justice John Barry into juvenile delinquency. Barry's report was released in July 1956, and made a sensible diagnosis of the issue, much to the chagrin of some of the city's newspapers. 'Serious though the problem is, we feel that occasionally it is presented in an alarmist and unnecessarily sensational fashion,' the judge observed.[44] Evidence supporting his view appeared a day later, when one newspaper represented one of Justice Barry's recommendations as 'banning the birch' for children under 16.[45] The other recommendations including requests for extending the school leaving age, initially to 15 and then to 16, and ensuring that only teachers with a state-accredited teaching qualification were allowed into the classroom. In the 103-page report there was only one mention of bodgies and widgies.

Before long, the community anxiety about 'juvenile delinquents' started to find a direct connection to the Olympics. Reports emerged of £1 million of damage to Olympic Park in August 1956. Les Coleman, as chair of the construction committee, was hard-line about the solution: to provide 'a strong armed guard' to protect the facility. 'The committee is seriously concerned at the wilful and thoughtless damage,' he said. 'If the police are unable to give us added protection for which we are prepared to pay perhaps private enterprise can help.'[46] Coleman's tone suggested a sense that something, somewhere, was going wrong that was beyond the Games organisers' remit. No one wanted to be caught unprepared.

Coleman's singular focus could now afford to be on the Games, as his political career was effectively over. He had lost his seat in the Victorian Legislative Council in the 1955 election, and although he was still on the Melbourne City Council, the Labor Party split meant the alliances he needed to rely on to become lord mayor were compromised.[47] The timing of his fall from political power was, in one way, fortuitous for the Olympics: it meant Coleman's forensic eye could concentrate on the Games. The breakaway party that Coleman had been part of had delivered its electoral poison to the federal ALP at the 1955 election, just as it had for John Cain seven months earlier. Anti communist party preferences were integral to Evatt's Labor losing ten seats in the 1955 federal poll. The split had not only torn Labor apart, it had eliminated much of its parliamentary talent, paralysing its capacity to regenerate.

*

On Sunday 9 September 1956 Betty Cuthbert set a new Australian record for the 200 metres when she ran 23.9 seconds. The meeting — the final Olympic trials — was on the cinder track at Sydney's Moore Park. Marlene Mathews had hurt a hamstring in the warm-up and was advised not to race. She had a history of leg injuries dating back to the Empire Games in Vancouver in 1954, when she was carried from the training track with a suspected thigh muscle injury. Now she was confronting a hamstring niggle just two months out from the Olympics.

Six days later, the MCG faced its own trial when the VFL Grand Final between Melbourne and Collingwood was held on what was about to become the home of the Olympics. With the ground awaiting the final touches, it was about to be tested by what turned out to be a record crowd. The old grandstand was demolished after the Queen's tour, and its replacement — called the Northern or Olympic Stand — started in June that year. It was to hold 41,000 spectators, 31,000 more than the stand it replaced. The ground had also been re-graded, 5,000 feet of drainage pipes had been installed, and the pitch where Sir Donald Bradman had thrilled thousands of spectators had been torn up. The Melbourne Football Club, whose home ground was the MCG, had spent most of the 1956 season at the nearby Olympic Park, and then at Albert Park, while the stand was being built.

Bruce Howard was there to photograph the Grand Final for *The Herald*, and it became one of the greatest spectacles he ever saw. The ground heaved with people, pushing to the edges of the boundary line, between the fence and the field of play. Fans scrambled to the top of the stairwells of the new Northern stand. Health department officials became so alarmed that they ordered the gates of the ground to be closed an hour before the match started. But those locked out became agitated; they knocked their way through the gates and found spots to sit or stand. Some perched in tree branches that over-looked the oval, and others used ladders to climb into the ground.[48] Ambulance officers treated 157 people during the game. A further six fans were taken to hospital — one had had a heart attack, another had collapsed, and four others had broken limbs. One estimate put the number locked out at 25,000.[49] The total attendance was 115,802. It was a massive, unpredictable crowd. And it forced the Olympic officials to wonder how they were going to cope in November.

The early diagnosis of the problem was that the old MCG stands were not the main issue — it was the new stand, where spectators had forced their way in to find a vantage point. Others recalled that the Olympic officials had promised everyone — locally and overseas — that the reconfigured ground could hold 120,000 people. On the evidence of the Grand Final, that was bunkum.

Sir William Bridgeford, who had taken over as CEO of the Melbourne organising committee in May 1953, interpreted the chaos as a warning of what could happen at the opening ceremony. 'We are anticipating a crowd of 110,000 for the opening ceremony,' he said. 'If the crowds are going to behave as they did on Saturday, maybe we will have to picket the whole area.' Fencing in an Olympic Games opening ceremony didn't seem like a great idea. But what were the options?[50] One Melbourne City councillor expressed the anxiety many other officials were feeling: 'The big thing we have to think of is that we will be in the eyes of the world, and we can't afford another episode like last Saturday.'[51]

Bruce Howard saw it differently: 'It was the first big event at the stadium with the new grandstand ... that was the curtain-raiser to the Olympics and the pictures that came out of there were: "Look at that stadium!" Or "That many people could get in!"'[52]

A meeting was called in the last week of September to discuss possible solutions. Booking seats for VFL Grand Finals would be considered, as would limiting the MCG's capacity and investigating whether the building regulations needed to be changed to accommodate such large attendances. The meeting involved police, the Health Commission, and representatives of the MCG Trustees. No Olympic officials took part.[53]

*

Marcus Marsden's office for organising the Olympic torch relay turned out to be his cramped digs in the geology department at the University of Melbourne. It was there that he planned a relay route that had not been fully inspected by anyone, had not had any of the distances checked, or even an itinerary compiled. He had one piece of largesse on his side: General Motors Holden donated three sedans and a panel van, plus their service network, for the team to drive from Melbourne to Cairns, and during the actual relay on the return journey. It was just as well, because it soon emerged that Marsden's task — to plan a 24-hour convoy that required a range of people to be involved at a range of locations down the east coast across several days — was an enormous organisational feat.

Marsden assembled his team, which consisted of his deputy (and University Athletic Club vice president), Peter Hoobin, and 16 student drivers. By mid-September the plans were in crisis. Marsden was unable to get confirmation from the Olympics' organisers on key initiatives, ranging from uniforms for the relay personnel, support from the Army, funds for the convoy, departure dates, accommodation bookings, and the possibility of a trial run.

The one attempt at a trial was organised by the NSW Amateur Athletic Association in 1955. It went from Maitland to Sydney, a distance of about 212 kilometres. The trial showed that most runners didn't require seven and a half minutes to complete their mile, but it also revealed the need for police support along the route (for traffic management and to ensure runner safety), and the value of having dedicated communication across the route. Police were engaged for the real relay, but Marsden was never given communications support — he would do it all without a walkie-talkie. One other recommendation emerged from the NSW trial: 'all those competing should have a haircut and shave shortly before running'.[54]

The one important thing Marsden didn't have to worry about was the torches. The approved number of 110 torches, made of a die-cast aluminium alloy, had arrived from England in July, along with 4,200 fuel canisters. The model had been trialled and worked efficiently during the Olympic equestrian competition that had been held in Stockholm during the European summer. Also included in the consignment were the ceremonial torch — to be used to light the flame at the MCG — and a spare.

Marsden was becoming more anxious, as a letter he wrote to his Olympic boss reveals:

> With the end of the academic year approaching, and examinations consequently almost here, my teaching duties are multiplying daily. Students are demanding tutorials and personal tuition, which they are entitled to receive as the top priority. If I can spread this work over a period of four weeks it will be possible to do it, but if left much longer it will simply be impossible to accomplish everything![55]

The letter was dated 25 September. Time was ticking on the torch relay.

*

Bruce Howard was puzzled. He couldn't believe there wasn't more publicity about the fast-approaching Games. There had been plenty of news about the wrangling, the discord, the arguments, and the delays, but where were the stories about the athletes and their preparation? He summoned up the courage to suggest to his boss, *The Herald*'s picture editor, that he do a series on people across the city getting ready for the Games. His boss agreed, on the condition Howard didn't neglect his other work.

Howard jumped into the project with youthful enthusiasm; no one else at the afternoon broadsheet had thought of it. Nor did anyone at Melbourne's other two newspapers do anything similar.

Three years earlier, the critical tone of the Melbourne press reports about the preparations for the Games had been cited as partly explaining the IOC's misgivings about the city's ability to deliver the Games. Later, Brundage thanked the press for helping him drive home his message about the urgent need for Melbourne to get its act together. Perhaps now, Howard thought, the time had come for that to end.

Chapter Eight
Clouds on the Horizon

When Colin Bednall walked into the old Heinz factory in Bendigo Street, Richmond, he saw holes in the cement floor where the giant boiling vats had once been, and drains still coated with sauces and jams. Hidden in the long grass outside was a foundation stone for the assembly of Wertheim pianos, laid by former prime minister Alfred Deakin. For the next two years, Bednall's office would be the anteroom off the toilet attached to the old staff canteen.

In December 1954 a company called General Television was established so it could bid for one of the two commercial television licences in Melbourne. The consortium behind the bid was made up of *The Age*, *The Argus* and *The Australasian*, J.C. Williamson, Greater Union Theatres, and radio broadcasters including 3KZ, 3UZ, and 3KY. Bednall, along with Arthur Warner, was one of the subscribers. Warner was a Victorian Liberal MP and former government minister, and had been something of a kingmaker for the leadership of Henry Bolte, who would become premier six months after General Television came into being. Warner's electronics business made the Astor range of products, including radios. Now it would make televisions. Bednall's involvement proved that he was putting his money where his mouth had been in the royal commission. General Television might have been built around Warner's business and wealth, but Bednall was integral to the company's licence application — he wrote it.

Television represented the next exciting phase of Bednall's career, but the move to the new medium disguised how hard he took the death of his mentor, Sir Keith Murdoch. '[It] deeply disturbed me and led me in to an unsettled, sometimes tortured life … From my days as a teenage reporter, I had refused every invitation to leave Murdoch,' Bednall later wrote.[1] Murdoch's sudden death in 1952 exposed Bednall in ways he had not expected, professionally and personally. Some rivals within Murdoch's Herald and Weekly Times told Bednall how advertising agencies were saying that now Murdoch was gone, Bednall 'will never be heard of again'.

Bednall's relationship with Murdoch was filial, but he was one of several young men Murdoch cultivated to aspire to the company's senior roles. Murdoch's model was British media tycoon Lord Northcliffe, who had bestowed his patronage on a young Murdoch. Bednall took all his big career decisions to Murdoch for ratification, but that didn't mean he was unaware of how Murdoch worked. 'To win men over to his side, he did frequently make promises he had not the slightest interest of honouring to gain wealth and power to himself,' he observed.[2]

Bednall found a way out of his despondency by joining *The Argus* in Melbourne, a once-venerable publication that had started in 1846 and had been bought by the Daily Mirror group of Britain. Under Cecil Harmsworth King, *The Daily Mirror* became the biggest-selling daily paper in the world. It was King who hired Bednall to be managing director of *The Argus* and *The Australasian* from 1 March 1954, six months before the royal commission's final report was tabled in parliament. Bednall was paid an annual salary of £8,000 (Australian), and had a £1,000 expense allowance. *The Mirror* was resolutely working-class in focus, but King had no such directions for Bednall. The political complexion of *The Argus* was to remain 'independent'.[3] The inevitable honeymoon did not last — there were a range of issues that London and Bednall had with each other. Despite Bednall's championing of the Menzies government during his time in Brisbane, and King's assurance of independence, King was soon telling Bednall that although there was no obligation to support the Australian Labor Party, '[w]e should have regard to the interests of the man in the street'.[4]

Perhaps most interesting was King's reading of Menzies' role on the world stage, which he had no hesitation in sharing with Bednall:

The impression here is that Menzies is a bit too assiduous in toeing the American line. In the last resort we are necessarily in the American camp but at times the irresponsibility of their politicians is frightening. I take the view that it is up to the wiser people of the Commonwealth to keep the Americans from doing something irretrievably foolish. And the way to influence Americans is not by subservience but by making them feel unpopular, which is more alarming to an American than most.[5]

King's observations about Menzies were an intriguing perspective on a prime minister who would have thought his acknowledgement of US power did not come at the expense of his Commonwealth affections. King was like most newspaper men and fancied the certainty of his opinions, even if some of them appeared contradictory. In a later letter he told Bednall that Australia had to look to the United States for defence support in the new world order. 'England's influence in the Pacific is now weak or non-existent and there is no point ignoring the fact,' he told Bednall. 'Financially and commercially, Australia has much closer links to England than with the US, but militarily this is not so.' In this King was spot-on, as the Suez Crisis would confirm. Finally, King reminded Bednall about the power of the Olympic Games: 'Nothing could damage Australia's reputation abroad more surely than a muddle over the Games.'[6]

King reassured Bednall that he was on track to re-establish *The Argus* as one of the world's great newspapers, but the resilience of competitors *The Sun* in the morning and *The Herald* in the afternoon was a challenge. Bednall managed to turn a loss of £92,623 at *The Argus* and *The Australasian* in 1954 into a modest profit of £50,233 in 1954–55.[7] In his first year Bednall also increased the paper's circulation — from 160,000 to 168,000 copies per day — which put it ahead of *The Age* (128,000) but still well behind *The Sun* (440,000). But his attempts to diversify and expand the product often fell on deaf ears in London. Bednall had a bold plan for *The Argus* to launch an evening paper to take on *The Herald*, with a pre-lunch edition and a 'mass' edition at 3 pm, but no one in London was interested.[8] It was no wonder that his enthusiasm started to ebb from newspapers and flow towards television, which seemed to offer limitless opportunities. He resigned from *The Argus* in 1955 and received a parting note from King at the end of the year, wishing him well in 1956. 'I am glad to hear you are likely to be the general manager of General Television,' King noted.[9]

On 18 April 1956 it was announced that the General Television Corporation (known as GTV) had been granted one of the two commercial television licences in Melbourne. The other licence went to The Herald and Weekly Times, confirming the suspicion that the established media groups were always favourites to pick up the licences. In what was another compelling example of the Labor Party's inability to unite on anything during its lowest point, an application by Doc Evatt and the Australian Workers' Union came up against a bid by the notoriously conservative Sir Frank Packer that also included the NSW Labor Council's 2KY radio station. Evatt's application was contrary to the royal commission's opposition to political parties holding a licence, which meant the bid was at best misguided, and at worst a demonstration of Labor picking a fight it didn't need to be in.

There were seven licence applications in Sydney but only four in Melbourne. GTV's secretary, V.G.H. Harrison, said: 'The great object of the corporation now that it has been granted a licence will be to get on the air in time to cover the Olympic Games for the people of Melbourne.' In Sydney the two licences went to Sir Frank Packer's TCN 9 and a Fairfax subsidiary, Amalgamated Television Services (ATN), ensuring that the first four television licences issued in Australia were awarded to organisations that already had media interests.

Bednall had got what he wanted. And as general manager of GTV-9, he would have to deliver the modest offering of only eight and a half hours of programming a week in the first year of its operation, 14 and a half hours in the second year and 27 and a half hours in the third. Its crosstown rival, the HSV-7 station, was far more optimistic, planning 35 hours a week in its first year and 50 hours in its second. Sir Arthur Warner's conservative approach was based on the forecast that only 8,000 television sets would be sold in Victoria in the first year.[10]

Warner took an almost defeatist air into the looming television battle. He told Bednall that he didn't need to get GTV on air first. He should take his time: HSV would dominate TV advertising anyway because of its newspaper interests, and GTV should accept that it would be a worthy second. Bednall didn't believe this and tried unsuccessfully to convince Warner otherwise. He gave up in the end, but he still refused to accept that GTV could not better its competitors. 'They don't understand these fellows ... newspaper advertising is a great promotion but word of mouth is more powerful and that's what we'll do,' he told one new employee.[11]

Bednall was up against a tough, cashed-up, buoyant rival which was committed to show almost four times as much content as his station. He had never run a television station, had never been on television, and had no one at his disposal who knew more than he did about any of it. Now he had to turn an old factory into a television studio in time to broadcast the Olympic Games.

*

The Empire might be in decline, but Britain was trying to hang on to its status as a world power. And during the Cold War, the best way to show that you were still pre-eminent was to have atomic weapons. The Soviet Union had done it with its own atomic explosion in 1949, and there was a determination in the United States to match and then outstrip the Soviets when it came to the power and range of its weaponry. Britain had opted in to the arms race, and if anyone had any doubts about the impact the first tests at Montebello had on the British mood, they needed only to look at the tabloid *Daily Mirror*. 'Today Britain is GREAT BRITAIN again — in the eyes of the world,' the front-page story stated.

> The orange-coloured flash of the explosion of Britain's first atomic bomb did more than signal the unleashing of a new and terrifying weapon of war. It changed a world still ruled by power politics. It signalled the undisputed return of Britain to her historic position as one of the great world powers. Today she stands alongside America and Russia in possessing not only the secret of the atomic weapon, but also the power to produce it.[12]

Australia had become Britain's handmaiden in its attempt to reclaim primacy in the changing world order. The Australian view, however, made it all sound like a Commonwealth mutual back-scratching exercise. When the time came to announce the Maralinga nuclear tests, the minister for supply, Howard Beale, made clear what was behind Australia's cooperation with Britain:

> It is a challenge to Australian men to show that the pioneering spirit of our forefathers who developed our country is still the driving force of achievement.
>
> The whole project is a striking example of inter-Commonwealth cooperation on the grand scale. England has the bomb and the know how; we have the open spaces, much technical skills and great willingness to help the Motherland. Between us, we should help to build the defences of the free world and make historic advances in harnessing the forces of nature.[13]

What Beale — and anyone else associated with the tests — failed to point out was that the Mosaic tests at Maralinga were not actually atomic tests — they were trialling the triggering devices for hydrogen weapons that were to be tested the following year.[14]

The omission was typical of the public discussion about the nuclear tests. There were limits on how much information was put in the public domain. There were 'D notices', which were security notices advising newspaper editors not to publish certain information because of the sensitivity of the details. These were a preventative measure, but they were supplemented by public and private rebuttals of any doubt, contrary positions, or even gentle inquiries about the tests. Objections were dismissed, and misgivings swatted away. Critics were marginalised and dismissed.

Some of this aggressive counterattack came from the politicians, but often it emanated from the scientists conducting the tests. Walter MacDougall, in the massive hinterland that most of the nation rarely thought about, traversed the intricate routes which many Indigenous Australians used and concluded that forcibly removing these communities from their traditional lands would be the end of them, as it would condemn them to an aimless wandering far removed from the food and water sources they knew so well. He wrote down his observations, which he planned to publish in an Adelaide newspaper in November 1955:

> Whenever the white man finds something of value to him in any Aboriginal area the Aborigines are pushed aside. I believe that what is happening to these natives is contrary to the spirit of the declaration of human rights in the United Nations charter. If no check is possible they seem doomed to increase the number of displaced persons in the work world — to become prideless, homeless vagabonds living by begging, stealing and government handouts.

The reaction to the proposed article became a stick to beat MacDougall with, and a means to prevent him from raising the issue again. After being hauled before the head of the Woomera range and told he had no right to speak publicly, MacDougall pushed back and refused to be intimidated. The matter was taken further, and the Australian department of supply's chief scientist, Alan Butement, weighed in: MacDougall 'had a lamentable lack of balance in his outlook in that he is apparently placing the affairs of a handful of natives above those of the British Commonwealth of Nations'.[15]

It wasn't an isolated example. When the British scientist Scott Russell was quizzed about the fate of Indigenous Australians at Maralinga, he responded that they were a dying race and were dispensable.[16] Later, the British-born scientist Ernest Titterton, one of the founding members of the Atomic Weapons Tests Safety Committee, claimed that if Indigenous Australians didn't like the tests, they could vote to change the government. Such ignorance was stupefying: Titterton failed to take into account that it wasn't until 1967 that Indigenous Australians even got the vote. This hubris was at the heart of the atomic tests to which Menzies signed Australia up; secrecy in the national interest was one thing, but misinformation, wilful ignorance, and sly character-assassination were just as dangerous.

In all the discussions, scientific analysis, and forecasting, the impact of the fallout from the nuclear tests on the Olympic Games barely got a mention. The earlier round of tests in 1956 generated anxiety across the country because radioactive rain fell as far afield as Queensland, but why was there no debate about the next round of tests, scheduled for September? Wasn't it possible that if the weather patterns were in the wrong place at the wrong time, there would be debris over Melbourne when the world's attention was on the Games? Patrick Sheehan, the head of mining and metallurgy at the Ballarat School of Mines, certainly thought so.

Sheehan studied rainfall after atomic explosions and noticed a pattern of freak rain soon after the explosion. He forecast rain for Melbourne for three to five days after the September explosion in Maralinga — 'just two months before the Olympic Games', he noted. 'If atomic explosions have no effect on weather, and are not harmful to humans, why are sites selected on the opposite side of the world to those countries which originate the tests?'[17]

It was a fair question, but not too many people were asking it and certainly no one was answering it. Yet weather did appear to be a factor when deciding to go ahead with the blast. One clue came from tests director William Penney's notes as he contemplated the final timing of the September blast: 'Am studying arrangements firings but not easy. Have Olympic Games in mind but still believe weather will not continue bad.'[18]

The British acknowledged that there needed to be a higher grade of information about the weather that could not only provide more certainty around the blast times but also give more reliable data about the prevailing winds for potential fallout. The best location for the weather station was identified as the Rawlinson Ranges, about 560 kilometres north-west of Maralinga. Butement believed the station was important in 'ensuring that no circumstances will arise which cause a change in the drift of the fallout to the east or south east centres of population'.[19] Regardless of what was said officially and publicly, there was no doubt the scientists were well aware of the how the fallout could be affected by prevailing weather conditions.

MacDougall opposed the station's location from the start. He believed the road to the station would not only intrude into the lives of the local communities but also open the way for others to follow, including miners. He was also concerned at the prospect of the station's staff having an impact on the Indigenous Australians' lives. MacDougall wrote to every relevant bureaucrat he knew to protest about setting up a station in a reserve: it was against policy and against common sense.

He received some initial comforting noises, but once it emerged that MacDougall was about to raise the issue with the Adelaide papers, all signs of support evaporated. He was described as 'making quite a fuss'; one of his superiors reminded him of his obligations as a Commonwealth officer, and also warned him off speaking to the press. But MacDougall was correct: the original agreement on

Indigenous protection made clear that no roads would be built into reserves or interfere with areas that were important to tribal life.[20]

The station went ahead anyway. Britain paid for it to be built and Australia agreed to pay for the running and maintenance costs for ten years. It named the station Giles after a British-born nineteenth-century explorer of Central Australia, Ernest Giles. Building the station meant carving a road through an Indigenous reserve largely peopled by Pitjantjatjara and Yankunytjatjara speakers, from Finke, just south of Alice Springs. The Finke River gave the place its name; although it was usually dry, it was part of a 350-million-year-old river system. It was ancient country, and it was to Giles that Robert Macaulay was sent on his first appointment as native patrol officer.

He started on his fiancée's Jean's birthday, 31 August. Although Macaulay was a Department of Supply employee, he was also given the titles of Protector of Aborigines in South Australia and Native Welfare Officer for Western Australia. He spent two weeks in Perth, acquainting himself with the files on Indigenous communities in the remote parts of the state, spent time with the relevant bureaucrats, flew to Adelaide, and from there flew on to his new job. MacDougall was waiting for him at the Mount Davies airstrip, half a day's drive from Giles.

Macaulay had never spent any time outside of Sydney. He arrived in a landscape that was harsh and subtle, confronting a brutal climate and a complex network of an ancient communities of Indigenous Australians, of whom he had only the most basic understanding. Giles was a building site: there were up to 30 construction workers putting the station together, and seven or eight meteorologists carrying out some preliminary testing. Macaulay saw an Indigenous camp very close to the station, but it would soon move a couple of kilometres away.

Macaulay slept under canvas and for two weeks was able to pick MacDougall's brain and hear about his experiences of the vast area the pair were about to share. There was no mention of the tests to come and what role Macaulay would play in them. Instead, he reminded himself of his two duties. The first task, from his bosses at the Department of Supply, was to help cushion the impact between the local communities and the people building — and, later, staffing — the weather station. The second set of directions came from Perth: that Indigenous Australians should remain in their traditional means of life as much as possible.[21]

Macaulay would implement these two goals with a firm adherence to protocol. He was not MacDougall, seasoned and able to draw on years of experience, who was prepared to grumble and agitate, but a young man trying to find his way in a bewildering and challenging environment. In time, some of the Indigenous Australians would think Macaulay was actually MacDougall's son: they were both tall and shared some Scottish antecedents, but that was where the resemblance ended. MacDougall made it clear that Macaulay was his junior. For the time being, Macaulay tried to settle in, with neither a vehicle of his own nor a radio to help him.

*

The chefs had finally arrived — from India, Pakistan, Hong Kong, and Singapore. There were ten cooks with experience of Muslim cooking who had been hired in Singapore by the Malayan Olympic Committee, the Royal Inter-Ocean Line, and the RAF. It was not a moment too soon, as the Olympic Village was about to undertake its first dress rehearsals.

On the first three weekends of September the athletes' village in Heidelberg was put through its paces, to see if it could cope with the 6,200 guests it would have in two months' time. The journalists went through on the first weekend; the other guinea pigs were 70 executive staff from Sydney and Canberra. The dress rehearsal was playfully called 'Operation Get Set'. The 70 'guests' slept in the beds, ate the food, and listened to the briefing about safety and medical facilities during the course of the weekend.

The Asian cooks were supervised by one of Melbourne's best

established Chinese chefs, Chinney Poon, who ran a cafe in the city's Chinatown. Poon had migrated from China in the 1930s, and believed that any Chinese cook would be able to handle the distinct cuisines of the 'Far East', whether it was Japanese, Siamese (Thai), Malay, Filipino, or Korean. And all offerings would be accompanied by Australia's 'world-class' rice.[22] While 92 per cent of the produce would be Australian — here indeed was the land of plenty — there was a shortage of certain spices. Nations were encouraged to bring along their own spice person to provide any additional flavourings required. Any other gaps in the menu would be covered by a selection of cookery books at the Village Catering Office.[23]

The simulations worked well enough for Melbourne's Olympic organisers to declare it a success. Now for the real thing.

*

Colin Bednall had plenty of ideas he wanted to roll out in the next few months, and the more time he had, the better. GTV would become the last of the four stations to launch. The first station was Frank Packer's TCN-9 in Sydney, which ushered in the first night of Australian television at 7 pm on Sunday 16 September. The opening footage was of a tall, elegant man wearing black tie. This was a gala occasion. Bruce Gyngell, the man in the dinner suit, then uttered the simple words: 'Good evening and welcome to television.'

Gyngell was speaking from TCN-9's studios at Willoughby, as two German-made television cameras transmitted his words to thousands of stunned viewers, some of whom were so unsure of what they were watching that they applauded. Although the introduction was simple, the rest of Gyngell's comments were more in keeping with the anticipation that surrounded the new medium:

> We feel very proud to be the first to give you television now and [a] preview of the exciting potential of its future in this country. Television, to millions of people overseas, is more than

mere entertainment: it has become a window to a wider and more fascinating world. It is our sincere hope that television in Australia will be the same.[24]

What followed was six weeks of programming, of about three hours a day, before the station formally launched in October with a full schedule. Gyngell, an erudite former Sydney Grammarian whose great-grandfather had organised the fireworks for Queen Victoria and Prince Albert's wedding, had become a favourite of Sir Frank Packer. He had been installed as the station's programming director, which meant a range of duties, including, apparently, introducing the start of television.

There was no doubt that those behind the introduction of television in Australia had grand hopes for the noble purpose of the medium. Those who owned a television set in those opening weeks were able to see a range of overseas programs, providing instant exposure to what was predominantly American popular culture. TCN-9 and Bednall's rival Melbourne station, known to some as Herald Sun Vision (HSV) after its owners, The Herald & Weekly Times, announced that they would be sharing the cost of those overseas programs, which meant advertisers could access both the Sydney and Melbourne markets. The stations' rate card offered advertisers the opportunity to sponsor a program on a one-off basis for £160 an hour.[25] The technical problems of broadcasting were to be ironed out by test transmissions — usually twice a day during the week — which would help TV manufacturers and retailers decide which type of aerial suited a particular region.[26]

Television was off and running. Bednall knew what he had to beat.

*

Robert Macaulay finally learnt about the new part of his job before the first atomic test at Maralinga, when MacDougall came back to Giles and told him that what was known as the Buffalo series was imminent. Even then, it wasn't made clear to Macaulay that a bomb was about to go off. Instead, he was asked to advise on the location of Indigenous Australians and whether any movement was likely within the next few weeks, particularly to the south.[27]

Macaulay's first patrol, with a driver while he awaited the arrival of his own vehicle, took him to the Tomkinson, Mann, and Musgrave ranges, along the northern border of South Australia. Whatever he found was as waste of time, because with no radio he lacked the means to contact anyone. Macaulay did meet some Indigenous Australians but, after speaking with missionaries and locals, concluded that they would not be moving.

With the date of the first blast looming, Supply Minister Beale submitted a report to cabinet: 'The Safety Committee point out that strict continuous ground and air patrols will ensure that there will be no natives inside the prohibited zone, but that there may be a few in the area immediately outside the prohibited zone.'[28] MacDougall and Macaulay were considered to be part of that 'continuous ground control'.

But the ground and air patrolling was neither strict nor continuous. Only two aerial searches were made of an area related to the intended explosion site — the first was 17 days before the first bomb, the second close to the firing of the fourth bomb, in October. One of the pilots involved thought that a single search of the area was enough because Indigenous Australians 'sleep most of the afternoon' and therefore didn't move around much.[29]

Another observer saw a group of 24 Indigenous Australians north-west of Maralinga, about four days before the first blast. They had left a mission and were heading south when they were picked up by a station truck. Another member of the Australian Radiation Detection Unit reported sightings of what he believed to be Indigenous Australians' hunting fires in the prohibited zone. MacDougall took the report seriously and went looking for them. No one else believed the ARDU member. Radio traffic derided what he had seen. 'A communication came back to me that I was going troppo. I had been up there too long; did I realize what sort of damage I would be doing by finding Aborigines where Aborigines could not be,' the officer said. His report was regarded with 'absolute disbelief'.[30] But MacDougall found them.

Neither MacDougall nor Macaulay could patrol the enormous outback hinterland to ascertain the Indigenous Australians' location, how many there were, and whether they were going to move into — or already were in — the prohibited zone around the blast site. MacDougall admitted to one scientist that his job was impossible. A member of the South Australian Aboriginal Protection Board later said that keeping Indigenous Australians out of the prohibited areas was a 'hopeless task'.[31]

One of the key British scientists involved, William Penney, later admitted he had no idea how the patrols operated: 'It was a very empty area. If there had been any Aboriginals I thought [MacDougall] would know about them and that sort of thing. If he was satisfied and he told me it was okay, then that was the best that could be done.'[32]

And so, on 27 September 1956, the first of the bombs went off.

*

On the same day, Colin Bednall's GTV network rolled out its first test program, a John Wayne western, to viewers in Melbourne and Geelong. The excellent quality of the images was courtesy of the station's transmitter, set at a height of 700 metres on Mount Dandenong, east of the city.

Bednall was delighted, and couldn't help spruiking the feedback GTV had received. 'We had scores of telephone calls, including calls from Americans visiting Australia who said they had never seen better transmission in America,' he said.[33] Better than America? That was saying something.

Chapter Nine
Lighting the Way

On 7 October the Russian ship *Gruzia* left Odessa, in Ukraine, on its way to Melbourne. On board was a stewardess called Nina Paranyuk. She was 34, single, and had no idea where the ship was going. All she knew was that she wanted to leave behind a peasant life of misery and hardship.

Paranyuk was born in the village of Hrushka, 200 kilometres north of Odessa. She had already endured two famines, the first of which claimed her father, while the second almost took her own life. Her two brothers were press-ganged into the Soviet army, and only one survived. Paranyuk's mother and younger sister were still at home, but she hadn't seen them in two years. She cherished the memory of her father telling her there must be better things in the world than their grim life in Hrushka. After years toiling on collective farms, Nina found a job at a new sugar refinery in Odessa. Then she became a receptionist and cloakroom attendant at a sanatorium for Communist Party officials. But grinding poverty dogged her steps — she worked six days a week, she did overtime without pay, and she had only two frocks (one for work, one for Sunday best), plus an old overcoat. 'Many nights I have gone to bed hungry and crying,' she later wrote. 'Always I kept praying I might get away.'[1]

Ukraine was not Russian by temperament or history — the country had only come under Russian control in 1793. There was a brief period of independence after the Bolshevik Revolution, but following the Nazi invasion of Poland in 1939, the western part of Ukraine that had been part of Poland soon joined the Soviet Union. Stalin's tyranny over the Ukrainians was total: he did all he could to extinguish their sense of identity and language. The Ukrainian distaste for Stalin and his regime was palpable and enduring.

Paranyuk applied to be a stewardess in East Germany but didn't get the job. Undeterred, she volunteered to work as a stewardess and go 'on overseas travel' from Odessa. In September 1956 she was summoned to the *Gruzia* and told to be ready to sail. She soon realised that the crew had been vetted by the Communist Party: they were all 'trusted people'. Before she could accept the job, she had to sign a document stating she had no relatives or friends in Australia. This was the moment when the anxiety of Paranyuk's uncertain future collided with her bitter-sweet memories of the past in Odessa. She clung to the image of the village's old stone church, where her family would go every week — until the priest was taken away, the church pulled down, and the stones used for Stalin's collective farming. 'Then ... the *Gruzia* sailed,' she recalled. 'I knew that the escape to freedom I had hoped for for so many years was getting closer.'[2]

Two days later, the Australian High Commission in London received a visit from a representative of the Russian embassy, who had a request to make. Australia had cut off diplomatic relations with the Soviet Union after the Petrov Affair in 1954, but this was a matter of some urgency. The High Commission sent a cablegram to Canberra explaining the request:

> The Russian minister called today [and said that he] consider[ed] it desirable to send to Melbourne, for the time of the Olympic Games, two Soviet Consular representatives for maintaining contact with the Australian authorities with the purpose of rendering them necessary assistance in questions connected with the stay of the Soviet sportsman in Australia during the Olympic Games.[3]

The Australian diplomats sought extra guidance from the UK Foreign Office, whose officers concluded that, though 'unusual', the request 'is not unreasonable and might be useful to us'.

Canberra agreed: 'We too have felt on balance that there could be advantage in having Soviet consular officers in Melbourne during Games. Our view will be that there is no connection between this arrangement and any discussions for resumption of diplomatic relations.'

The director-general of ASIO, Brigadier Charles Spry, advised that if the Soviet officials did come, it should only be for the duration of the Games: 'If such a Consular office were permitted to remain open indefinitely after the Games, it would defeat, to a large extent, the measures that have been planned regarding movement restrictions on Soviet Embassy officials when they return to Canberra.'[4]

Menzies considered the arguments and agreed that the USSR could resume diplomatic relations with Australia for the duration of the Olympic Games. The two officials would be given accommodation at the Savoy Hotel in Melbourne. It could only be two bedsit rooms because accommodation had become so tight. The Soviets agreed. The two men they sent were Dmitri Zaikin, 45, from Kiev, and Yuri Filimonov, 31, from Moscow. It is almost certain that Filimonov was a KGB agent. Zaikin was a seasoned diplomat who had been at a range of important Soviet posts, including New York during World War II, then Havana, before arriving in Melbourne.

The Australian Security Intelligence Organisation did its homework on each of them. Zaikin was '[of] typical Russian build ... short and stocky ... full face, sallow complexion, receding hairline and short closely cut dark hair, starting to turn grey. Widely spaced light blue eyes nose slightly hooked wide thin lips gently receding chin.' Filimonov presented a stark physical contrast: '[M]edium height, slim build, was a clerk at the Soviet Embassy in London and was also at Soviet Ministry of Foreign Affairs.'[5]

By the time the *Gruzia* arrived in Melbourne, the two Soviet diplomats had checked in at the Savoy.

*

The torch convoy team held a meeting on 10 October at the University Amateur Sports Club to get to know each other. Marcus Marsden had received some bad news during the day: the time of the torch's arrival in Cairns on 9 November had changed from 9.41 am to 1.09 pm. The three-and-a-half-hour difference threw every piece of scheduling Marsden had done out the window. It meant he had to significantly revise what he called his 'time and distance' charts — and he had only 30 days before the relay started.

Marsden's consolation was that he had already been in contact by letter with the four main state-based organisations — in northern Queensland, southern Queensland, New South Wales, and Victoria — and each had started selecting and training their torchbearers, and planning their civic receptions and local transport, with support from local police and ambulance. It would largely devolve to these state-based athletic associations to organise the relay in each state, but local councils, especially in northern Queensland, were integral hubs for community cooperation.

Darwin would be the Olympic torch's landing spot in Australia, after a journey of 13,672 kilometres — and 33 hours in the air — from Greece. The torch would then be flown to Cairns, where the running relay was to start. Cairns was therefore central to the plan. It was from here that the torch relay in north Queensland would be coordinated, including stages through Townsville, Mackay, Rockhampton, and Bundaberg.

Cairns had special requirements because of its remoteness and the conditions. In November the town is warm, often humid, and has a kind of tropical hum that is part of the build-up to the wet season. There can be downpours followed by warm and brilliant sunshine. It is verdant, rich country, but it can be challenging for anyone who isn't a seasoned runner.

In Far North Queensland Thelma Kahl and her husband, Ray, were busy raising a family of three children, all of them under five.

Ray was a canecutter. He went to work early, and started cutting at 6 am. The cutters would knock off for lunch and have a break as the heat reached its peak, then resume later in the afternoon, and finish at 5 pm. Ray would come straight home: there wasn't enough money for a beer at the pub. There were friends nearby but no extended family to call on when things were difficult. Thelma didn't have a driver's licence and so went everywhere on foot or took the bus. It wasn't until 1957 that Cairns had a supermarket. Until then, Thelma got her provisions from the corner store, or ordered her fruit and vegetables to be delivered. The family had a fridge but no hot water.

Ray and Thelma had grown up in Far North Queensland. They'd worked for the same company for a while and finished up meeting properly on a blind date. Thelma had always wanted to be a primary school teacher but life intervened. 'It just wasn't possible,' she said. 'I didn't know anybody who had done that.' The three kids were given their Sunday School teaching in a nearby house because there was no church close to the family home. Ray had a car, but it didn't get much use, except on some weekends when the family would go to a nearby beach and Ray would teach the kids to fish.

Ray had been cutting cane around Cairns for four years, mostly in a gang of two with a mate. They'd sign on in June and keep going until November, before the wet came. Cyclones would play havoc with the cane, and make it regrow crooked. The knowledge and skill the job required was slowly being lost. In Queensland in 1956 there were 8,700 canecutters like Ray and only 400 machine workers. Twelve years later, there would be 4,600 machine workers in the Queensland canefields and only 2,800 canecutters.[6] The work was hard, the temperatures hot, and Ray would come home to Thelma and the kids exhausted and dirty at the end of the day.

He was cutting cane at Enmore Estate, in west Cairns, for Jack Warner, an accountant in the town, when Warner's son John appeared on site. Ray had been thinking about the Olympic Games, knowing there would be no way he would be able to get down to Melbourne to see them because the cane still needed to be cut. Then

John turned up with an offer. Did Ray and his mate want to be part of the Olympic torch relay? Too right, Ray said.

But as fit and trim as Ray was after spending all day in the canefields, he knew it might not be enough to run a mile carrying a torch. Ray got some information about the size and weight of the torch. He did some rough calculations: it turned out that the torch was around the same dimensions as a bottle of beer. Ray filled an empty longneck with water, measured out a mile in his car, and then, after work, in the dark, ran the distance on a gravel road holding the beer bottle. The dogs barked and Ray's neighbours came out see what all the fuss was about while Ray did two laps around the block, every night. After a few weeks of training, he reckoned he was ready to carry the torch.

*

The Australian Olympic track and field team was due to be named on Sunday 21 October. There were a number of events, though, that would determine the team's final make-up. There was an Olympic squad competition at Moore Park, in Sydney, and then the final trials over two weekends in Melbourne.

Marlene Mathews believed her hamstring issue was behind her, but now she had a new problem, and her name was Betty Cuthbert. It was a small circle of excellence that was all too familiar to Mathews. Cuthbert's coach was June Ferguson, who as June Maston was one of the Fort Street Olympians who had inspired Mathews. Maston and Mathews had been at the Western Suburbs Athletics Club together before Maston left to set up a club in Cumberland, which Cuthbert made her athletics home. In 1954 Maston had predicted that Cuthbert would actually beat the great Marjorie Jackson's sprint records, a kind of heresy at the time. Cuthbert, at just 18, was doing her level best to prove her coach's forecast correct, and was building momentum ahead of the Games.

At Moore Park on the first weekend in October Mathews and Cuthbert both recorded 11.2 seconds for the 100 metres to break

Shirley Strickland's record, but Cuthbert crossed the line first. In Melbourne the following weekend Cuthbert stitched up the sprint double, beating Mathews in both races.

The two sprinters combined several days later, at Lidcombe Oval, for a special invitational meeting, when they were part of an attempt on the world record for the 880 yards and the 800 metres relay. Mathews, Cuthbert, and Fleur Mellor were part of the original team, but Nancy Fogarty, a promising sprinter, pulled out before the race with a leg injury. Hurdler Sylvia Mitchell replaced her and ran the first leg. She was uncertain with the baton and struggled with the handover to Mathews for the second leg. Normally such moments are accepted as risks of a relay race. But this incident, with the Olympics looming, perhaps seemed to hold greater importance. Mathews, Mellor, and Cuthbert motored through the last 600 metres and fell 0.3 seconds short of Great Britain's world record.

Mathews once again confronted Cuthbert in a 100-yard invitational, and won in an impressive 10.7 seconds. It was the first time she had beaten Cuthbert since her leg injury. Mathews told reporters that she felt in perfect condition, and the win had restored her confidence.[7] Both women were announced in the Australian athletics team for Melbourne, where they would resume their rivalry. This time, the prize would be gold.

*

Despite Eisenhower's intervention scuppering Menzies' Suez negotiations, Colonel Nasser was continuing to keep his options open. He sounded out the Soviets: would they provide 'volunteers and submarines', should Egypt come under attack? At the same time, he sent two envoys to start discussions with the CIA about the United States protecting Egypt from British military incursions and Soviet penetration.[8]

Menzies was perplexed at Eisenhower's intervention. 'It is all very well for people to denounce the idea of force, but in negotiations of this kind, it is good sense to keep the other man guessing,' he said.

The intervention also emboldened Nasser, who consolidated his hold on the Suez Canal.[9] Menzies flew back to London, briefed Eden, and then flew out to the United States, where he met Eisenhower and Dulles. The meeting with Eisenhower was strained, and the president gave Menzies little satisfaction about why he had publicly criticised the option to use force in the canal.

Menzies returned to Australia after 16 weeks abroad, and soon after delivered a 70-minute speech to parliament outlining the Suez predicament and denouncing Nasser's rejection of the proposal Menzies had put on the table. Users of the canal should not only reserve the right to impose economic sanctions on Egypt, he said, but should also use force, if necessary, to restore international control of the canal.[10] But events were already moving beyond Menzies' role in the crisis.

The diplomatic niceties disguised a far more dangerous strategy. On 22 October representatives of the French, English, and Israeli governments met in secret at a villa outside Paris to plan what would become known as Operation Musketeer. The details were agreed two days later. The Israelis would attack the Egyptian army near the Suez Canal. It would effectively be a pretext for an Anglo-French invasion.

Although Israel hadn't been one of the key nations taking part in the diplomatic negotiations over Suez, it had legitimate grounds for seeking redress. After the Jewish state was established in 1948, Egypt had refused passage through the canal to any Israeli-flagged ships or any ships bound for Israel.

After the Israelis invaded the Gaza Strip and Sinai Peninsula to move towards the canal, Anthony Eden told the UK parliament that there was an Anglo-French ultimatum to demand both nations withdrew from the conflict. A joint Anglo-French force would be sent to Egypt to separate the two combatants and ensure there was no problem for shipping using the canal. If Nasser didn't agree to these terms, Eden told parliament, the Anglo-French forces would go in to ensure compliance.

It was a dumb plan, based on a secretive piece of collusion. Not only that, but it was predicated on the false premise that Nasser was the one behaving badly by using his troops to defend his country from a foreign invasion. Not surprisingly, Nasser rejected Eden's 'offer', so Eden sent in the troops. It was a bizarre and ill-fated expedition. After the RAF practically destroyed its Egyptian counterpart, the Anglo-French campaign was halted after eight days, looking ham-fisted and counter-productive.

Menzies knew nothing about the plans for the military operation, and received no information from Eden other than urgings for him to publicly support what Britain was doing. Menzies obliged. 'You must never entertain any doubts about the British quality of this country,' he told Eden.[11] Menzies was happy to back that up with Australian military support if required. He had already told the British Commonwealth Relations secretary, Lord Home, that if force had to be applied, 'Australia would certainly be in this'. Menzies suggested it could take the form of air and naval support but no troops, because Australian soldiers were already committed overseas.[12]

The main concern was the extent of Australia's interests in the region, and whether Menzies' actions were actually aiding those interests. There was no doubt Menzies believed that by supporting Eden, he was also representing Australian interests. But the Suez Canal was less important to Australian trade than to British, and it was increasingly clear that Eden's desperate strategy was flawed and dangerous. Even so, Menzies' support for Britain never wavered.

Central to the West's anxiety about Nasser was his apparent willingness to deal with the Soviet Union. If anyone had any doubts about the Soviets' intentions within its own backyard, they were quickly confirmed when an uprising broke out in Budapest on 23 October. The Hungarian capital was in the grip of rising anti-Soviet feeling, driven by a suspicion that Moscow was ripping it off, especially on the bargain prices it was paying for the country's uranium. In the countryside hardship was increasing, from a poor harvest and shortages of fuel, driving discontent and disillusionment. The presence of Soviet troops was a constant reminder to Hungarians of Russian oppression. In neighbouring Poland a new leader, Władysław Gomułka, had emerged with the promise of distancing the country from Soviet control. Some Hungarians hoped their nation would take a similar path.

Students gathered in Budapest and endorsed a 16-point plan that demanded major economic reforms, restored the freedom of the press and of speech, free multi-party elections, total equality in relations between Hungary and the USSR, and the removal of all Soviet troops. More than 200,000 protestors marched on the parliament, and later in the evening toppled the huge bronze statue of Stalin that had been erected in 1951.

An attempt by the insurgents to capture the radio station so that it would broadcast the 16 points turned ugly, and as night became dawn, a battle between the secret police and the revolutionaries left 21 people dead. The government fell, and a new administration under the liberal Imre Nagy emerged. There were several days of comparative calm, and initial agreement in Moscow for this new regime to exist within the Soviet orbit, but reality was about to show otherwise.

Some members of the Hungarian Olympic team in Budapest were alarmed and profoundly moved by what had happened. The uprising's practical consequences for the Olympic team was that the two French planes chartered to take them to Australia could not land at the Soviet-controlled airfield in the capital. The planes went to Prague instead, and the team members had to find their way there. The Hungarians climbed aboard five buses that took them to Bratislava; from there they took a train to Nymburk, not far from Prague.

Once there, they held a team meeting to discuss what they should do. Some of the athletes thought the revolutionaries had finally seen off the Soviet troops, and they should go to Melbourne under the new Hungarian flag which the students had carried in Budapest. There was no doubt, the team decided after a vote, that they should continue on to Melbourne. But in the five days it took the two French planes to get to Melbourne, the situation in Budapest deteriorated. By the time the Hungarian Olympic team arrived in Australia, the Soviet army had re-established bloody control of the city.[13]

In Egypt Nasser was encouraged to see that the international reaction was increasingly on his side. Eden desperately cabled Menzies and asked him to express his public support. In parliament Menzies described the Anglo-French action as proper. Eden cabled back: 'Dear Bob, I cannot tell you how much your message has heartened me.'[14]

Eden needed all the help he could get. Many parts of Africa and Asia made it clear they didn't support the action. Indonesia even denied Britain's BOAC airliners refuelling rights at Jakarta airport. New Zealand was conflicted about the situation because it was supportive of the United Nations playing a role, while Canada's prime minister, Louis St Laurent, told Eden he regretted that the British prime minister had found it necessary to follow such a course of action. US president Dwight D. Eisenhower, who was in the final week of his re-election campaign, was even more direct: 'Those who began this operation should be left ... to boil in their own oil.'[15]

Richard Casey was shocked at the breakdown in relations between the United States and the United Kingdom. 'The almost physical cleavage ... was one of the most distressing things I have ever experienced,' he wrote.[16] Menzies' support appeared to have been given with a degree of sorrow, bordering on remorse. He was reluctant, even in private, to question Eden's determination to show that Britain was still an international power. Eden's problems were largely of his own making; a thin-skinned egotist with a yearning for the Empire's past glories was not the man Britain needed at this time of significant social and economic change. Eden's actions in Suez confirmed just how far the British Empire had declined.

The Suez Crisis was a chastening experience for Menzies, and one that subtly underlined the risk associated with retaining his devotion to a nation that was being overtaken by other countries and a more complex diplomatic order. Years later, Menzies explained why he had taken on the role Eden and Dulles had offered him: 'When your friends are in great difficulty and ask for help, you don't let them down.'[17] For all Menzies' pragmatic appreciation of the need for Australia to be friends with the United States, his acknowledgement of the importance of embracing Asia and Australia's near neighbours, and his wisdom in seeing that the Commonwealth was inevitably a changed organisation post-Empire, his heart belonged to Blighty. He could not escape his deep faith in Britain's pre-eminence, or his nostalgia for its moral and intellectual leadership. To Eden's successor as prime minister, Harold Macmillan, Menzies wrote:

> [D]eeply as I respect the Americans and realistically as I understand their immense power and significance, I have for a long time felt that they are not yet ripe for the intellectual and spiritual leadership which many people have assumed they can give. Great Britain still has the major resources in this field.[18]

On Suez, though, Menzies found himself on the wrong side of history.

The United Nations brokered a ceasefire in Suez, but by then Nasser had scuppered 47 ships in the canal and blocked the waterway. Eden's folly emboldened the Soviets, adding a new layer of instability to a notoriously complicated region. Colonel Nasser conflated the Suez Crisis with the looming Games: 'Nations guilty of cowardly aggression should be expelled from the Games.' IOC president Avery Brundage, unsurprisingly, was having nothing of it: 'We are dead against any country using the Games for political purposes, whether right or wrong. The Olympics are a contest between individuals not nations.'[19]

It was not the first instance, and certainly would not be the last, of an Olympic executive adopting a studied indifference to political reality. Nasser decided to withdrew Egypt from the Games. Lebanon followed.

*

On the calm waters of Ballarat's Lake Wendouree Merv Wood and Murray Riley cruised to a convincing win in the Olympic trial for the double sculls, easing their way to the finish line three and a half lengths ahead of their competitors. The win ensured that Wood, at the venerable (sporting) age of 39, qualified for his fourth Olympics. It would be Riley's second Games. Since teaming up in 1949, the pair had been beaten only once, when they were stuck in a poor quality shell and got swamped in the Parramatta River. This time the word was out that the Europeans, including the Russians, were coming to the Olympics with narrow, sleek double scull shells with a cutaway stern. They promised to be lighter and quicker. Even so, Wood and Riley had experience on their side. The Australian press thought the pair could do it.

Melbourne was starting to come alive with anticipation, putting the negative stories behind it as the final elements of the Olympic party were put in place. A 20-metre-high replica of the Olympic torch was hoisted into place at the corner of Swanston and Flinders streets, and seven other city intersections were decorated with Australian-themed images. This burst of activity meant that Andor Mészáros was in demand again.

The State Electricity Commission architect Bill Gower had the job of decorating the corner of Russell and Bourke streets in the city. Gower and his deputy, Bill Eales, went to see Mészáros to talk about what they were planning, but Mészáros wasn't impressed by their designs. He offered them something else, a design that managed to transform images from an Indigenous wall painting into something that gave the impression the Indigenous women were running. 'These beautiful runners had a fairy quality, a lightness and grace rarely accomplished,' Mészáros said.[20]

Mészáros assembled the required materials — the steel cables for the truss that framed and supported the figures, aluminium tubing for the figures themselves, and the plastic ribbons that wound around them, all of it anchored by the Olympic rings, which hung in the middle of the decoration. Mészáros, Gower, and Eales worked over several nights at the SEC architects' office to ensure the new design worked. The decoration was tied to one corner and tightened at the diagonal corner, giving the large Indigenous Australian figures — which were 4 to 5 metres high — an imposing yet stylish presence. 'It was certainly *the* decoration of the Games,' Mészáros declared proudly.

When the time came to add a plaque identifying the work's creators, Gower, according to Mészáros, listed it as 'W.G. Gower and Associates'. Mészáros' contribution remained anonymous. Perhaps Gower's ownership was merited by hair-raising work one evening during the Games when a ribbon on the decoration came loose. Gower borrowed a 20-metre ladder from the fire brigade so he could climb up and re-tie the ribbon. Mészáros called it a 'fantastic feat'.[21]

Bruce Howard's boss thought it was high time the young man went over to the MCG to scout for the best position from which to photograph the lighting of the Olympic cauldron. He also had to work out how to get the image back to *The Herald*. The MCG was only a ten-minute stroll to The Herald and Weekly Times' offices, in Flinders Street, but this job was all about time — a leisurely walk wouldn't cut it. Speed mattered.

As it was an afternoon broadsheet, all of *The Herald*'s main editions would be on the street by the time the cauldron was set alight late in the afternoon. The paper's executives decided to hold the presses in the midst of their final edition to ensure Howard could get a picture into the paper. But it would need to be a different picture to what everyone else had, and it would have to be delivered within minutes of the torch being lit.

Howard thought *The Herald* had made a good decision in not relying on an official image, which would have arrived much too late for the paper's deadline, but it put the pressure on him to deliver a crisp, evocative, and unique photo, on the tightest of deadlines.

'I needed to find somewhere I could take the picture unimpeded,' he recalled. 'So the top deck of the new Olympic Stand looked down on the cauldron. There was a gap between the [row] of seats and the grandstand, in no one's way and close to the stairs,' he said.[22] That would be where he would set up for the shot. Then he had to work out how he was going to get it back to *The Herald*. The stairs were his only way out, and he counted every one of them — 98 steps to the ground.

What would he do after that? And just who would be carrying the torch? That was always one of the Olympics' best-kept secrets. It was two weeks to the opening ceremony. Howard went back to the office to ponder his options.

*

It was 24 October and the torch relay convoy was finally ready to leave Melbourne. It had grown to ten vehicles. Marcus Marsden not only had his Holden vehicles, but the Army had also stumped up two three-ton trucks, a utility vehicle and officer, four other ranks, and relief drivers in each state, plus accommodation at Army camps as required on the journey. The Beaurepaire Olympic Tyre & Rubber Company was resolute in its involvement, even after Sir Frank's death, and provided tyres with gold lettering and a list of 20 outlets in three states that would provide replacement tyres.

By 2.30 pm, Marsden and his deputy, Peter Hoobin, eased their Holden sedan into traffic on the first part of the journey. Friends farewelled them, some even pointing out that it had only been a short distance away in Royal Park that the explorers Burke and Wills had started their own journey years earlier.[23]

*

Nothing seemed to be more Australian than Ned Kelly. The bushranger's story reflected the history of the nation's white founders: from their convict migrant past, downtrodden and angry, striking back against authority. To some, Ned Kelly's outlaw ways made him a hero. To others, he was a thief who killed honest policemen. Either way, Kelly's story stood at the centre of the nation's imagination — myth, legend, and fact conspired to shape the idea of who and what Kelly was.

The distinguished poet Douglas Stewart had written a play about Kelly that was first performed in 1942. Now, in the build-up to the Olympics, the Australian Elizabethan Theatre Trust decided to make the play its contribution to the Games. Sidney Nolan, whose extraordinary series of Kelly paintings captured some of the complexity at the heart of the Kelly story, was engaged to help with the design. Former Sydney actor Leo McKern, who was making a name for himself in London theatre, was hired to return home and play Ned. Fresh from his success with *Summer of the Seventeenth Doll*, John Sumner would direct. The play would open at the trust's Newtown theatre, in Sydney, before moving to Melbourne in time for the Games.

Sumner had his initial doubts about the combination of verse and prose in Stewart's play, and after he spent time with Stewart, the play was cut back and a new ending written. The playwright would later call it the 'ending to end all endings'.[24] Sumner was more optimistic after the rewrite. The positive build-up to opening night was only enhanced when photographer Helmut Newton flew up from Melbourne to take the pre-production images.

McKern was deeply absorbed in the role. He was 36, and stockier and shorter than Kelly was believed to be (he wore special heels for the role), and he started growing a beard soon after he returned to Sydney. McKern's research led him to adopt a strong view about Kelly:

> His enemies regarded him as a brute, a murderer, a wicked pig and a real criminal. I don't see him that way. I believe those remarks come from propertied classes of the time whom he opposed. But I do not see him according to the nonsensical modern legend which hails him a great hero, a nineteenth century Robin Hood. The truth, I feel, lies somewhere between. Kelly was no

uneducated bushman. You have only to see his handwriting and read some of his amazing speeches he made during his trial.[25]

The opening night, on 3 October, went well. The reviews were generous. But the bookings didn't follow. The show lost £1,000 a week.[26] Sumner concluded: 'If the subject does not appeal, people will not come. The attempt to make a folk hero of Ned Kelly, and the poetical treatment, was anathema to most.'[27] The play's commercial failure became the perfect reason for the Olympic organising committee to get cold feet.

A view emerged that it was the Melbourne arts establishment — deeply conservative and highly sensitive to public judgement — who decided that a dramatic depiction of a bushranger's life and times was not the kind of fare the rest of the world was ready to see, especially during the Olympics. The show was 'banned' from Her Majesty's Theatre in Melbourne after being scheduled to open on 4 December. 'This was a dreadful blow to the cast and all the professionals in the [Australian Elizabethan Theatre Trust],' Sumner said. McKern explained several weeks later that the show was a success in every way, except financially. Nonetheless, he thought the play should have come to Melbourne.[28] Instead, the trust brought *The Doll* back for a return season, from 3 December.

If Australians didn't want to watch a story about their most famous bushranger, what would they go to see? An international opera? Well, they might have, but not in Melbourne, and not during the Olympics. In September representatives of the Chinese Classical Opera Company turned up in Melbourne to get their first look at the Princess Theatre. The opera company was booked to perform for 19 days, from 21 November. The 85-person company had already been booked to stay at Ormond College and Janet Clarke Hall at the University of Melbourne. It all appeared to be set to become a fine addition to the city's cultural fare — before it wasn't.

The official reason was that Olympic officials had contacted the federal government and suggested that the Chinese appearance in

Melbourne during the Games could cause international embarrassment. Yet journalists contacted a range of local Olympic officials, all of whom denied any knowledge of such a rationale. Government representatives asked the company's Australian agent to reschedule, and the company said it was happy to perform elsewhere during the Games. There was a suggestion that theatrical agents had actually moved the original Melbourne performance from September to coincide with the Games, but no one could be sure.

Perhaps the real reason for the sudden decision was to do with a Queensland Liberal Party member who had written to her local MP to protest about the appearance of the Chinese company in Australia. Mrs Gladys Edwards, of Windsor in Brisbane, was dismayed at what her government was doing:

> I hang my head in shame when I realise that a Party I support is granting visa's [sic] to Red Spies to enter this country, as to any thinking individual this is clear. Has any move been made by any Member of the Government, to object to this serious state of affairs?

Mrs Edwards continued in her neat typewritten letter:

> One could expect these moves from the Opposition maybe — but its [sic] a real and wounding shock to realise Red Spies have friends in the Government also ... but you, being my representative in the Federal House, I do request you to raise your voice in protest of any more visits from 'Reds' under any disguise, to this fair land.[29]

The letter was sent from the local MP to Richard Casey, who passed it on to Harold Holt, who was the minister for labour (and immigration) at the time. The matter was then raised in cabinet on 16 October, when the decision was made to postpone the opera company's visit.

Condemnation came swiftly. Theatre agents with the company in New Zealand when the announcement became known were 'mystified'. The Victorian government admitted that no one in Canberra had consulted them before making the decision. Peter Russo, a seasoned and highly respected writer on foreign affairs, condemned the move, pointing out that going ahead with the performances would have been an example of Australia's growing cultural awareness:

> We could perhaps get away with this sulky, spiteful behaviour in our colonial infancy or even our Dominion days, but if we now want to move about among the big boys of international society, we shall have to show considerably more poise and less priggishness. The embarrassing international implication of this Chinese opera ban is that it will appear abroad as such a little man's gesture.[30]

A former Olympian turned sports journalist, Judy Joy Davies, took a slightly different but equally critical perspective:

> At the Olympic Games nobody cares what country a competitor, performer or entertainer comes from, nor do they worry about their politics. So would somebody please explain to me why the appearance of a Chinese opera company in Melbourne during the Games would cause 'inevitable controversy' or why it would be 'undesirable' [sic].[31]

Even the churches got in on it, with an Anglican priest in Prahran adding his voice to the condemnation, and affirming his faith in the power of the Games to bring some peace to the world. 'In the ancient Olympic Games, the spirit of the Games was sufficient to stop wars that were in progress,' he wrote. 'Surely the spirit of the Games will be sufficient to stop the cold war in Melbourne.'[32]

Menzies explained to parliament several days later: 'It would be more in accord with the spirit of the Olympic Games, we believe, if controversy was kept in the healthy rivalry of the arena, and that we should avoid anything that would cause differences or acrimonious dispute outside the arena at that time.'

Labor leader Doc Evatt got closer to the nub of it than he had for some time when he rounded on the government for bringing the nation's international reputation into question. 'It brings Australia, first of all in its cultural and international relations with the world, and as host country to all nations of this great Olympic Games, into ridicule and contempt and the Government ought to be ashamed of itself,' he responded.[33]

So this was what the Cold War looked like.

*

Little ripples found their way into the Olympic debate. After years of tub-thumping, arguments, dramas, big egos, and clashes of ideas and finance, there was an eruption of spotfires in the final few weeks before the Games began.

Why was Tasmania not shown on the map of Australia that adorned our athletes' official clothing, some observers asked. Well, if Tasmania was put on the map, there would need to be Heard Island, Flinders Island, Norfolk Island, even Mud Island too, according to an Olympic official. And it had always been like that — apparently, there just wasn't sufficient room for the sixth state of the Commonwealth to be included on the official Olympic clothing. 'Tasmania has not been left off with any intention,' the Australian Olympic Federation's Edgar Tanner explained. '[If it was included] we would have an atlas on the clothing instead of what has always been the badge of Australia in the Olympics.'[34]

Here was a nation which couldn't acknowledge its past, which wasn't sure how to engage with its neighbours, and which wasn't even convinced of its own geography. And it was about to hold the biggest international event in its history. Was Australia ready?

Chapter Ten
The World Waits

Nina Paranyuk was given orders on board the *Gruzia*. 'When you go to Melbourne, you will meet strange people,' a Communist Party official from Moscow told the ship's staff. 'You might meet a few of your people living in Melbourne. But don't talk to them or tell them anything. They are our enemies.'

Although Paranyuk didn't know it at the time, Melbourne had a small Ukrainian community that was united in its hostility to the Soviets. They would be watching when the *Gruzia* docked. Paranyuk and her colleagues were told not to even think about deserting the ship. One sailor had already deserted, but the ship's captain knew where he was, and he would be punished. Deserters, the party official said, were enemies of Russia. Nina Paranyuk didn't care — the thought of freedom was too powerful.[1]

Two weeks out of Odessa, with the *Gruzia* making progress through the Indian Ocean, the ship suddenly slowed down. Some of the crew told Paranyuk that the ship had changed course and was observing radio silence. Australia might not be their destination after all; they might finish up in a safe port, in China. The problem was Hungary: the *Gruzia* was waiting on directions from Moscow. Should they proceed? Would international reaction to the uprising — and its violent aftermath — mean the Soviet team would leave Australia and return home?

Several days later, a crew member told Paranyuk that the ship had been told to proceed to Melbourne. Radio silence had been broken. The *Gruzia* anchored at Appleton Dock, in Melbourne, on the evening of 7 November, six days late. Sixteen Hungarian trainers, cooks, and drivers immediately disembarked and were taken to the Olympic Village. Paranyuk, for the moment, stayed on board.

*

The torch relay convoy had a few hiccups from Melbourne to south-east Queensland, but not enough for Marcus Marsden to get too worried. Halfway around the world, the subject of his anx-iety and planning was about to start its own journey. Amid the rutted and weedy ground of a hill near Pyrgos, in Greece, Salteris Peristerakis, a 47-year-old physicist, positioned a reflector and put a torch on its hotspot of reflected light. A flame flared to life, just as in the legend.

From there, what was now the Olympic flame of the XVI Olympiad was carried by runners for 217 miles to Athens, where a plane was waiting. The flame was put into a miner's lamp and the plane set off. The Suez Crisis meant the torch couldn't go south, to Egypt, where bombers were active. Instead, it diverted across Karachi, Calcutta, and Singapore. Indonesians upset at Britain's role in Suez refused to service any British plane, so the flame had to bypass Jakarta and fly on to Darwin.[2] It all took more time.

Marsden's concern was Far North Queensland, where a combi-nation of heaving tropical rain, bad roads with potholes, loose soil, and washaways was wreaking havoc with his plans. Heading slightly away from the coast, Marsden's convoy left Rockhampton, bound for Mackay, along the Bruce Highway. It was a horror stretch. One of the sedans had skidded into a tree, and the Dodge utility was in danger of overturning, even at the cautious speed of 15 miles per hour. Nine times convoy vehicles were caught in storm-driven creeks, some for up to 45 minutes. Marsden could almost hear the clock ticking as he assessed the situation. The weather was getting worse: towns ahead of them were inundated with rain. One of the roads he had planned to take would be closed for two days. Marsden worked out three different routes. Each was eliminated as more rain fell and police closed roads. The convoy was marooned.

There was only one solution, and that was to get the convoy on the train to Sarina, near Mackay. Marsden rang Melbourne to get approval. There was resistance because moving the convoy onto rail tracks was expensive. Marsden persisted: there wouldn't be a torch relay unless they could get through. After a 90-minute phone call, Marsden was told he could use the train.[3]

Nagging at Marsden was the bigger problem: what the hell were they going to do on the way back, when they had the actual torch and dozens of runners? If this weather kept up, there was no way the torch would make it back to Melbourne in time.

The train finally reached Sarina in time for the convoy to embark for the last part of the scheduled trip, to Mackay, as the light faded. Then the rains came again, and one of the sedans got bogged. The convoy had lost a day, then made it up again. They pressed on in constant and torrential rain. Not for the first time, trying to coordinate an event, without a proper trial, at the start of the wet season in Far North Queensland looked like madness. Marsden clung to the hope, forlorn though it seemed, that if the rain stopped by Tuesday 6 November, the relay might be able to use the coast road.

*

Colin Bednall had been working on what would be the first telecast of a sporting event in Australia. Bednall knew how important sport was to Australians, and reasoned that covering a live outdoor event was the best way of getting GTV-9 prepared for the Olympics. He chose a trotting meeting at the Melbourne Showgrounds for practice. The station did a closed-circuit test on the Saturday night and then delivered the real thing.

Bednall was building his technical understanding and confidence as the Games approached, and had a few ideas up his sleeve. That was just as well, because his competitor was already on air and building an audience. On Sunday 4 November HSV-7 had launched, airing a speech by Premier Henry Bolte, a live broadcast from the Tivoli, a game show, the news, and an episode of the serial *Robin Hood*. There were also appearances from overseas 'stars', including the woman dubbed 'Miss Hollywood 1956', Jean Moorhead, and British comedian Richard Hearne.

Overseas stars were a feature of Australian television's first weeks, adding a touch of glamour and sophistication to what was otherwise a tentative foray into the medium by the new stations. Moorhead had a CV that was not fully revealed to the HSV-7 audience. She had actually been named Miss Hollywood in 1953, when she was just 18, and had appeared in *Playboy* two years later. It's hard to know how many viewers actually realised this, because the men's magazine was banned in Australia. In the absence of her magazine history Moorhead was given a breathless blurb promoting her appearance as a guest contestant on *I've Got a Secret*. 'Miss Moorehead [her name was spelt both ways] is one of the six most beautiful models in the United States,' *The Listener-In* cover gushed over a glamourous photo of the American.[4]

Richard Hearne was considered something akin to a serious artist because of his comic creation Mr Pastry, and therefore worth interrogating about what he thought of local performers. On his arrival in Melbourne he observed it would be 'selfish' for Australia to hang onto its acting and performing talent and not let them explore their opportunities overseas. 'Let them go out into the world and let others enjoy them,' he said. 'It's good for Australia and good for the world. Look at all the big Australian names in British show business. They're a wonderful advertisement for the country.' In case anyone doubted the authority behind Hearne's views, it was pointed out that he had appeared a record 14 times on *The Ed Sullivan Show* in the United States, and Sullivan was a notoriously pernickety judge of talent.[5]

Melbourne's radio shops accommodated the interest in the HSV-7 launch by remaining open until 10.30 pm. It was a big concession to the crowds of interested onlookers, who came in to watch the shop's television sets, all tuned to the launch. Eric Pearce hosted the event and made a solemn pledge at the end of the formalities: 'We dedicate this station to the full service of the community. To Australian life — the happy families in the homes — we promise to serve you faithfully and well.'[6] After that, the station crossed to a live performance from the Tivoli that went off flawlessly, except for a few moments of blank screen.

The station management measured their success by how far afield the images carried to underline the quality of the transmission. Reception in Maffra, 231 kilometres away, was excellent, and it was good at Lorne, Cola, Warragul, and Ballarat. Three hundred inquisitive souls were turned away from the Prahran Town Hall, where 32 television sets had been set up for the evening.[7]

Mrs Norm Everage had spent most of the year in Sydney, where she found that what seemed like a particularly Melbourne view of the world was not unfamiliar to Sydney audiences. Barry Humphries had been warned before he left Melbourne to work at Sydney's Phillip Street Theatre that Edna shouldn't go with him. 'I wouldn't take Edna to Sydney if I were you, she's too Melbourne. They've got a funny sense of humour up there,' he was told. Sydney audiences turned out not to be too different to their southern cousins, and Mrs Everage's desire to become an Olympic hostess resonated there too.[8] Back in town for the Tivoli show that appeared on the HSV-7 launch program, Mrs Everage's Olympic party piece was even more timely. Her accomplice from her debut 12 months earlier, Noel Ferrier, was replaced by Gordon Chater for the broadcast, but little else had changed. It looked like Mrs Everage was here to stay.

*

Four Dutch athletes, an official, and a coach were already in Melbourne when their country's national Olympic committee sent a telegram: 'At extraordinary meeting the Dutch Olympic participation to withdraw due to Hungary. Leave Olympic Village. Find other place to stay. Wear civilian clothes — if impossible remove [national Olympic] badge ... Cancel all hotel reservations but reserve Hotel Windsor ... Sorry all the best.'[9]

It was a sudden end to the Dutch athletes' dreams. Some were in tears, but there was no doubt about their nation's motives for their withdrawal: to emphasise the point, they donated 100,000 guilders to the victims of violence in Hungary.

The Swiss, legendarily neutral, had a harder time reaching a decision. The country's Olympic committee required unanimous support from its national sports federations to agree to send its team to Melbourne, but that didn't happen after the events in Hungary, so the Swiss decided not to attend. The country's most senior Olympic official, Otto Mayer, was the IOC chancellor; he called the withdrawal a 'disgrace'. The Swiss changed their mind, but it was too late to send the whole team so they withdrew anyway.

Five Nordic countries — Denmark, Finland, Iceland, Norway, and Sweden — prevaricated. Nine days before the opening ceremony, they agreed to compete.[10] There was also a 'new' team on its way — a united German team, which meant both East and West Germany would compete under a common flag and uniform but with no anthem for combined gold medal–winning teams and only an anthem from the country of an individual gold medal winner. Spain went out in solidarity with Hungary, implying that it didn't relish the prospect of fraternising with communists.

Then came the big one: Communist China pulled out too, because the Republic of China — known at one time as Formosa, and now generally known as Taiwan — was going. The official government mouthpiece in Beijing stated: 'This artificial splitting of China cannot be tolerated.' It had stressed that only one China could be recognised at Olympic level, and it was not Chiang Kai-Shek's little domain. Formosa, according to Beijing, was no more than a province of China.[11] But the circumstances on the ground revealed how a low-level mistake could feed into a high-level diplomatic stand-off.

At the official opening of the Olympic Village the Australian Army corporal in charge of the national flags was approached by a Chinese journalist and told that he was preparing the wrong flag for Nationalist China. Taking this in good faith, the corporal went off and returned with another Chinese flag — that of Communist China. When it was hoisted on the flagpole allocated to Formosa, all kinds of hell broke loose within the Formosa team. 'It's inexcusable. We will protest,' one of the Chinese Nationalists exclaimed. The contrite corporal admitted his ignorance: 'I didn't know the difference in the flags, but I certainly do now.'[12]

The correct flag was then reinstated, but not without offending a Peking journalist, who confronted Wilfrid Kent Hughes because he was insulted by his country's flag being taken down. Kent Hughes had just finished apologising to the Republic of China representative and now found himself trying to placate the other China. He told the journalist that the Communist China flag would be raised when the team arrived in the village. The discussion continued, without resolution.

Kent Hughes told the journalist he was too busy to continue the discussion but was happy to resume it the next day.

'This is a free country and I am entitled to talk to you,' the Chinese journalist said.

'Yes, it's so free I don't have to listen to you,' Kent Hughes replied, and walked off.[13]

The next day Communist China announced it would not be taking part in the Melbourne Olympics.

That made seven nations that were no longer coming to Melbourne. None of it had anything to do with how far away Australia was from Europe or Asia. It had little to do with the calibre of the competition, the weather, the time of year the Games were held, or the cost. It was about the Cold War and international sensitivities. The consequence for Australia was that Melbourne became the first Olympic Games affected by international boycotts. It was a legacy that no one in Australia wanted, especially after the controversies about having to transfer the equestrian competition to Stockholm because of Australia's quarantine rules, the fall-off in the predicted number of overseas visitors, and the fraught construction timetable around the Games.

The tenor of how Melbourne would respond to the Russian presence was set well before Suez or Hungary, when the organising committee made it clear that no Iron Curtain countries would be given special treatment in Australia. The Melbourne Olympic committee's CEO, William Bridgeford, told the international press that Australia had made it clear to the Russians that they would be treated just like everyone else in Melbourne. 'That's the only way we'll have it and I anticipate no problems,' the former brigadier general said. 'We couldn't segregate them if we wanted to. The Olympic Village is the only place where we can house and feed the athletes.'[14] The statement was a sensible and practical response to the anxiety surrounding the biggest bear in the Cold War woods. No one had the time or inclination to show the Russians any favours. The events in Hungary only confirmed that treating the Russian athletes like every other athlete was the best policy.

That wouldn't prevent one arm of the Australian government having special plans for them. ASIO had been preparing for the Games for more than 12 months. It was well aware of the potential dangers of having so many communists in the country at the one time. The fallout from Suez and Hungary, although never part of ASIO's original planning, added another layer of complexity to the task.

There were three areas that ASIO believed it needed to monitor. One was the possibility of communist agents using the Games as cover for their own intelligence operations. Another was the potential assassination threat to Vladimir and Evdokia Petrov from Russian agents seeking retaliation for their defection of two years earlier. The couple were moved to Queensland for the duration of the Games, and into a safe house, just to make sure they were out of the way. And the third concern was the possibility of athletes and officials seeking political asylum, a likelihood that increased in the aftermath of the Hungarian uprising.

After liaising with the Department of External Affairs and several others, ASIO got cabinet approval to establish a process for dealing with potential defectors or 'refugees'. A safe house and flat were set up in Victoria — other states were told to have a similar arrangement in place in case it were needed — and ASIO officers were put on rosters to ensure there was always someone available to activate the plans.[15]

Towards the end of October, a meeting was held in the office of ASIO director-general Charles Spry between protocol officers and ASIO representatives — including the legendary Japanese codebreaker Captain Eric Nave — to discuss the likely communist presence in Melbourne, ranging from the *Gruzia* to the two Russian consuls, Zaikin and Filimonov, plus the three 'Iron Curtain Ministers' from Poland, Hungary, and Romania. It was resolved that the Victorian police commissioner, Selwyn Porter, should appoint an officer who would be given ASIO's 'special silent number and asked to contact us as soon as possible regarding any matters concerning us, e.g: requests for political asylum'.[16] ASIO itself would try to photograph as many Eastern Bloc visitors as it could, and then check with overseas intelligence agencies to see who was who.

Surveillance of possible Soviet spies was a routine part of ASIO's activities during the Games, but it meant bringing in agents from Sydney and Adelaide, and using the full strength of the Melbourne office. The plans revealed an organisation that was becoming increasingly indispensable to the nation's security. The Petrov Affair gave ASIO significant cachet within government, and confirmed to Menzies the organisation's value. The Labor opposition, though, was hostile and quick to link ASIO's activities to Menzies' political bidding. The best way to protect ASIO against any change of government and the potential risk of being dissolved was to make it a statutory authority. Labor's Ben Chifley had summoned the organisation into existence in 1949 at the stroke of pen, but ASIO had enjoyed no statutory independence since then. Menzies needed little convincing from Spry that ASIO's status needed to change, and introduced a bill to parliament just two weeks before the *Gruzia* docked at Melbourne that guaranteed the agency's future.

There were expressions of outrage about the Suez and Hungarian crises in Melbourne. The left-wing Labor MP, Jim Cairns, managed to rally some students to Parliament House and told them that although there were some sensitivities about making political statements because of the Games, they should do it anyway. Even such small demonstrations were considered contrary to the impression authorities wanted to convey. Commissioner Porter was determined that no one visiting Melbourne should have to put up with such demonstrations:

> This is a time when Australia and Australia's reputation as host to the visitors from all parts of the world should be foremost in people's minds. We have assumed an obligation to honor the Olympic tradition, not only from the point of view of making the Games a success, but for the sake of Australia. Irrespective of class, creed or political thought, demonstrators will not be allowed to damage the reputation of Australians as open-hearted hosts.

In case any one of these demonstrators had a desire to persist with such expressions, Commissioner Porter suggested police may come down pretty hard. 'Normally, police take a broadminded view of demonstrators, but particularly during the Games, they will be ready and capable to deal immediately with any ill-considered expression of feeling on the part of any section of the community,' he said.[17]

More cynical types in Melbourne might have thought Commissioner Porter's recipe for quelling protest owed more to the

Soviet system of government than the Australian, especially on the recent evidence from Budapest. His view, though, was common: there was an anxiety about Melbourne and the nation being seen in the wrong light. Everyone, it seemed, had to be on their best behaviour. It was the attitude of a nation whose lack of certainty about its place in the world drove a desperate sense of trying to impress everyone.

*

Athletes had started to arrive at the Olympic Village in Heidelberg West, in the city's north-eastern suburbs. One of the first teams to arrive were the Nigerians, led by chief Joseph Randle, who disembarked from the plane at Essendon airport in yellow and scarlet robes, accompanied by 12 athletes.

By the time the Games were due to start, the village was to hold 4,700 athletes in what was considered a brave experiment in replacing old-style dormitories with houses that had unlimited hot water. Men and women lived next to each other, separated only by a wire fence. There were two beds in each room, featuring 'thick inner-spring mattresses and collage-weave bedspreads'. The women's quarters, however, were different to the men's, where you could find electric razors. The female athletes were provided, instead, with washing machines, electric steam irons, and sewing machines.[18] Male athletes didn't apparently need to wash their tracksuits, iron their T-shirts, or mend their socks.

Marlene Mathews arrived at the village nursing a secret. Ten days earlier, over breakfast, her mother had said to her: 'Have you looked in the mirror this morning?' When Mathews checked, the face looking back at her was covered in a red rash. 'I think you've got measles,' her mother said. Mathews was horrified. 'I really couldn't believe it ... I really flew in to a flat spin,' she said. A doctor confirmed the diagnosis, but there was no way Mathews could take a few days off. She had too much at stake to let the illness interfere with her preparation for the Games.

It wasn't just about the impact the measles might have on Mathews' performances. She had made great sacrifices in order to compete in Melbourne, giving up her job in the New Zealand Trade Commissioner's office in Sydney; like every other athlete at the Games, she was not permitted to combine work and sport.[19] The rewards and security of the professional era were still some years away. Mathews had also taken a modelling course with the doyen of Australian style, June Dally-Watkins, which had led to the prospect of a photo shoot for the department store Grace Bros. Once that became known, Mathews was told she couldn't do it because it would compromise her amateur status. But missing the Olympics, the Holy Grail of amateur sport, was simply not an option.

'I don't think too many people realised that when I went into the village I was just getting over this bout of measles,' Mathews said. 'I was through the infectious period, so there was no way that I was going to pass the infection on to anybody else. It was just inconvenient at that stage.'[20]

Mathews' bigger worry was how she would handle the expectations of success. Many observers thought she was Australia's best sprint medal hope going into the Games, but the view wasn't unanimous. Leading athletics coach Franz Stampfl had watched the Olympic trials two weeks earlier and predicted it would be Betty Cuthbert, not Mathews, who would win gold in the Olympic sprint double. Cuthbert, he said, was even better than the 'fabulous' Marjorie Jackson.[21] It was a big statement, given that Mathews had a history of running world-class times. Cuthbert was young, and was untested in international company.

*

When the Hungarian Olympic team left Europe, the revolution they had seen in Budapest appeared destined to deliver the nation independence from Moscow. By the time the team reached Darwin, all was lost. Miklós Martin, a water polo player, read English and came across a newspaper at Darwin airport. The Nagy government had been overthrown, and 200,000 Soviet troops had swept into Hungary. The death toll was a grim reminder of Moscow's determination to snuff out any signs of resistance. One of Martin's teammates, István Hevesi, could not forget the news that Martin shared with him: 'By the time we got on the plane it had turned in to a counterrevolution — meaning they had begun to shoot us, goddam them.'[22]

The Hungarian community in Melbourne had followed the events back home closely. They turned out in force at Essendon airport to meet the team when it arrived in the evening of 12 November. Joseph Csonka, the head of the local Hungarian Association, declared that he and others would ask every Hungarian on the team if they intended to stay in Australia. If they said yes, he would submit their names to the government to be considered for political asylum.

The Argus didn't care for such messages at all, declaring in an editorial that Csonka had 'dismayed' Melbourne:

[Csonka's actions] risked the whole success of our Games. The Hungarian Olympic team comes here at our invitation to compete in the Games and NOT to be exposed to political pressures ... It is dangerous impertinence for Dr Csonka — speaking for people who themselves are guests of Australia — to provoke a political explosion that could so deeply embarrass us. It's plain bad manners for him to try to set friend against friend in the Hungarian team — and incite angry hostility against other competitors who are also our gests ... SO STAY AWAY FROM OUR VISITORS, DR CSONKA AND FRIENDS.[23]

The message revealed a superficial understanding of what exactly had happened in Hungary, and underlined a naivety that overseas politics was something you declared at Australian immigration control and surrendered at the gate. At the village the communist flag of

Hungary had been replaced by a new flag, one ordered by the Nagy government. At the airport the gathered Hungarians sang the old national anthem that had existed before the communists, and tears were shed. In Canberra the prime minister pledged Australia would take 3,000 Hungarian refugees.

*

Nina Paranyuk was working when the *Gruzia* docked at Melbourne, so she saw nothing of the reception that the locals gave the ship. Her colleagues, though, returned to the cabin cradling flowers, sweets, and gumleaves. Some had exchanged the souvenirs for postcards and pamphlets, as a gesture of goodwill. The Australians sang, and so did the Russians.

But the ship's captain was anything but happy. 'You acted like beggars,' Captain Elizabaz Gogitidze told the crew. 'You were warned how to act when you arrived in Australia ... You were running up and down the gangplanks like monkeys to get presents for the capitalists.' The captain said Russia would have been ashamed of how the crew behaved. He made sure the crew were given the real picture of what they had just seen: 'Everybody was wearing his best suit. They have no more than one suit like that. All those cars you saw are owned by the Government. They were given to the people for publicity for Australia during the Olympic Games.'

Nina doubted many of the crew actually believed their captain. But she was excited to be told that she would be given £14 as spending money, and there would be opportunities to go ashore and sightsee. 'The news stopped me from sleeping at nights,' she wrote. 'I prayed all the harder and thought now that I had been answered.'[24]

Local Ukrainians could barely contain the offence they took at the arrival of the *Gruzia*, which carried Ukrainian athletes under the Soviet flag. It was a bitter reminder of how Russia had tried to nullify the Ukrainian identity, and absorb the nation into the vast USSR. The Ukrainian newspaper in Melbourne addressed the issue:

[N]obody from the Ukrainian community welcomed them [the athletes] with flowers, flags or the dinging of the national anthem. They probably didn't bring with them Ukrainian flags. Local Ukrainian immigrants were unable to welcome them to their homes, or to organise an official welcome. Why? Because the Ukrainian athletes from the USSR are under the strictest control of 'big brother', they are not allowed to speak with Ukrainian immigrants, or to visit them in their homes or in any Ukrainian community centres or organisations.[25]

A new layer of disappointment had been added to the years of historical oppression when the IOC decided to deny Ukraine's bid to send its own Olympic team to Melbourne. Between the Helsinki and Melbourne Games, a group of expat Ukrainians set up an office in Washington to lobby for their own team. The idea hinged on Ukraine being one of only two Soviet 'states' (the other was Belarus) that had their own United Nations membership. They argued that the USSR actually comprised 14 different nations, and each should compete under its own flag. The idea was sensible, but it was a precedent that Avery Brundage and the IOC could not accept.[26] The decision did nothing to quell the fierce nationalism that was fundamental to the plan. And the Ukrainians who had migrated to Australia after World War II kept their anti-Soviet feeling alive.

*

For a couple of years, Wilfrid Kent Hughes had been suspicious of the impact television would have on the Games. 'I feel that television has introduced a new problem,' he confided to Brundage.[27] He was right to be wary, especially with the aggressive desires of US television interests, and Australia's lack of knowledge about the technology.

Kent Hughes had effectively appointed himself as the Games' custodian for future generations, which meant he acted as a bulwark against the overseas television networks' push for more concessions on their coverage. In practice Kent Hughes was trying to hold back a massive tide of television investment in the Games. The networks argued that the Games were news, not entertainment, and therefore they shouldn't be charged for the privilege of televising the events. Kent Hughes reasoned that if he allowed that approach, he risked any interest from a film company wanting to shoot a feature-length movie on the Games. He offered to limit the networks to three minutes' coverage each day of the Games, a doomed attempt at compromise that eventually denied Melbourne the international publicity only extensive television coverage of the Games could provide. A boycott by the overseas television networks soon followed. 'The Olympic Games as an institution, Australia as a nation and television as a medium of the free world, all have suffered from the consequences of the extensive blackout,' a *New York Times* journalist noted.[28]

The blackout compounded Melbourne's anonymity. A US Gallup poll found that only one in five Americans knew the Games were to be held in Australia. Although more people in Britain knew the Games' destination — 58 per cent — they were less likely to afford the trip.[29]

Kent Hughes was stoic in the face of some extraordinary pressure from the US networks, and he received no help from Brundage, who kept himself at arm's length from the process. Brundage's feelings about television's investment in the Games were at best ambivalent — he felt they tainted the amateur spirit, but the businessman in him saw the great commercial potential that would bring revenue to the Olympic movement. That was yet to come.

Colin Bednall found an alternative model for cheaply televising an Olympic Games:

> I persuaded Wilfrid Kent Hughes … that television could successfully flog a mountain of tickets left unsold for what were then ranked as the minor Games. I passed a share of both rights and the barter deal on to the other stations. It was the first

and last time in the world that television ever got access to an Olympic Games without paying an enormous sum of money for the right to do so.[30]

The linchpin was getting the Australian petrol company Ampol to turn 120 of its service stations in Sydney and Melbourne into television showrooms for the Games' coverage.[31] With a publicist's eye for detail, Bednall promoted the idea by reassuring the potential audience that he had thought of everything: 'Mobile generators will be available in case of power breakdowns and every inch of television cable will be patrolled night and day to prevent accidents.'[32] Yet Bednall wasn't letting on was just how rudimentary his operation really was. He had no money to pay his staff overtime, and no money to pay for any performance rights. The equipment had not been approved for use, as was required by government inspectors. And the camera crews, not surprisingly, were still in training. Bednall directed that studio equipment be put in the back of a utility truck to make an outside broadcast van. The station managed to get two such vans working in time for the Games, which gave GTV-9 the advantage of being able to broadcast from two Olympic venues.

The local stations were given the right to televise from any Olympic site that was a sellout, which, given the popularity of events at the MCG, meant there was action from the main stadium on a daily basis. The fee for this was effectively a donation to the Games organising committee, calculated on the small number of television sets in use. Three television stations — GTV-9, HSV-7, and the ABC — managed to show more than 20 hours of daily coverage to Victorian viewers for ten of the 15 days of the Games. Those in Sydney and parts of New South Wales could watch the 16-millimetre film of the day's events that was flown to Sydney each night.[33]

Bednall, in an echo of his resourcefulness as a cadet reporter in the outback, saw an opportunity to make the most of not being shackled to a programming schedule. As stations built up to their formal broadcast launch, they were allowed to replace their test patterns with the occasional film or other footage to provide their technical staff with real-time broadcasting experience. As GTV-9 was still weeks away from launch, Bednall filled his transmission test time with Olympic footage from his two outside broadcast vans.[34] It was cheeky, and meant that when Bednall's rivals at HSV-7 and the ABC crossed back from the Olympics to their own programs, Bednall's Olympic coverage continued.

*

The Olympic torch relay organising team managed to enjoy a day's swimming and fishing before the torch was scheduled to arrive in Cairns. Marcus Marsden sent groups off to Innisfail and Cardwell. He immersed himself in the final preparations for the torch's arrival, and the first eight-hour relay stint that would follow. 'To me this was the scary part. (Was it going to work?)' he wrote.[35] Marsden was chastened by the experience of getting to Cairns. Little did he know how close the whole relay had come to falling apart in what had looked the easiest part of the torch's journey, from Darwin to Cairns.

The flame arrived safely in Darwin on the evening of Tuesday 6 November, as 3,000 locals crammed into the airport for a view of the Sacred Flame of Olympia. In the two days before it was due to arrive in Cairns, the locals held an unofficial torch relay of their own; unlike the real thing, it featured eight women among the 31 runners, each of them carrying a locally made torch. There were three Aboriginal runners, including the first runner, Billy Larrakeyah, who had competed in the 1954 national athletic championships as a javelin thrower.

On the morning of Friday 9 November the flame was taken from the RAAF jail cells, where it had been kept, to Darwin airport and into the custody of the pilots who would fly it to Cairns in three Canberra bombers. One of the bombers would have the flame, a second would have the backup, and the third was an escort plane.

Although the bombers regularly cruised at 40,000 feet, carrying the flame meant they needed to fly lower, at 20,000 feet. And that meant using more fuel. The bombers would have to refuel at Cloncurry, Queensland, making the flight time to Cairns around three hours and ten minutes. So far, so good.

The bombers left Darwin early that morning. The flames were suspended from the aircraft roof by a piece of rigging wire, and a bungee cord anchored it to the floor. The planes and the flames arrived safely in Cloncurry, and the bombers drew up alongside each other. The pilots hopped out to check with the control tower about the weather conditions and any other important information they needed for the final leg of the flight. The ground crews went about refuelling.

When the time came to resume the journey, one of the pilots noticed that the main wheels of the lead bomber were sinking into the decrepit tarmac. A tractor was summoned to pull the bomber out of the tarmac, which was slowly collapsing. Locals were also enlisted to press upwards on the wings' tanks, in order to lighten the plane. Neither ploy worked. The tractor's tyres spun and started to catch fire.

Desperate measures were called for. The decision was taken to use the lead jet's thrust to loosen the tarmac's hold on the plane, and that soon started to work. The bomber broke free, but it also managed to shower the other two planes with splintered tarmac, dust, and gravel. Some of the material lodged in the bombers' engines, meaning they couldn't fly. The backup flame was taken to join the first flame in the only airworthy bomber left.

In Cairns the anxiety was rising. Heavy rain had fallen in the morning, and bruised clouds remained around the airstrip. Visibility would be a challenge for the pilot in such conditions. By 1 pm there was still no sign or sound of the Canberra bomber. Minutes later, it emerged from the clouds and made a flawless landing. The two torches had arrived in Cairns, and only one Canberra bomber. It was 1.09 pm. Marcus Marsden breathed a sigh of relief.[36]

226

The first person to officially carry the Olympic flame in the Southern Hemisphere was a 22-year-old Greek-Australian, Constantine Verevis, a Cairns council worker. Verevis's parents hailed from Kastellorizo, an island in the southeastern Mediterranean. George Verevis had migrated to Australia when he was 14, and for a time was a canecutter. He married Despina Lazarus in Cairns, and they had five children. Con was a lad of five-foot-six who was a fine surfer and a budding footballer. He passed the torch to Anthony Mark, an Aboriginal man from the Mitchell River mission, on the western coast of Cape York. The mission was three hours away by plane from Cairns, and free flights were arranged to ensure he was there for the run. Mark worked for the mission superintendent, doing a range of jobs, including delivering the mail. He'd left his wife and three children behind for two weeks for the trip to Cairns.[37] Mark ran barefoot, taking his time, and travelling the mile in nine minutes. On that first night the rains came again, and the torch was blown out three times; each time it was reignited from the miner's lamp that Marsden kept in the back of one of the trucks.

It was raining on the morning Ray Kahl was to run his mile. He was due to run just near Cardwell, in the third major section of the relay after Cairns airport. A few weeks earlier he had received a letter asking him to be at the Cairns Council Chambers at 1.30 am on Saturday 10 November. About 20 runners assembled there in the dark, and then climbed into the back of the waiting Holden utes. They pulled a tarp over their heads and set off for Cardwell, between Tully and Ingham. Thelma Kahl remained tucked up in bed, the kids asleep, the rain pattering on the roof.

At around 10 am Ray loosened up and took his place on the road. He was just south of Cardwell. The rain had stopped and the air was fresh but still heavy with moisture. Ray lit his torch and set off. He didn't change hands and kept his arm out in front to avoid getting any burns. Ray felt the tiredness kick in after a while, but he finished his mile in seven minutes, as expected. Then all the runners in that section were picked up, had some lunch, and headed home. No one took a picture of Ray with his torch.

*

Nina Paranyuk's day off was scheduled for Sunday 18 October. It was the day she made her dash for freedom. At about 10.30 am she joined the other sightseers at the bottom of the *Gruzia*'s gangplank and boarded a bus that would take the group around Melbourne's attractions. The first stop was Captain Cook's cottage, but Paranyuk couldn't find an opportunity to slip away, especially after the rain came. Then it was on to the MCG, around the city, and into some of the suburbs. The next stop on the itinerary was the Melbourne Zoo. 'I thought I might not get the chance again,' Paranyuk said. 'I knew I must get away from the party this time.'[38]

Her first attempt to lose herself in the crowd was foiled when the bus driver came back to the bus and saw her. So she changed tactics and tailed the Russians towards the koala cages, stopping to admire a bird that she thought was a lyrebird but was actually a macaw. When she saw the last of the Russians disappear behind the hedge, Paranyuk turned and walked slowly back out of the zoo. 'I knew I wouldn't get another chance if the party missed me before I had got well away,' she said.

The next stage of her bid for freedom involved extraordinary luck. She started walking along the road and then ducked behind a tree when she thought she saw her Russian colleagues returning to the bus. She decided to flag down a car, and managed to stop a vehicle with two men, but neither could speak Ukrainian or Russian. Paranyuk had no English, so amid constant questions from her driver and his passenger, she kept pointing forward, although she had no idea what was up ahead. Before long, the driver stopped by a busy road — she later learnt it was the corner of Sydney and Brunswick roads — opened the rear door, and ushered Paranyuk out. She didn't want to leave because she didn't think she was far enough away from

228

the zoo, or the *Gruzia*. The two men let her get back into the car.

So what Paranyuk later called 'the freedom drive' continued, taking her further north, before her driver finally stopped at the train station in Broadmeadows. Paranyuk offered him ten shillings, but he declined. Then they drove off.

By now Paranyuk's anxiety was getting the better of her:

> The people I had seen since I arrived at the Zoo looked friendly and most were smiling. But I thought some of them could have Russian sympathies and take me back to the *Gruzia*. I was thinking like a mad woman. I was working myself up so much that I was almost helpless to think properly.[39]

In what turned out to be a remarkable stroke of luck, Paranyuk had been dropped at Camp Road, where many migrants from the old Broadmeadows Migrant Camp had settled. She worked up sufficient courage to approach a woman walking across a paddock. The woman was German but understood some Ukrainian. She pointed Paranyuk towards some houses, where she heard children playing and the sound of Ukrainian voices. Within a few moments, she was taken in by the children's mother: 'The woman ... opened the front gate and took me by the arm. "Don't be afraid: you are among friends now," she reassured me and I followed her into the house.'

Word had got out that Paranyuk was missing. Two people stopped at the house that night to ask if there were any strangers there. Paranyuk's new protectors sent them on their way, but another Ukrainian arrived later and offered to help. At 8 pm a taxi arrived to take Paranyuk to a safe house. No one would find her for another two months.

Her ability to remain hidden was helped by one important factor: the physical description of her was woefully inaccurate:

> A policeman standing at the gangplank with my passport photograph in his hand and the description circulated would

have possibly missed me. The description said I was 5 ft 8 in tall, but that's inches out. The coat I was wearing was black and not blue. It was a full-length coat, not a 'shortie'. I was wearing grey high-heel shoes and not black high-heel shoes.

Soon after moving on from Broadmeadows, Paranyuk was given a haircut and wave treatment. New clothes and sunglasses completed her new look.

The Russian response was swift. It was now only two days before the opening ceremony, and Paranyuk's disappearance seemed suspicious. The Russians suspected she was holed up somewhere, at a place known to the Australian authorities. There were strenuous official denials about that, but it seemed unlikely that she had disappeared completely.

The Russian consuls who had been given last-minute clearance to represent the Soviet Union during the Games now had an issue of diplomatic importance to resolve. And ASIO's pre-Games planning would be tested after all. But no one, from Menzies down, wanted any of it to detract from the opening ceremony.

Summer
1956–57

Chapter Eleven
Let the Games Begin

In late November 1956 Melbourne police intercepted a letter addressed to Prime Minister Robert Menzies and handed it over to the nation's chief spy. Dated 18 November, it was written in Russian. 'Mr Menzies,' the letter began, 'I desire to settle in Australia and I am appealing to you as I would to my father to allow me to remain here. I have nobody left except you now.'

It was accompanied by another letter, this one simply addressed to 'Immigration Office, Elizabeth St, Melbourne'. That letter was written in Ukrainian. Neither letter had a return address, only the words 'Free Australia Nina'.[1]

Those Australians who had been following the news would have known that 'Nina' was the stewardess who had gone missing from the Soviet ship *Gruzia*, anchored at Port Melbourne for the Olympic Games, a few days before. Already her disappearance was shaping up as an international incident.

Her letter to Menzies was pleading:

I beg you to save me from the Russians with whom there is no life. Throughout my whole life, I have not known freedom and I hated communism. I ask you very much not to refuse my application to remain here. If you hand me back to be shot by a Russian bullet I prefer to be shot here by your bullet. I have decided to remain here for the rest of my life.

The anti-communist message of Paranyuk's letter was a powerful endorsement of Menzies' opposition to the 'socialist menace', which was so strident he had tried to outlaw the Communist Party in Australia.

But ASIO director-general Brigadier Charles Spry was unmoved. He advised the prime minister that there was no evidence Paranyuk was the author of the letter, and that a formal response 'would only result in unseemly haggling and unwelcome publicity':

My own opinion is that these letters have been despatched — if indeed they are from the lady in question — at the instigation of her 'harbourers' in an attempt to precipitate an issue which has been overshadowed by the Games. I have no doubt that it is their hope that action will be taken on these letters and that she will be granted political asylum. Such a precedent would then be used by them to provoke others.[2]

Spry's message was clear: this could well be an act of opportunism rather than a legitimate plea for help. The world's attention was on Melbourne. The Soviets already believed that ASIO was planning to provoke defections among its team, and Spry knew Australia had to proceed carefully to ensure no one jumped to the wrong conclusion.[3] A false move could trigger a Soviet withdrawal from the Olympics, and spark a diplomatic incident that would wreck the Games and imperil the nation's security.

If Paranyuk was to trying to defect, the ASIO chief knew, the matter had to be handled with delicacy and tact. Spry's overriding priority was to ensure that nothing political interfered with the Games. 'I would recommend that where such a course is practicable an applicant for political asylum should be encouraged to defer his final break until all the competitive events are over,' Spry told Menzies. The prime minister was in firm agreement. Nina, however, had upset those plans: she had gone missing at a time when the world was looking at Australia. It was the scenario Spry had feared, and the *Gruzia* was at the centre of his anxiety.

'The individual concerned might already have compromised himself with his fellow countrymen when he makes his application for asylum and it might be unsafe or unwise for him to return to them,' Spry wrote ahead of the Olympics. 'The presence of a Soviet ship in Melbourne during the Games, to which any Communist national might be transported and detained, is of real importance in this connection.' In anticipation of such an outcome, where it became impossible for a member of the Soviet team or its operation to return to the ship, Menzies gave Spry the authority to act, with minimal consultation. But the problem for Nina's case was that no one could find her. No one knew exactly what her circumstances were, what she had to offer, and if she was genuine.

The situation turned theatrical. 'I have decided to commit suicide on the day [the] *Gruzia* leaves Melbourne,' one of Nina's letters claimed. 'I shall be in the port and as soon as the *Gruzia* signals her departure, I'll jump in to the sea to help the Russian people.' It was the promise of a desperate woman. To the public, it seemed that no one was willing or able to help her, let alone believe her. Nina Paranyuk was apparently abandoned to her fate while the country she wanted to call home watched the curtain rise on the biggest sporting party in its history.

*

Five days before the Olympic Games opened in Melbourne, the other Olympic festival was launched at the city's National Gallery. The opening of the Olympic Arts Festival was the moment when Melbourne's high society met high art. The women wore gowns, furs, jewels, and, in one case, a tiara. The men's attire was all black ties, sashes, and medals. The Victorian governor, Sir Dallas Brooks, stood in front of a large group of international Olympic officials, local VIPs, and a smattering of city council officials to open the festival.

His tone was downbeat, verging on the apologetic. 'Our national treasures have not been brought forward in any spirit of boastfulness,' he said. 'We simply offer the best we have.' The British playwright and wit Noël Coward once described Dallas Brooks as 'a typical Royal Marine officer, which means he was efficient, sentimental and had perfect manners'. Perhaps it was the manners — pointing out that Australian culture was not quite good enough — that came to the fore in the governor's next remarks: 'Australia is only a young country and we are very proud of our achievements. But we are also fully conscious of our shortcomings. So we hope you will find something to enjoy and admire in the exhibitions and we all look forward to learning something from your friendly criticism.'[4]

Sir Dallas's sentiment chimed with Melbourne's mood: it was trying hard to be worthy of the world's attention but expected to come up short of providing the sort of international experiences visitors were used to. This feeling found its strongest expression in the arts festival. Not only was it a secondary and largely forgotten adjunct to the Games, but the caution surrounding it was in stark contrast to the anticipation — and confidence — which attended the nation's athletes. Sir Dallas had metaphorically put the nation's writers, artists, architects, and musicians into a collective act of self-abnegation. No one publicly challenged his view of the cultural offering; no one seemed particularly interested. The festival of sport was where the real business of national promotion was going to be done. And that party was just getting started.

*

A heady mix of Olympic VIPs, international visitors, and national and local dignitaries became regulars at the social whirl around the Games. Mrs Brundage admitted to 41 social engagements during the Games, and the prime minister at least ten parties in the first week.[5]

There was even a frisson of pride when the Marchioness of Landsdowne — from a family of British peers dating back to the country's first prime minister — had to shop locally for a new frock. 'I brought only short evening dresses with me from England, but I'm so impressed by the glorious clothes your women are wearing to all these Olympic festivities, I had to hurry out and buy something more befitting a gala,' she said, with the impeccable manners of the upper class.[6] The locals purred. Even Avery Brundage's impact on the Games was celebrated in a particularly Australian manner: a cocktail was named after him. The Brundage Buster had brandy, sweet vermouth, vodka, some maraschino, and apricot brandy (just a dash).[7] There was a squeeze of lemon, topped with ginger ale and soda. Here was a drink that packed a wallop, just like the man himself.

Spectators keen not to miss any of the opening ceremony camped outside the MCG the night before to ensure they could get a place in the standing-room section of the ground. Some were women who came straight from work, while others brought chairs, flasks, and even a Davy Crockett hat to keep themselves comfortable during the night.[8]

Bruce Howard felt there was an overriding sense of doubt that Melbourne would pull the Games off. 'I think people were nervous, the attitude that we've bitten off more than we can chew here,' he explained. Many felt that if Melbourne made a good fist of the opening, everything after that would be all right. Howard made his way to the MCG, mingling with the crowd.

By midday on 22 November 1956, three hours before the opening ceremony was to start, the MCG was already half-full. The weather had been cool and wet in the lead-up to the Games, which not surprisingly had contributed to a growing sense of anxiety in Melbourne. It had been a sunny morning, but still many male spectators were in suits and ties. By midafternoon the temperature hit 27 degrees.

The mood in the stadium was heating up too: the torch was not far away. It had taken a remarkable journey down the coast after the dramas of getting to Cairns. More than 30,000 people had gathered at Sydney Town Hall to await the torch's arrival, but it was almost upstaged by a hoax torch made out of a plum pudding tin and a chair leg. The tin contained three pairs of Army-issue men's underpants and a quart of kerosene. The bloke who finished up carrying it was a Sydney University student called Barry Larkin. Even though he was wearing long grey trousers, a white shirt, and a green tie, rather than the white T-shirt and shorts of every other relay runner, Larkin was given a police escort for the final stage of his run. He bounded up the steps to hand the 'torch' to Lord Mayor Pat Hills, who took it and embarked on a short speech to the 30,000 people thronging around the Town Hall. But the silver paint on the fake torch was still fresh and came off in Hills' hand.

Marcus Marsden, who was standing next to the lord mayor, recognised Larkin from when he was studying at the University of Melbourne. Marsden tapped the official on the shoulder and told him that he wasn't holding the real torch. '[That] was a trial run by our friends at the university who apparently think this is funny,' Hills said to the crowd, trying to save the situation. Minutes later the real torch arrived.

Now, in Melbourne, the torch was making its final approach towards the MCG. Earlier that day, the teenager who would carry the torch into the stadium and light the Olympic cauldron had been picked up at his home in Essendon by a chauffeured car and taken to the MCG. He was given a balaclava and an old Army pullover to disguise him from the press and officials at the ground. Secrecy about the identity of the final torch carrier was paramount. There had been much speculation about who it would be, but the suggested names didn't include the runner finally selected for the honour. At 10 am, before the general public was admitted, the runner had set off on a test lap of the MCG, carrying a torch fired by a magnesium flare candle. This was a different mechanism to the relay torches, which were designed to burn with a low flame for only seven or eight minutes. The magnesium flare created an almost pyrotechnic effect, sparking and arcing from the torch. By the end of the trial lap, the sleeve of the Army jumper was lacerated by sparks.

One person had worked out who was under the balaclava: radio station 3AW's Norman Banks, who had come to the MCG early and recognised the runner's stride during the rehearsal lap. Banks broke an exclusive story about the Olympic torch carrier's identity several hours ahead of the event.

The torch had one more hurdle before it reached Melbourne. Marsden's convoy of helpers from the university medical school had been promised all-venue passes to every Games event when they had joined the relay. The passes were to be distributed when the torch team reached Brisbane, but the passes hadn't turned up — and they weren't in Sydney either. Once the convoy crew reached Bendigo, the students let Marsden know that unless they received the passes the following morning, they would strike and the torch would have to find its way to Melbourne without them. The ultimatum worked and the passes reached Bendigo in time.[9]

Relay runners' police escorts had to be strengthened to cope with the massive crowds lining the streets when the torch reached Melbourne. The final route went along Spencer Street, up Collins Street, past the Town Hall, right into Spring Street, and left into Wellington Parade, at which point the MCG almost came into sight.

At Clarendon Street, in East Melbourne, Victorian steeplechase champion Doug Eales took the torch for the final stage of the relay. Eales would actually finish at the Richmond Cricket Ground, where the athletes were being marshalled for the march into the opening ceremony. Eales was then to enter the MCG through the players' race leading to a small green wooden door and then to a room in the Olympic Stand, where he would complete the final handover.

Eales got changed in a room beneath the Olympic cauldron, donned his relay uniform and donated white Dunlop Volley shoes, and went to receive the torch. Once he had it, he ran along Wellington Parade, down Vale Street, through the park, and then into the Richmond ground. He was due to be there at 4.24 pm. An attendant at the Richmond ground spotted the torch and went to give Eales entry through the gates, so that Eales could continue on to the MCG. But someone had mistakenly padlocked the gates and the attendant didn't have a key. After so much time and so many miles, a padlocked gate now threatened to end the 1956 Olympic torch relay at its most critical point.

Eales was desperate. Could he get around the gate somehow? Would that make him late delivering the torch? How long would the flame last? He set off around the ground and saw a ticket booth. He slid in through the booth, galloped across the adjoining park, past the milling Olympians, and headed off to the green door that led him back to the room underneath the cauldron.

The 4,594-kilometre torch journey was practically at an end. The deadline had been 4.32 pm on 22 November, and the torch had made it.

Eales' flame was transferred to the ceremonial torch and handed to Ron Clarke, the junior world record holder for the mile, who was about to take the Olympic flame into the MCG.[10]

By the time Clarke was ready to emerge from the bare concrete room where he had been waiting, the clouds had rolled in and it had become humid. Bruce Howard had gone to the position he had identified a fortnight earlier, and was set up for the moment when the cauldron would be lit. His instructions were clear: get an upright shot of the moment Clarke lit the flame. He had his Speedgraphic camera and standard lens ready. The shot was in Howard's head.

After the second round Salute of Guns at the opening ceremony, Clarke emerged with the torch, sparking and firing, creating its own fireworks against the bruised sky. The sudden change in weather had created the perfect backdrop for the torch's pyrotechnics. Nearby athletes ran alongside Clarke, trying to get their own pictures, but Clarke kept on running, completing the lap, not pausing to brush away the sparks that were falling on his arm. He disappeared from view to mount the steps to the cauldron. After the cauldron had been slow to ignite at the morning trial, the gas had been turned on well in advance.

Clarke emerged on to a platform near the cauldron and paused, holding the torch aloft. The crowd roared, and Howard thought for a moment that the young man looked like a statue of sport. He was captivated by the image: it would make a wonderful photograph. The temptation to shoot a frame was hard to resist, but Howard knew that if he took that shot, he may miss the image he had been sent to take. Clarke was about 30 metres away and down in front of Howard.

Now Clarke took a step towards the cauldron. Howard readied himself. Clarke stepped onto a stool and touched the torch into the cauldron, and the Olympic flame roared to life, pushing Clarke back for a moment before he regained his poise. At that moment Clarke felt 'an eerie sensation of omnipotence'.[11]

Howard squeezed the shutter button. It was one frame, no more — no time.

He secured his camera in his camera bag and bolted down the stairs, out of the stadium, and out onto Wellington Parade, where a motorcyclist was waiting for him. He climbed on and was driven straight to Flinders Street, where a lift was being held to take him up to editorial and the darkroom. The processing trays were ready — the developer had been warmed to speed up the processing — when Howard rushed in. He was vaguely aware of there being more people in the darkroom than he had ever seen, but nothing distracted him. From processing the film, he then made one print and handed it to *The Herald*'s production team. It was just 15 minutes from taking the photo to handing over the image.

In the meantime, Clarke was having treatment for burns to his arm from the torch sparks. The torch kept burning for more than five minutes, despite the best efforts of Marsden and his team to extinguish it. It even briefly set fire to the bitumen roof of the building that was the cauldron's base.

Clarke, his parents, and Clarke's girlfriend, Helen, would take the train home that evening. Along with 102,000 other people who left the MCG, they were able to buy the special final edition of *The Herald* that featured Bruce Howard's picture of Clarke lighting the Olympic flame.

*

The international reaction to the opening ceremony was the sort of publicity the organising committee had been craving. One UK reporter, who had been to three Summer and two Winter Olympics, declared it at least the equal, if not the best of those he had seen.[12] The Canadians were told the Games opened 'in a riot of colour, music, pageantry and brotherly love'. The somewhat acerbic but always engaging US sportswriter Red Smith likened the MCG's 'double decked old stands with weathered red brick suggest nothing so much as a brewery in south St Louis. Grafted on to them is a sleek new addition of battleship grey, triple decked and as modern as penicillin.' He found the whole torch and Olympic flame routine a little tired. '[Clarke] tossed his torch in to a gilded gaboon that looked a little like a trash incinerator. Thanks to the gas and fuel corporation of Victoria flame leapt from this dingy urn and will leap until the gas man turns it off.'

Smith's greatest criticism was saved for the emerging Cold War narrative that came to characterise the 1956 Olympics:

Beneath this effluvium from the founder of the modern Olympics was a reminder to the jingoists who try to picture this muscle dance as a head on collision of democratic and communist ideologies: 'Classification of points on a national basis is not recognised.' In other words, this is for fun, and no death struggle between the United States and Russia.[13]

Smith's idealism was catching. The *Manchester Guardian* reporter observed: 'Melbourne is happy tonight and full of peace. Furore and the Middle East seem not only far away but something in another world.'[14]

The dignitaries at the opening ceremony had addressed the fractured international situation directly. The old Olympian and devoted amateur Kent Hughes told the packed MCG at the opening ceremony that the Olympic spirit outrode the storms of international 'misunderstandings'; he hoped that the festival of sport would rekindle an enthusiasm for nations to uphold the Olympic spirit. At the Olympic banquet that night Prime Minister Menzies admitted that the world was not an easy or comfortable place: 'I believe that the Olympic organisation will do much to bring about that balance, that sensible and human understanding of men and affairs which the world has only to learn to usher in the greatest period of peace we have ever known.'[15]

Avery Brundage was similarly optimistic about the spirit of sportsmanship and fair play. It was their absence, he said, that helped explain why there were international tensions. Brundage went on to praise Australia and the Melbourne organising committee: 'British Commonwealth members do not know how to spell words like "program" but when it comes to sport and amateurism they know not only the spelling but also understand the spirit.'[16] Brundage was playing to the head table: the Duke of Edinburgh, who opened the Games, and Menzies.

For those who weren't interested in Brundage's soft soap, there was always the Duke's ringing endorsement of the organising committee. 'The committee can relax. For once it is not going to be abused,' he said. 'I have the most profound admiration for the organising committee ... People have come from all over the world to see athletes compete in peace and brotherhood.'[17]

Indeed they had. The Games of the XVI Olympiad, in Melbourne — miles away, out of season, and a basket case of missteps and broken promises — had delivered the first day of its great sports festival. Just how deeply this feeling of brotherly love went would become clearer on the first day of the track competition.

*

Vladimir Kuts had survived famine and the loss of many relatives and friends in Ukraine, slave labour under the Nazis, and regular beatings with a club — all before he was 16. He escaped his captors and became part of the Soviet Army's fight against the Germans while he was still a teenager. There was no doubt that Kuts had forsaken Ukraine for Mother Russia. 'He lived with a gun in his hand and death at his shoulder in the battle for the Soviet Union,' one observer remarked.[18]

Kuts came to Melbourne with his eye on the 10,000 metres and 5,000 metres double. With the legendary Czech distance runner Emil Zátopek still recovering from hernia-related injuries and fit perhaps only for the marathon, Kuts' biggest rival would be Englishman Gordon Pirie. The 10,000 metres gold medal would be decided on the first day of the athletics.

Kuts had a coxcomb of blond hair, a steely look, and a remorselessness to his running that extinguished hope from his opponents. Not even a car accident outside the village in the days before competition interfered with his preparation. At the MCG Kuts surged and stalled, surged and stalled, taunting Pirie, and eventually leaching the spirit from him. With four laps to go, Pirie thought he could still win it, but Kuts was unbreakable, and Pirie felt the soft, yielding surface at the MCG slowly sapping his strength. There was no way back for Pirie, and the Russian surged to the gold medal.

Kuts' performance provoked an extraordinary crowd response. There was no sense of animosity, no cavil about communism, nothing but enthusiasm for an athlete dominating his event. The Cold War hostilities appeared to have been suspended. Bruce Howard felt the hair on the back of his neck stand up as the crowd roared their support for the Russian. 'When you consider the tension in the world in advance, the Russians doing what they did and him coming to Australia and everyone probably being anti-Russian, it was a classic case of sport transcending everything,' Howard said. 'When Kuts did those victory laps, everyone stood.'[19]

The victory meant Kuts was the first male Russian athlete to win an Olympic gold medal. Kuts pointed out that the running track 'was very bad on the inside', but not even this mild criticism could detract from the bonhomie generated at the MCG. Several days later, Kuts told the Australian communist newspaper *Tribune*: 'Sport has found a common language out here in Melbourne. They have helped the cause of peace … [Australian crowds] are wonderful. It is a pleasure to run before them. The Australian people are very sporting. I like their attitude.'[20]

*

It wasn't quite so warm at the *Gruzia*, where Nina Paranyuk's absence was becoming a problem.

Filimonov and Zaikin were immediately involved after they were told of her disappearance. The pair called on the minister for external affairs Richard Casey's head of protocol, Francis Stuart, to find out what the Australians were doing about her disappearance, and to gauge how much the locals actually knew about her whereabouts. Not content with the answers they received, they rang Stuart three times later that day, seeking more information. They suspected Paranyuk had been lured into leaving the ship by people on the dockside who encouraged her 'to come over', and that she was in the clutches of white Russians, and therefore associating with those who were no friends of Moscow. These elements, they told Stuart, would exploit Paranyuk and harm Australian–Soviet relations.

The Soviet officials also thought it worthwhile to give Stuart a snapshot of Paranyuk's personality: she was a nervous type, prone to despondency, timid but a good worker, although slovenly in her personal habits. The implication was that Nina Paranyuk was not an ideal citizen.

Stuart discerned a larger agenda lurking behind all of this bluster: he told Canberra the two consuls were close to making a threat about Russia pulling out of the Games.[21] This was the scenario Spry had warned cabinet about months before. The Soviet consuls let the threat hang in the air while they pursued the more mundane aspects of the investigation.

Filimonov alerted Special Branch to a person who had offered the *Gruzia*'s crew some idea of where Paranyuk might be. The informant was someone who was loitering around the ship, and he claimed to be able to show them a house and a car that could help the investigation. Detective Sergeant James Rosengren went to Appleton Dock but had no success in finding the informant.

Publicly, Menzies said there had been no application for political asylum — whether this was accurate depended on your reading of Nina's letters to the prime minister. This wasn't the only instance of public statements appearing to be at odds with private information. ASIO had been at the Melbourne Zoo and taken photographs of the group that Paranyuk was part of: it appeared she was among them. In another odd omission, the Russians didn't even contemplate using the *Navigation Act*, which would have enabled them to charge Paranyuk with desertion. The catch was that it would only have the power of law while the *Gruzia* was in Australian waters. So, who would blink first: Paranyuk or the Soviets?

*

In the village there were attempts to promote an atmosphere of détente. Bruce Howard spent many hours there, especially before competition started, and saw little evidence of tension. He took a photograph of a Russian lifting an American on his shoulders during one training session at the village, an image contrary to the narrative of the day. Red Smith observed something more compelling when he came across US sprinter Andy Stanfield and Russian hurdler Boris Stolyarov playing chess. 'He's a nice guy,' Stanfield told Smith. 'You should have seen him dancing with the girls last night.'[22]

But there were tensions, about the Hungarian flag and erroneous reports in the Melbourne papers that the Czechs had threatened to put the Hungarians in concentration camps if they refused to attend the Games. When Andor Mészáros visited the village, he was struck by his countrymen's listlessness in the face of the tragedy in

Budapest. 'The poor Hungarian athletes did not know what to do — go home or stay,' Mészáros said. After he had handed out some of the medallions he had designed, he noticed how few of the athletes thanked him. '[T]heir mind was so preoccupied. It was a sad sight to see them lifelessly linger about.'[23]

For Marlene Mathews, the village was a different experience: this was her first Olympics and it all seemed novel. '[T]here was no sign of racism and there was no sign of any political differences whatsoever, irrespective of whether you were Russian, Chinese or whatever, everybody belonged to everybody else,' she said.[24] Getting to know your own country men and women was a bit more of a challenge. The men and women were separated by a wire fence, and although Mathews knew John Landy, she had no chance to socialise with anyone. The separate accommodation meant the athlete you roomed with was the person you saw the most of. Mathews didn't know the women in the Australian field team, or any of the swimmers. But for the moment, her biggest challenge was preparing for the heats of the 100 metres.

Mathews got nervous before every race. Maybe it was genetic — her father, who developed a heart condition, put an angina tablet on his tongue whenever his daughter was about to run. The heats and semifinals of the 100 metres were to be held on the first Saturday of the Games, 24 November. There were six gold medal candidates across the six heats: Mathews, Cuthbert, Giuseppina Leone, from Italy, the Soviet Union's Galina Popova, and Germans Gisela Köhler and Christa Stubnick. On previous performances Leone and Popova didn't have the speed of the Australian girls, and Popova had injured her leg a week before the Games. Köhler had some good times, but her form was patchy, and she was a far better hurdler. That left Stubnick as the most likely challenger.[25]

Mathews admitted that the Australian athletes' knowledge of their overseas rivals was limited. There was hardly any sports coverage of international athletics in the Australian newspapers or on the radio. She certainly knew about Cuthbert's form: they spent just about every weekend competing against each other in club, state, or national competition.[26]

The 100 metres heats were run in a testing headwind. Leone won the first heat in 11.8 seconds. Mathews was the clear favourite in the second heat, and ran impressively to win easily, equalling Marjorie Jackson's Olympic record of 11.5 seconds. Cuthbert dominated the next heat, and pipped Jackson and Mathews' mark by 0.1 of a second, setting a new Olympic record. Popova won the fifth heat in 11.6 seconds, and Stubnick won the sixth in 11.7 seconds. Köhler, too, qualified for the semifinal after finishing second in her heat. So all the favourites progressed through to the next round.

Cuthbert and Mathews were drawn in separate semifinals. The wind was stronger later in the day, and no one expected the fast times to be repeated. Stubnick won the first semi in 11.9 seconds, with Cuthbert 0.1 seconds behind her, and Leone third. Mathews narrowly won her semifinal, ahead of British runner Heather Armitage and Isabelle Daniels of the United States. The women had a nervous 48-hour wait, with the final not being run until 5.20 pm on the Monday.

Mathews was toey in the build-up — she had nothing else to do but prepare for the final. There was also an expectation now. If not the outright favourite, she was one of them. Marjorie Jackson had won the gold in the 100 metres in Helsinki: surely an Aussie girl could do it again? Mathews always felt she ran better in her second race of the day — a final after a heat — but she wouldn't have that chance in the final. It was one race, lasting a little over 11 seconds, and you had no chance to fix any mistakes or change your strategy.

The next day, she was calmer than she had expected as she got on the blocks. A firm breeze blew in her face. The crowd was pulsing with anticipation. The gun went off and the crowd roared. Mathews looked up and saw five women already in front of her. Her notoriously slow start had come back to haunt her. Betty Cuthbert had burst from the blocks. Daniels too. At 30 metres Cuthbert was in front. At 50 metres her lead was a metre. Marlene was last. She vowed to herself that was not where she would finish.

Daniels tried to match it with Cuthbert in the last half of the race, but Marlene had found her groove, as had Stubnick. The pair of them raced up to Daniels but still couldn't catch Cuthbert, who crossed the line 1.2 metres ahead of Stubnick. It looked like Daniels had finished third, but a photo-finish image showed that Mathews had just got the bronze. Cuthbert's time was 11.5 seconds.

Mathews' disappointment was almost tangible. 'It was the worst race of my life,' she said. 'You just rely on what you practise,' she explained — but a slow start was never part of the plan. She had trained on the blocks to help her overcome her difficult starts, but, at the key moment, it didn't happen.

In time, Mathews would reflect on what had made Cuthbert an Olympic champion: Betty had a killer instinct. Mathews liked winning but Cuthbert thrived in the competitive environment — and she had a gold medal to prove it.

*

The Olympic Arts Festival failed to find an audience. The problem was not the art; those who saw it discerned something contrary to Sir Dallas's opening remarks — there were signs of a local culture worth celebrating. No, the problem was that Melbourne — and the rest of the nation — had other things to look at.

The Age lamented that the festival was 'held in an atmosphere of hushed calm and has attracted few visitors'. A reviewer, Alan Nicholls, wrote in the same publication: 'The exhibitions are so fine in themselves and mark such a significant turning point in the Australian arts, that this lack of interest is astonishing.'[27] Nicholls blamed a lack of publicity for the patronage problem, and could not contemplate any other reason for the audience being 'only a thin sprinkling of students'. 'There was hardly anyone present over 25,' he continued, 'and I did not once succeed in identifying an Olympic visitor.'[28]

Nicholls was right to argue that it would be a long time before

Australia got the chance to put on a national cultural exhibition again. The most popular elements of the festival program were the public music performances, which included a sellout concert featuring a combined Sydney Symphony and Victorian Symphony orchestras, conducted by Sir Bernard Heinze at the Olympic pool. Menzies and a host of other dignitaries turned up and enjoyed what *The Age* appropriately called 'communal arts'.

In truth, the arts festival was doomed from the start. The budget was limited, there was little appetite for it among the Melbourne Olympic organisers, and it was supervised by someone who had little interest in the end result. The festival was under the overall coordination of Maurice Nathan's civics committee. Nathan was a businessman, with extensive connections to the football fraternity, but save for his successful push for the outdoor Melbourne festival that became Moomba, he was neither a patron nor a purveyor of high culture. And yet he opened the architectural and sculptural sections of the arts festival. Australia was on firm ground celebrating sport. But art and culture? That was another matter entirely.

The festival exhibitions were critically applauded, but their inability to engage audiences spoke loudly about what people in Melbourne wanted to see at that time. Not surprisingly, the man behind the festival, Avery Brundage, refused to see it as anything other than a success:

> When [the Olympics] first began in ancient Greece, there was only one athletic event. More time was devoted to composing music, writing odes and making sculpture. Melbourne has done very well in this regard also. We are very happy about the music and the grand opera and the museum exhibition of art which has been put on as part of the Olympic festival.[29]

As long as Brundage was happy, then everyone in the Olympic movement was happy. The rest of the country had other distractions — in Sydney and Melbourne it was called television.

Television's arrival had been preceded by a range of vested interests making sure that any misgivings about the new medium did not undermine it in the eyes of the audience. The evidence from other television markets in Britain and the United States was applied to the Australian consumer, with an attempt to reassure them that television was not the bogeyman that critics, including some churches, were suggesting.

Bold statements about television's capacity to make 'happier homes' became part of the general discussion. Home had become increasingly important: it was the focus of family life. The emergence of new jobs that didn't entail unsociable shifts in noisy factories meant that families were able to spend more time together. Although jobs in manufacturing were still growing, there was also a sizeable increase in white-collar jobs, across the property, finance, retail, professional, and entertainment sectors during the decade.[30] The worries about what young people were up to — whether they were listening to rock'n'roll, or, worse, hanging out with bodgies or widgies — ensured that teenagers' behaviour was a frequent topic of discussion when it came to TV. The Church of Scotland argued that television had a positive impact on teenagers. 'Many more people, and especially young people, are prepared to spend the evening at home when the TV programme promises to be attractive, rather than go out and seek entertainment,' the church claimed. 'The increase of this habit may possibly play a really important part in the restoration of the family.'[31] It was a nice idea, and might even have been true.

Beyond doubt was that television had an impact on how families decorated their lounge rooms and what forms of heating they used. The British Coal Utilisation Council found that a quarter of those who had bought TV sets had improved the comfort of their 'viewing room', with more comfortable chairs and small tables for their snacks. A further 40 per cent of TV owners changed their heating arrangements, because their source of warmth was in the wrong spot for them to watch the television.[32]

In Australia the advent of television forced families to make a choice about their next domestic purchase. The early evidence was that those who were buying TVs were sacrificing a new refrigerator or radio set for their television. Television sets were made locally, which was a useful antidote to the nation's balance-of-trade problem, and families were comforted to know that both their car and their television were made in Australia. By the end of 1956, there were 40,000 Australian-made TV sets. The number was expected to grow to 300,000 by the end of 1957, driven by the boom growth in the number of manufacturers, which reached a giddy 23 at one stage.

Even so, televisions were not cheap. An Astor Table model — a standalone television, with a 17-inch screen and 'high fidelity sound' — cost 95 guineas, or almost £100. It was a fair indicator that televisions had some social cachet when the price tag came in guineas, as it was a currency that was usually only used for something of substance. Fridges could be more expensive, but they still only came in pounds — £166 for a unit of 7¾ cubic feet.

Another thing that made the television different was that only 20 per cent of customers took up the offered terms and bought their TV on a 'hire purchase' scheme. Most consumers paid cash.[33] This was a significant departure from the growing tendency for Australian consumers to use hire purchase: at the end of 1955 Australia had a hire purchase debt of £200 million, twice what it had been only three and a half years earlier.[34] The Menzies government was not best pleased with the frequency of hire purchase, blaming it for contributing to inflation, but the truth was it enabled many consumers to buy whitegoods, furniture, and, of course, cars. But in this instance, televisions were the kind of purchase that most Australians were happy to pay for up front. There was something fundamentally different between the necessity of owning a fridge and buying a piece of technology that delivered entertainment into the home.

If you didn't get to the Games, and you weren't able to access a television, there was no way you could see any other moving vision of Olympic events, as private filming was outlawed at the Games — with one exception: the president of the Australian Olympic Federation, Prime Minister Menzies. Menzies was a keen amateur filmmaker, who took his camera to the Games even though only accredited newsreel filmmakers were technically able to do so. The issue, for everyone else, was spelt out very clearly when the organising committee realised that some newspaper photographers were shooting movie film when they were not accredited to do so. The committee stated those caught shooting movie film would be asked to show their accreditation cards.[35] Menzies had already compiled footage of the London Blitz, of the British royal family, and even of the Churchill family. He took his 16-millimetre movie camera, and from his privileged position — slightly elevated and in close proximity to the finish line for the track events at the MCG — shot a number of events, including Betty Cuthbert's heat in the 200 metres.

The film showed the ease of Cuthbert's win: she was almost 1.5 seconds quicker than her nearest rival. Marlene Mathews knew Cuthbert was an outstanding 200 metres runner, and it was a distance that Mathews didn't much like. But her disappointment in the 100 metres drove her to do better in the 200 metres. Her previous form over the distance meant that she came into the event outside the world's top six performers; her best time was 24 seconds dead, while Cuthbert's record, set in September, was 23.2 seconds, a huge difference in a sprint race.

Cuthbert's heat was the quickest by a long chalk, with Mathews winning her heat in 24 seconds. The other four heats were won by women recording slower times. Once again, the two Australians were the fastest qualifiers. Cuthbert ran another swift race at 23.6 to finish in front of Stubnick in the first semifinal. In the other semi Britain's June Paul beat Mathews, with both of them recording over 24 seconds. On the face of it the race was Cuthbert's to lose: she was 0.3 seconds quicker than Stubnick, and more than half a second ahead of everyone else who qualified for the final.

Cuthbert drew lane five in the final. Stubnick was outside her. Paul, who on the semifinal performance looked a likely bronze medallist, had Mathews on her inside. Queenslander Norma Croker qualified in the same time as Mathews, and was the third Australian in the field.

The start was delayed twice to shoo photographers away from the area, but when the gun went off for the third time, Marlene got away better than in the 100 metres final. Cuthbert, though, had got to the front early and opened a good lead on Stubnick, with Mathews some distance behind. Stubnick narrowed the gap on Cuthbert, and Mathews was threatening for the silver, as Paul, who had been holding her position, lost her rhythm and started to fall away through the bend and into the straight. Croker started to surge into contention for a medal. Mathews ranged up to Stubnick, but Cuthbert was too far in front for both of them. Cuthbert crossed the line for her second gold, four metres ahead of Stubnick and Mathews, who were almost locked together. Mathews' bronze medal performance was her fastest ever time in the 200 metres, 23.8 seconds, just 0.4 seconds slower than Cuthbert's.[36] Croker finished just behind Mathews.

Her second bronze of the Olympics came with an epiphany. Mathews had treated the 200 metres as a race in which she should start flat-out, coast around the bend, and go hard from there. The 1956 Melbourne Games taught her that there was another, better way. 'That was the first time I realised that I had to go flat out from start to finish, and that changed my whole aspect [on the race],' she explained.[37] But Mathews still had her greatest disappointment to come.

*

The time had come, Merv Wood said, to give up rowing. He and Murray Riley took the bronze medal in the double sculls, beaten by the Russians, who took the gold, and the Americans, with silver. 'I'm now too old to row in first-class events,' Wood said after the race. 'I'm 39 and my time has come.' It was a pragmatic end to a glorious career that had started 20 years earlier, at the Berlin Olympics, and ended with his third Olympic final, at Lake Wendouree, in Ballarat. Murray Riley gave no hint of his future plans. No one was sure if he would continue rowing without Wood's stability and strength to guide him.

*

The captain of the *Gruzia*, Elizabaz Gogitidze, embarked on a charm offensive, inviting local journalists and some left-wing unionists on board. 'I have never been aboard a craft more friendly than the *Gruzia*,' *The Argus*'s journalist enthused, praising the captain as a 'laughing, chunky and gravel-voiced' man. The ship was 'immaculate' and the captain's hospitality — Russian cigarettes and cognac — was exemplary. 'All Melbourne people can come to my ship and see my people,' the captain said. 'We want to buy from you and sell to you, then everybody can work and eat and be happy.'

Perhaps keen to dissuade the locals from getting the wrong idea about communism, Captain Gogitidze volunteered that his salary was £650 a month, and admitted that he and his sailors were 'not so poor'.[38]

The welcome, though, was not unanimous. Gogitidze confessed to representatives of the Seamen's Union that 'about 25 per cent' of visitors to the *Gruzia* had been 'very bad types' who abused the crew and made their anti-Soviet feelings known. There were also what were described as 'New Australians', who stood on the wharf and abused the crew until 10 pm. The situation forced Gogitidze to institute a system of official passes for those visitors who wanted to tour the ship.

The union contacted the wharf police, threatening to man the wharf to protect their fellow seamen from the USSR if the police could not restore order. In a reflection of just how sensitive the issue was — and with Nina Paranyuk already missing — the authorities moved swiftly. The official organ of the union reported: 'The response was immediate and the police called for a daily report, and the captain in thanking us, said "everything was good, no trouble at all now".'[39]

*

Five days before the Games ended, planes carrying Hungarian refugees landed in Sydney. The 90 men, women, and children were just the first of the initial 3,000 Hungarians for whom Australia had committed to find homes — and there was growing evidence that this would not be enough. Austria was struggling to deal with the refugee crisis, where 200,000 Hungarians were living in camps at the border. The United States announced it was boosting its original figure of 5,500 refugees to 21,500. The new Hungarian government was vigilant at its border with Austria and reports emerged of between 1,800 and 2,000 Hungarians being caught at the border every day and taken to Hungarian camps.

The group that landed at Mascot airport on the morning of 3 December was made up of 36 men, 28 women, and 26 children aged under 16. There were several family groups, and many of the men had either trades or valuable qualifications — agronomist, chemist, geologist, lawyer, engineer. They would be easy to employ.

They all had stories to tell. One couple was reunited after being separated for eight years — the man had stayed in Budapest getting ready to join his wife in Melbourne, but it took the uprising to sweep away all the barriers to their reunion. A diminutive resistance fighter named Fereno Ritter, who was married to a double-bass player in a Hungarian orchestra, hid in his double-bass case to ensure they crossed the border into Austria safely. For Professor Islvan Pavlovitz, there was also the incentive of coming to a country where barracking at a football match was allowed. The professor of bacteriology at Budapest Technical University had been arrested, put in jail, and dismissed from his university post for barracking too loudly in support of a Hungarian soccer team playing a visiting Soviet side. When he was talking to Australian immigration officials in Vienna, the professor asked the question: 'Is barracking at football matches banned or restricted in Australia?' When he was told that barracking was fine, Professor Pavlovitz decided Australia was for him.[40] Another refugee said: 'It was such a heroic but hopeless fight. Boys as young as 13 with few arms and ammunition joined in the fight with whatever weapons they could find. I think conditions will be a little better as a result of the revolution, but it still won't be real freedom.'[41]

The United Nations' deputy high commissioner for refugees, John Read, outlined the extent of the humanitarian challenge: 92,000 Hungarians had arrived in Austria after the uprising, but as of the start of December, only 22,000 could be accommodated in new homes around the world. What was to become of the other 70,000? Two days after the first group of Hungarians arrived in Australia, the government announced it would take another 2,000 under assisted passage agreements. More would need to follow them.

World events were starting to have an impact on Australia's migration. The requisition of ships, including the 'migrant ship' New Australia, for troop movements in the Suez Crisis, had an immediate impact on the number of British migrants coming to Australia. The crisis actually drove interest among non-British migrants, and the number of applications to emigrate lodged at Australia House increased. Australia was still seen as a safe haven in troubled times.

The chairman of the Federal Immigration Planning Council, Mr A.S. Hulme, praised Australia's quick response to the Hungarian situation: 'The plight of the Hungarians has aroused the sympathy and interest of all Australians ... No other country, except America, has acted as quickly or in such a positive and practical way.'[42]

Just as ASIO director-general Charles Spry had anticipated, a sizeable number of Hungarian athletes didn't want to go home. Hungarian officials had been coy in the build-up to the Games about whether there would be any defections, but it became clear as the Games went on that there had been discussions among the team and with local supporters who were prepared to help some athletes stay. In line with Spry's advice, the Hungarians received no encouragement from Australian officials or government representatives to defect. Just as Nina Paranyuk's pleading fell on deaf ears, so too did the Hungarian entreaties.

Not everyone was happy about this. The man who had seen the reports in Darwin about the atrocities at home, Miklós Martin, was upset at the Australian response. 'The Australian authorities would have nothing to do with us,' he said.[43]

The deadline for a decision was looming: 7 December was the date the plane carrying the Hungarian team was to leave Melbourne.

Chapter Twelve
The Worst of Times, the Best of Times

Four years earlier, at the Helsinki Olympics, the Australian women's 4 x 100 metres relay team was in a good position to win gold when disaster struck. The team comprised gold medallists Shirley Strickland and Marjorie Jackson, as well as Verna Johnston and Winsome Cripps. In the heat they had set a new world record. Cripps, running the third leg, was in front when she prepared to hand the baton to Jackson, but they were too close, and as Cripps went to make the pass, her knee hit the baton. The baton spilt free and hit the ground. Jackson managed to pick it up and keep running. She regained some ground to finish fifth, but the US team took the gold. It felt like a gold medal lost. The incident was still being talked about four years later, before the women's relay in Melbourne.

Australia named a relay team of six after the Olympic trials: Cuthbert, Mathews, Fleur Mellor, Shirley Strickland, Norma Croker, and Gloria Cooke. Later, Cooke was told her only event would be the 80 metres hurdles, which left five women competing for four spots. All five were still training up to the day before the first heat of the relay.

Strickland, at her third Olympics, was the most senior runner in the squad. The West Australian had won her first gold in the 80 metres hurdles in Helsinki, and her victory over the same distance in

Melbourne meant she became the first woman in Olympic history to retain her title. At 31, Strickland wasn't interested in playing games or soothing egos. She simply wanted the best Australian team out on the track, and told the relay coach, Nell Gould, that they needed to settle on the final team so they could have the order of runners established. Gould, who also coached 20-year-old Fleur Mellor, explained that not finalising the team was a tactic to confuse the press. Strickland replied that the only ones who were being confused were the girls in the relay squad.[1] Strickland believed the way the final selection was being handled originated in New South Wales, Gould's home state, and where the decision-making in athletics was centred.

The final of the 200 metres final was on Friday 30 November. The relay heats and final were the next day. After taking bronze in the 200 metres, Mathews was told she wouldn't be part of the relay team. Mellor would take her place as the fourth runner. Mellor later acknowledged that she was lucky to be selected, but she also believed she should have been part of the original 100 metres selection. She was certainly a promising sprinter, ranked just below Cuthbert and Mathews in New South Wales. Like Mathews, she had given up her job — as a stenographer in Lithgow — to come to the Games. If she wasn't in the sprints, then at least the relay gave her a chance at the gold.

Mathews tried to mask her disappointment. On the Friday night she and her fiancé, Barry Willard, went out to dinner together, and Mathews spoke about having 12 months off, before preparing for the Empire Games in 1958. The press was more explicit about her non-selection. *The Age* declared:

> If Marlene Mathews had been chosen for the relay, Australia could be classified as a certain winner, but the selectors have left her on the sidelines — despite her bronze medal in the 100 metres. No other country would have the third fastest woman in the world looking over the fence.[2]

Strickland, too, was horrified, calling Mathews' absence 'totally unfair'. 'In fact, it was a disgrace,' she said.[3] Norma Croker, who did make the team, years later called it 'criminal'.

Mathews had no real inkling about what was behind the decision. 'I've had no explanation, except for the fact possibly that they said I wasn't reliable enough when changing the baton, but that was the only excuse they gave me,' Mathews said later.[4] But there was no evidence that Mathews was unreliable with the baton; Nell Gould, who had been the women's athletics coach at the Empire Games in Vancouver two years earlier, had declared that she had not seen any female athletes 'to touch' the relay team, which at that stage included Mathews.[5] Mathews then had to withdraw from the team after suffering leg cramps, leaving Jackson, Cripps, Gwen Wallace, and Nancy Fogarty to win the gold medal. Since then, Jackson had retired and Cuthbert emerged, but nothing else appeared to have changed. Strickland later debunked the idea that Mathews' baton change was a problem, describing her as being 'as good as anyone'.[6]

The Australian athletics team manager from the 1952 Helsinki Games, Keith Donald, wrote a short time after the event that Mathews' omission 'bewildered many':

> She was quite clearly the second fastest sprinter in the team. Why then was she omitted? Some had said she couldn't run well around a turn. But she had won a bronze medal in the 200m and in any case could have run either the second or the fourth leg in the relay with no turn to negotiate. Some had said that her baton passing wasn't reliable. But the Australians had not done any intensive baton practice and 'reliability' was therefore only a relative term. This argument was weak and could not be proved in any case. It meant Mathews had been omitted because of a weak supposition.[7]

Others speculated that it wasn't so much about Mellor but Croker being a Queenslander — if Mathews replaced Croker, it would have given the team three NSW representatives. Mathews understood she was never going to run the last leg because of Cuthbert's outstanding form, but any doubts about her capacity to run the bend could certainly have been overcome by giving her the second leg, along the back straight. Mathews believed Cuthbert thought her omission was the right decision, but Mathews was never sure why Cuthbert was so certain.

The other issue was baton technique. There were two schools of thought on the best method: the old-fashioned hand-on-hip receive, and the modern, but riskier, extended-arm take. The Australians had been trying the old way, but Strickland wasn't at all happy about it, and, after some discussions and some covert training, she got her way. She later said:

> I didn't say no [to the old method], but I did a bit of arguing, and with the support of the girls, because I knew what relay changing was about. And I knew that if we were going to do the change that they were suggesting we were going to be laughed at, because all the European teams were doing a better change. So we managed to politically work our way around that one, and did the change we wanted to ...[8]

There was no clear favourite for the gold medal, because the USSR, German, and British teams were all in excellent pre-Games form. Australia narrowly won its heat against Germany, while Great Britain had a similarly close victory ahead of the United States. The two heat winners inevitably became the main contenders in the final, with Australia and Britain in adjoining lanes.

Strickland started Australia off, and was level with Britain when she passed to Croker, who fell several steps behind. But Mellor, running a good leg on the bend, made up some of the distance and passed to Cuthbert with the Australians only about 30 centimetres behind Britain. Cuthbert, mouth open, arms pumping, took off, with Britain's Heather Armitage in clear view. Cuthbert surged to the front but then felt Armitage come again and seize the lead halfway down the straight. Cuthbert made one last effort and powered past Armitage to regain the lead for long enough to cross the line, winning the gold medal in a world record time of 44.5 seconds.

In the grandstand Marlene Mathews sat and watched the Olympic gold medal that could have been hers disappear. She was in tears. It was the biggest disappointment of her career. That night, Betty Cuthbert, Shirley Strickland, Norma Croker, and Fleur Mellor went to Luna Park to celebrate. They remain the only Australian track sprint relay team to have won Olympic gold.

*

Nina Paranyuk had been taken in by members of the local Ukrainian society, one of whom owned the house that became her sanctuary. Their plan was for her to come out of hiding only after the *Gruzia* left Melbourne. The Ukrainians believed that it would be bad publicity for Australia if she gave herself up during the Games. It would also potentially affect the Australian relationship with the Soviet Union, and raise significant questions about Paranyuk's status — was she a defector, a refugee, or something else?

The Ukrainians knew about the *Navigation Act* and told Paranyuk that she could be charged with desertion if she was found and taken back to the *Gruzia*. Laying low seemed the best option. But she was nearly discovered when police searching for her embarked on a doorknock of the houses in the street where she was staying. The next day Paranyuk was moved to a farm near Geelong, where for the first time she felt the freedom she craved. It wasn't intended to be a long stay, but the Ukrainians heard that the *Gruzia* may turn back to Melbourne after it had left, so they had to be careful.

Paranyuk marvelled at the differences between the collective farm she knew and the bounty that surrounded her. 'My friends on the Geelong farm know life in the Ukraine, and they know how lucky they are,' she noted. 'They are producing more than under the

Russian collective farming system.'[9] For the first time, for instance, she had water from a tap — not collected from a well.

She was constantly vigilant, never going out at nights, staying in her room when those who were hiding her had guests, and only spending a couple of minutes a day outside in case she was spotted. In the meantime, she made two dresses, two blouses, and two skirts. Her hosts translated the stories in the papers about her, which she found amusing: 'Theories were advanced that I was in one district and then another — and even as far away as Adelaide — but all the time I was in one of two houses. I was amused by these theories and felt quite important.'[10]

The two Russian envoys didn't find it so funny. Zaikin badgered Francis Stuart and Special Branch, trying to find out if there were any breakthroughs. No one knew anything.

*

The international tensions, which had all but disappeared amid the spirit of goodwill at the Games, finally erupted on Thursday 6 December in a water polo match between Hungary and the USSR. The match became the most memorable demonstration of Cold War tensions in the Games.

Few observers had thought it would become so willing. The timing was important: the match occurred only days after the Hungarian refugees had arrived in Australia. That event alone would have brought reminders of home, and increased the intensity of feeling among the Hungarians. The game itself was a spiteful and nasty contest, which Hungary — the defending Olympic champions — won by four goals to one. But it was the 'blood in the water' moment that gave the match a heightened sense of drama and intrigue.

A Hungarian player, Ervin Zádor, was punched off the ball by a Soviet opponent, and left the pool with blood streaming down his face. The Hungarians claimed the Soviets had made offensive remarks during the match, but the Hungarians denied they had been provocateurs. They claimed the instruction they had been given before the match was to avoid physical confrontation. 'We were told we must win, but don't fight, don't box and don't play rough,' Hungarian captain Dezső Gyarmati said afterwards. The crowd at the Olympic pool quickly identified who they thought were the sinners and the sinned against, cheering the Hungarians and booing the Soviets when they left the pool at the end of the game.[11]

Those who weren't at the pool but had access to a television would have been able to see for themselves what was going on. All three networks — the ABC, HSV-7, and GTV-9 — were there to record the match. But only Colin Bednall's station had the compelling footage of what was happening under the water. 'We had put all our cameras in the hands of our fledgling producers and one of the most enterprising of them discovered there were glass portholes on the sides of the Olympic swimming pool,' Bednall explained. 'We secretly put a camera lens to one of the portholes.' The lens was in place for the water polo match, and it revealed just how hard the Hungarians worked on provoking their Soviet opponents. 'Those parts of the body the Hungarians worked on were well below the surface of the water,' Bednall revealed.[12] Hungary went on to win the gold medal, and the team was roundly cheered at an emotional medal ceremony.

The crowd response at the pool was a rare instance of Melbourne spectators picking sides. At the fencing at St Kilda Town Hall, Soviet fencer Lev Kuznetsov was roundly booed during his bout with Hungarian Pál Kovács. The Russian was gracious in conceding the points he lost to Kovács, but he put his hand over his face in protest at the predominantly US jury that ruled on some of the hits. The booing was at its height just as Avery Brundage walked into the hall to present the medals. Kuznetsov won bronze, and even then there was a section of the crowd who were determined to drown out the boos with the sound of applause.[13] While Vladimir Kuts' extraordinary running had won over the local crowd, even he could not escape one eccentric protest. A woman managed to infiltrate Kuts' press conference after his 5,000 metres gold medal, hissed, 'Red rat!' at him, and tipped eight red-painted rats on to the table between them.[14]

No matter how Australian crowds reacted, for the American and the Russian press, the final medal tally offered the best propaganda they could get from the Olympics. Brundage might hate it, but where the main Cold War combatants finished on the medal table was the real game in town.

*

Wilfrid Kent Hughes was not the sort of person who entered public life for reward or praise. It was a job to be done. No one could argue that his Olympic year had been easy: he'd been sacked from cabinet in January, and had then faced the extraordinary pressures the international situation brought to bear on the Games at the last minute. Kent Hughes could have been forgiven for basking in some of the glory that came with the Games' sense of success.

'Kent Hughes has applied his restless energy to such concentrated purpose that the Melbourne Games are achieving what even the United Nations cannot achieve. They are causing competitors to forget on the field and in recreation rooms the hatreds which some of their homelands feel for each other,' Sydney's *Sunday Telegraph* opined — before the water polo match.[15]

While this notion of international brotherhood wasn't strictly true, there was sufficient goodwill for Kent Hughes to feel he had done all he could to make the Games function as an international event. The ideas of mutual tolerance, the soft diplomacy of sport, and the supposed civilising influence of amateurism was what Kent Hughes was all about. It made him receptive to an anonymous letter he received from a 17-year-old Chinese-Australian student in Melbourne, who had come up with a new way to present the Olympic closing ceremony.

John Ian Wing was the grandson of a Chinese migrant who had come to Victoria with the thousands of others during the gold rush and stayed. Wing's mother had died when he was a baby, and he'd been raised in a Methodist children's home, while his father worked at all hours of the day in his restaurant, the Kwong Tung, at the top end of Bourke Street. His father remarried, and while the rest of the family — a younger brother and sister — stayed with their mother in Balwyn, John, aged only eight, moved in above the restaurant. For years, he would look out of his window at the passing parade of people, watching, thinking, and wondering.

Three days before the end of the Games, Wing sat down at a table above his father's restaurant and hastily composed a letter that would finish up in Kent Hughes' hands. 'Before the Games I thought everything would be in a muddle,' Wing wrote, 'however, I am quite wrong, it is the most successful Games ever staged. One of the reasons for its great success is the friendliness of Melbourne people. Overseas people would agree with me that Melbourne people are the most friendly people in the world.'[16]

Wing outlined his idea: that the teams should depart from the closing ceremony's standard practice of marching in their national groups, and instead march as one, mingling with each other:

> The march I have in mind is different than the one during the Opening Ceremony and will make these games even greater, during the march there will only be 1 NATION. War, politics and nationality will be all forgotten, what more could anyone want, if the whole world could be made as one nation. Well, you can do it in a small way … no team is to keep together and there should be no more than 2 team mates together, they must be spread out evenly, THEY MUST NOT MARCH but walk freely and wave to the public … It will show the whole world how friendly Australia is.[17]

There was something both naive and appealing about Wing's idea. At its heart was an idealism that harked back to a gentler time, before the suspicion and hostility of the Cold War and even before the two world wars. Without knowing it, Wing had hit upon an idea that chimed with Brundage's own desire for the Olympics to transcend nationalism and division.

Given how hard Melbourne had tried to stick to the Olympic rule book — and how regularly he had been reminded by Brundage about the conventions of being the host city — it was extraordinary that Kent Hughes embraced Wing's idea. But he swiftly saw the appeal of the march, and found Brundage to be a willing ally.

What made Wing's idea possible was the spirit that had infused the Games. A fractious and confronting two weeks would have made it almost impossible to schedule a closing ceremony that was a celebration of goodwill. Melbourne's success was that it had created an environment in which athletes felt comfortable to swap their national loyalties for an innocent celebration of sport. Brundage's endorsement of the plan came at a cost, when he was censured by the IOC executive for acting unilaterally. But his hold on the top job was so secure that such criticism was only a minor impediment. Once Brundage had approved it, Kent Hughes told his Friday-evening meeting with the chefs de mission about the plan.

When the closing ceremony arrived on 8 December, it set the precedent for every Games' closing ceremony to come: athletes from all 67 nations mingled, waving to 102,000 spectators, farewelling what had become known as the Friendly Games. John Wing had not been able to afford any tickets to the Games, and so all he knew of the closing ceremony were the pictures he saw in the newspapers. It was, for some time, his secret. He didn't even tell his parents. 'When you are Chinese, being young you probably would get into trouble,' he said years later. 'And I didn't tell my mates. They wouldn't have believed me anyway.'[18]

The athletes found the new approach invigorating. 'The inter-mingling of the athletes in the [closing] parade typified the brother-hood of sport which the Olympic Games had developed,' Strickland wrote later.[19] Australian sprint pioneer Marjorie Jackson was equally moved. 'Perhaps the true Olympic spirit was more evident in the closing ceremony when all the competitors from various nations marched in to the arena in one group,' she said.[20]

Wing had achieved something rare. In a time of war he had found a way to create a sense of unity. It was a strange, unpredicted, and compelling legacy for the Melbourne Games.

*

On the eve of the *Gruzia*'s departure the captain tried to shrug off Nina Paranyuk's absence. 'If she is not here when we sail tomorrow morning, never mind. We are not worrying about that,' Captain Gogitidze told reporters. He had refused to make out a warrant for her arrest if she was found. He didn't care that he would forgo a £100 bond if his employee didn't rejoin the ship. But he promised Paranyuk that no harm would come to her if she did come back to the *Gruzia*. All she would lose was the pay she had been entitled to.

'I have no bad feelings towards Nina,' he said. 'I am not worried by her disappearance. She is just a silly young woman who has made a rash decision.'[21] Moscow wasn't even worried about Nina's disappearance. 'If Nina chooses to stay, she is being foolish. But that is her decision and I wish her luck in Australia. We do not want ill feeling with Australians over her disappearance.'[22]

Paranyuk and her friends read this with an appropriate dose of scepticism. 'The people sheltering me and I know better. I would have been branded as "an enemy of the people" and anything might have happened to me,' she said.[23]

Captain Gogitidze wanted to make sure all the bridges of diplomacy were firmly in place before he left, regardless of his missing staff member. 'I have been at sea 22 years and I have visited many countries, but this is the friendliest port I can remember,' he said. Tucked away on board was Vladimir Kuts, now the owner of two Olympic gold medals. All the Soviet Union's gold medallists had been promised an airline flight home, but Kuts, inexplicably, was put on the *Gruzia*. He spent the next three days getting drunk.[24]

On the same day that the *Gruzia* was preparing for its return to Vladivostok Dmitri Zaikin and Yuri Filimonov visited Francis Stuart for the final time. Zaikin had a letter that he asked Stuart to pass on to Richard Casey about Nina Paranyuk. Stuart told the two consuls that he still had no information about the woman's whereabouts but that he would deliver the letter immediately. It outlined the Russians' hopes that 'all expedition will be used to do something about' the missing Ukrainian.

For all of the bluster, there was a sense that the Soviets were going through the diplomatic motions. They seemed reconciled to the fact that Paranyuk would not be found while they were still in Australia.[25] Menzies had only a few days earlier confirmed to Spry of ASIO that all approaches that purportedly came from Paranyuk should be ignored 'until there is more substantial evidence of her whereabouts and intentions'.[26] That wasn't going to happen any time soon. The police didn't suspect anything sinister had happened to Nina but appeared to have no clues to her whereabouts. And the government, just as it had shown with the Hungarian athletes, was in no hurry to offer her political asylum.

Once the *Gruzia* had left Melbourne, Paranyuk started to move about more freely. She left the farm and went back to a suburban house. She even went to the movies, with someone who could translate the dialogue for her. Paranyuk was amazed that there was no propaganda in the films she saw, but *Rock Around the Clock* puzzled her. 'Some of the young people went almost mad during "Rock Around The Clock",' she said. 'I was waiting for the police to throw them out. That's what would have happened in Russia.'[27]

*

The Games' success could be measured in many ways: how many medals Australia had won, how many spectators had attended, and what the response from overseas visitors and the world's press had been. How everyone else saw the Olympic city and the host nation had been such a concern in the build-up to the Games that it threatened to turn Melbourne into an anodyne destination, and Australia into a bland, remote, and featureless island. The results, though, pointed in the other direction.

It was Australia's most successful Olympics (surpassed only by the Sydney Games in 2000), collecting 13 gold medals and 35 medals in total, behind the United States and the USSR, and in front of Hungary.

Attendances had been high, across all venues, not just at the MCG, and reached a total of 2 million for the first time in the Games' history. There was no doubt that the Games had galvanised the Melbourne and national audiences. In years to come stories would emerge among athletes of the next generation who had found their inspiration in being at the Games as children. Adults confessed to enjoying the excitement, colour, and buzz of the two weeks. It even seemed to move the notoriously hard-to-please Avery Brundage, who praised the commitment of local fans who had packed out the Games' stadiums in record numbers.

Harold Abrahams, the 1924 Olympic 100 metres champion, lauded the spirit of Melbourne's Games. 'This was in no small degree due to the magnificent hospitality of our hosts, which set the right tone throughout,' he observed. Abrahams didn't believe the crowds were particularly knowledgeable about athletics in particular, '[b]ut the generous recognition of fine achievement by overseas athletes gave an example which one hopes will always be followed at future Games'.[28]

For some international visitors, what stood out was how familiar Melbourne was to where they had come from. Associated Press's Murray Rose labelled Melbourne a 'hustling, booming city': 'An American feels right at home here: American movies, American records almost predominate. Milk bars dot the streets as well as pubs. Fine, large department stores have full stocks of most items anyone can desire.'[29] The suggestion was that Australia had already fallen into the embrace of the American way of culture and consumerism:

if a visiting American felt it was like home, then perhaps Australia was already travelling swiftly away from the Empire and the Mother Country into the arms of someone else.

Television was perfectly placed to accelerate that trend. If there was one element that every visitor agreed upon, it was the nation's love of sport. 'This town is sports crazy,' Rose said. Brundage declared Melbourne the world's capital of sport. Red Smith took a more insightful approach:

Wherever you turn in Australia you see playgrounds ... football fields, cricket grounds, race courses, surf beaches, footracing tracks, grass tennis courts and these [lawn] bowling lawns. The Australian's enthusiasm for sport is a consuming passion and it gives him high marks for intelligence. He is smart enough to prefer playing to working: he is jealous of his leisure and he makes use of it.[30]

There were some observers, though, who were determined to present a different picture of Australia. The correspondent for French newspaper *Le Figaro* was pointed in his critique: 'Australians suffer from a naive, jealous boastfulness, which is a national disease.' What might have been a legitimate point of discussion about the national character became tenuously connected to fascism in the correspondent's argument when he suggested that such boastfulness had its origin in the behaviour of Italian dictator Benito Mussolini, when he invaded Abyssinia. Kent Hughes did his best not to engage, and responded: 'It's too silly to worry about.'[31]

Desmond Hackett (an appropriate moniker in the circumstances) wrote in London's *Daily Express* about what he perceived to be the lack of Australian support for Britain:

No other Olympics has ever been so fiercely parochial. Australia has had a joyful cause to raise its voice to for her athletes and swimmers. Americans were almost in the idolised class. Russians were fawned and feted. Hungarians, Czechs and the rest were all highly commended. But no bravoes for Britain. In the most peaceful and probably the most tame Olympics ever, Britain was the only victim of political taint.[32]

If the *Figaro* observations were silly, Hackett's seemed downright implausible. Of course, the Australian media rushed to find — without too much difficulty — alternative views to discount Hackett's whinge. Or maybe Hackett was onto something — was he detecting a small shift in the Australian consciousness? Could it mean that the old apron strings were starting to loosen, just a little? Was the exposure to the rest of non-Empire world a little exciting after all?

Other criticisms of the Games were more practical. Some athletes identified issues with the MCG track, which shifted underfoot and posed particular problems for runners in lane five. Bruce Howard saw spectators scraping the cinders off the top of the track and putting them into their handbags at the end of competition. Harold Abrahams pointed out errors in timekeeping and problems with the quality and timeliness of some information provided to the press about events and athletes.

But Roger Bannister, the first man to run a sub-four-minute mile — and the great rival of Melbourne's own John Landy — wrote in *The Sunday Times* that it had been the atmosphere of friendliness so successfully created by Australia that was one of the outstanding features of the Games.[33] Friendliness became the shorthand for the Melbourne Games, two weeks of calm amid the international turbulence.

That might have been what many of the athletes and observers remembered, but by the end of the Games, 61 athletes and officials, including 48 Hungarians, refused to return home. Many of the Hungarians travelled to the United States on what was billed 'the Freedom Tour', underwritten by magazine *Sports Illustrated*, a publication owned by fervent anti-communist Henry Luce. A few stayed in Australia, while some found their way to other democracies, including Sweden, Canada, and Israel.

Brundage used the Games' success as a basis for his own grander plans. Revealing that the limits of his ambitions were not confined to sport, Brundage suggested after Melbourne that the IOC should be awarded the Nobel Peace Prize. (In the event, there was no peace prize awarded in 1956.) Brundage's belief in sport as an elixir of international harmony never really dimmed, nor his odd logic that sport could achieve this by remaining separate from international politics.

The reality showed just the opposite. The Press Association in Moscow carried reports about the Soviet press crowing about the Russian Olympic team capturing more medals than the United States. The Communist Party organ *Pravda* devoted a remarkable two columns to the Soviets' Olympic victories. 'It was a day of reckoning for Uncle Sam as medals and points were totalled up on the adding machine and, for the first time in history, we found ourselves in second place on two counts,' one US journalist wrote. 'The Reds had us beaten on our own scoring system — [counting points for placings, from first to last]. They also topped us in gold medals, 37–32.'[34] The USSR also won more medals overall, 98 to the United States' 74.

The athletic competition did not end in Melbourne. Betty Cuthbert, Marlene Mathews, and the rest of the runners moved to Sydney to take part in a one-off competition billed as the British Commonwealth vs the United States of America. Moore Park was crammed with 24,000 spectators, and the women's relay team — Strickland, Croker, Mellor, and Cuthbert — set a new world record for the 4 x 110 yards relay, its second world record in five days. Once again, Cuthbert anchored the team and brought home the win. Mathews replaced Strickland in the 4 x 220 yards relay, which the Australians also won, in another world record.

Mathews had left Melbourne with a new attitude. The disappointments had provided her with some fresh insights into how to tackle her future.

Melbourne made me realise 'Yes, if you can run fast, you can win' but that there's more to it than just running fast. I became more determined after that. I'd had a fair amount of success up to then and Melbourne put a brake on me. And I realised that I wasn't going to remain a top athlete unless I changed my attitude — my attitude was good, but I realised you get out of it, what you put in to it.[35]

After Melbourne, Mathews set her own world records. In 1958 she defeated Cuthbert at the Cardiff Commonwealth Games to win both sprint gold medals.

*

Everyone was asked again if Nina Paranyuk had been found. The prime minister's office had nothing to say. Premier Bolte said there had been no progress. His deputy premier, Arthur Rylah, who looked after the police, had no comment. The police still couldn't shed any light on the situation. The next question wasn't whether Paranyuk would be found but what her status would be when she was.

Special Branch's Detective Sergeant Rosengren said Paranyuk would be detained 'as being a person suspected of being a prohibited migrant'. But a government spokesman had a different view: 'Nina will be allowed to stay here and will have exactly the same privileges and safeguards as the ordinary European migrant to Australia.'[36] The statement sounded like a gesture of reassurance: the *Gruzia* had sailed, and it was time for the Ukrainian refugee to come in from the cold.

Paranyuk kept her own counsel and remained hidden.

*

On the other side of the country a document was tabled in the West Australian parliament that peeled back another layer around what had occurred less than three months earlier at Maralinga. The report was the work of a parliamentary select committee led by Liberal MP Bill Grayden, a World War II veteran and former federal MP.

Only 27 when he entered state parliament in 1947, he later shifted to federal politics, and then returned to state parliament in 1956 as the member for South Perth. He had a rugged face, was pugnacious in style, and was known for his independence, crossing the floor on several occasions.

Grayden had a long-standing interest in Indigenous Australians' welfare, and pushed hard for an inquiry into what had been happening around Maralinga. His campaign for an inquiry began with a series of pointed questions to the minister for native welfare, John Brady, five weeks before the first Maralinga test:

> What I want to know from the Minister is this: What assurances have been given by the Commonwealth ... that steps have been taken to see this particular danger zone [around Maralinga] has been cleared of natives and what steps to ensure after the test the area is not contaminated, and to see that the natives do not wander back to the area after the tests.[37]

No one officially associated with the nuclear tests had been adequately able to answer Grayden's question, and Brady was not about to start now. He passed the question to the federal minister for supply, Howard Beale, whose response was tabled in the West Australian parliament after the One Tree explosion launched the Maralinga tests.

Beale once again maintained the fiction he deployed in every other instance when the issue of Indigenous safety was raised. He started with the usual line of doing nothing to jeopardise 'the welfare and precarious living of the native', and went on to state that 'two or three mobile ground patrols' were keeping a check on the location and movement of Indigenous Australians; scientific teams were also keeping an eye out for any Indigenous Australians in the area and alerting Robert Macaulay to their proximity; 'low level aerial reconnaissance' centred on Maralinga and 'extending out about 200 miles from the firing area is made with meticulous care'.[38] All of which was subsequently found to be, at best, open to question; at worst, it was a complete misrepresentation. Grayden politely acknowledged Brady's and Beale's responses, and pushed on with plans for his select committee.

Grayden knew the test location hinterland after spending time in the Rawlinson Ranges three years earlier, searching unsuccessfully for the remains of the ill-fated 1848 expedition of explorer Ludwig Leichhardt. He knew when he posed a rhetorical question — 'What chance would a patrol have of contacting these people?' — that the answer was: 'Not much of a chance at all.' Grayden was worried about the scientists' faith that winds would blow the radioactive particles away from the so-called uninhabited areas. 'But there are thousands of natives living in those parts,' he pressed. 'It is not possible to travel anywhere there without seeing the smoke from native fires on the horizon.'[39] Grayden stressed he was in favour of the tests, but precautions needed to be taken to safeguard the local communities.

In November 1956 Grayden and three other MPs flew to Giles, where Robert Macaulay picked them up in the vehicle that had finally arrived for him. Grayden and his fellow MPs spoke to a range of people, including Indigenous Australian communities in the area. They didn't appear to interview Macaulay or Walter MacDougall; neither man was mentioned in the committee's 18-page final report, either. The oversight is hard to explain. Although Macaulay had only been in the area for just over two months, MacDougall was an experienced voice. There was a suspicion, however, that Grayden did spend some time talking to MacDougall on an off-the-record basis; the report's final assessment of Giles's negative impact on the local communities' access to water and game mirrored MacDougall's own reservations about the station.[40]

Grayden and his committee's final report was a devastating critique of how abandoned, bereft, impoverished, and debilitated the Indigenous Australians of the area had become. Its conclusion was as devastating as it was concise:

The Committee has arrived at the conclusion that the plight of the aborigines [sic] in the Warburton-Laverton area is deplorable to the extreme. The natives lack even the most basic necessities of life. Malnutrition and blindness and disease, abortion and infanticide and burns and other injuries are commonplace. Game is extremely scarce on the reserve, water supplies for drinking precarious, and adequate medical attention far beyond the resources of the Warburton Mission. Employment opportunities for mission educated children are hopelessly insufficient and in the circumstances, education only serves to leave them more poorly fitted for fending for themselves when thrown back on their own resources at the completion of that education. Immediate food and medical aid are urgently necessary for these people and permanent provision for them a pressing obligation on the State.[41]

And as for Maralinga, the committee concluded: 'The necessity for keeping the Maralinga Testing Ground free from natives has interfered with the normal way of life of the natives who frequented the area east and south of the Warburton Mission, inasmuch as a large area of their tribal grounds is now denied them.'[42]

It was a simple denunciation of the most basic impact of the nuclear tests on the local Indigenous Australians — yet again, in a new and disastrous way, their land had been taken away from them. The logical consequence was to ask just how safe the communities were from the nuclear tests, but that query wasn't raised. Instead, Grayden's priority was to focus on the general circumstances of Indigenous Australians in a specific area. He took a movie camera with him to record what he saw. Together with the report, he had made his own kind of explosive device. But it would be some weeks before it detonated.

*

On 6 December, two days before the Games closed, news had broken about Vladimir and Evdokia Petrov. Two months earlier, in a secret ceremony at the immigration department office in Elizabeth Street, Melbourne, Australia's two most famous Cold War defectors had become Australian citizens. The naturalisation offered some reassurance to the couple, who had become, in the months since their defection, hostage to their own anxieties and misgivings, wondering when the government would provide them with the comfort of being able to call Australia home.[43]

The Menzies cabinet had started discussions about the idea in July, and proceeded carefully to ensure there were no leaks. Cabinet's deliberations captured the need for a nuanced approach to the Petrovs' naturalisation, not just to ensure their needs were met but so as not to compromise potential trade deals between Australia and the Soviet Union. The cabinet submission stated:

> As to the question of naturalization I suggest we have no alternative but to accord it to the Petrovs despite whatever mixed feelings there may be about their reasons for staying in Australia. It has been contemplated in various official pronouncements that they will become permanent residents of Australia and naturalization cannot be withheld indefinitely. Because of their past unhappy history they are entitled to whatever peace of mind such a decision will give them.[44]

The other consideration was residency. Five years' residency in Australia was considered the basic qualification, but cabinet agreed that the Petrovs' time in Australia working for the Soviet embassy would count. Even so, a decision was taken to delay the naturalisation for several months, in order to give the department of trade 'an uncomplicated opportunity' to extend trade talks with the USSR. ASIO boss Charles Spry supported the move because he believed naturalisation would confirm the Petrovs' loyalty to their new home. It might also encourage them to go on providing service and information.[45]

On 17 October the couple were naturalised, and cabinet was informed six days later. By the end of November, the Petrovs had been moved out of one Queensland safe house and into another, in Caloundra, after Vladimir, an aggressive alcoholic, had been locked up for the night in the Southport cells following a run-in with some locals.[46] It was one way to celebrate becoming an Australian citizen.

*

As the year drew to a close, stories emerged about Menzies' health. On 20 December the prime minister turned 62, and he was quick to discount any suggestion of fatigue or illness. The truth was that it had been a challenging year: the shearers' strike, the mini-budget, the Commonwealth Prime Ministers' Conference (and his extended time overseas), the atomic tests, the Suez Crisis, and the Olympics. Such an agenda would have been taxing for any politician, let alone one such as Menzies, who so dominated his government.

He was not the picture of youthful energy and brio anymore. Menzies was a stout, white-haired, middle-aged man, the gentle parabola of his stomach suggesting a long exposure to official lunches and dinners. He walked at a stately pace and did little to indicate that anything was either urgent or exciting. Many found his stature and demeanour reassuring. He sailed on, the imperturbable ship of the Australian state.

The Suez Crisis had already undermined British prime minister Anthony Eden's fragile health: he and his wife headed off to Jamaica towards the end of November, to a house called Golden Eye on the island's north coast, for 'rest, rest, rest'. He was there for three weeks. Menzies' own holiday plans were far less global: some time in Adelaide watching the Davis Cup challenge round, and some time in Melbourne. But the year couldn't end without one unexpected honour. The British tabloid newspaper, *The Daily Sketch*, announced Menzies as its 'Man of the Year'.

The Sketch's right to confer such a title on a political figure was tenuous. It was a tabloid 'picture' paper that was fast losing circulation to its rival *The Daily Mirror*. But its politics were firmly on Menzies' side of the ledger, and it was ever keen to prosecute a conservative agenda to the masses. The paper could be easily shocked, and sometimes bent itself out of shape to make its point, or indeed to avoid making one. Most famously, the paper's photograph of a prize-winning bull had the bull's anatomy rendered invisible, by request of the newspaper owner's wife. The decision caused great offence to the bull's owner, who sued the paper for damages to the bull's stud potential.[47] These eccentric moments did little to deter the newspaper from trying to set out a distinct ideological cart that led it — not surprisingly, in the climate of the time — to Menzies and a hyperbolic rendition of his physical and political qualities. 'He is a burly, vigorous man. Even the way his white hair floats in the wind is energetic,' the paper said. It went on to discuss Menzies' response to persistent rumours that he was resigning his post in Canberra and coming to London as Australia's high commissioner.

> If Menzies ever comes permanently to London it will not be as a spokesman for his own Dominion. It will be as a spokesman of the whole Commonwealth. There are qualities of supreme leadership in this man. He has everything it takes. His qualities were shown during the Suez crisis. From start to finish he was there at Britain's side. Menzies has been violently attached in his political career in Australia and will no doubt be violently attacked again … Love him or hate him: nobody disregards him. He is a sticker.[48]

The Sketch's take on Menzies was a nostalgic echo of a time when the Commonwealth was made up of Empire men who had Britain's interests at heart. If the events of the year had revealed anything, it was that something seismic was occurring across the world. Politics, diplomacy, economics, and sport were in a state of flux. *The Sketch* would close just three years later, a victim of changing tastes in Britain. For the moment, though, the newspaper saw Menzies as a vital figure on the fast-revolving world stage. But it was a rear-vision view. The picture ahead was far more challenging.

Finale

The post-mortems started immediately. One of the most telling assessments, from Maurice Nathan and Don Chipp's civics committee, also contained a specific challenge: 'The Games were successful but is this fact a signal to rest on our Olympic laurels or is it a glorious opportunity to merely commence the tremendous task of raising our city, state and nation into a position commanding world prestige and acknowledgement?'[1] Putting aside the rhetorical flourish, the question was pertinent: how could Melbourne and Australia convert the Olympic success into something lasting?

There was no obvious answer. What echoed back from the various columns of reflection in the nation's press was how important the Games were to Melbourne's sense of itself. 'It is now clear that what the world may gain from adjusting itself to Melbourne is nothing compared with Melbourne's gains from adjusting itself to the world,' a *Herald* columnist observed.[2]

Perhaps one reason for this was that the Melbourne message had not been communicated overseas as effectively as many in the city would have liked. The Games' press and publicity committee blamed international tensions and 'other reasons' for fewer journalists turning up. One consequence was unused accommodation, rooms that had been booked — and secured by a £5 deposit — by journalists who were intending to be in Melbourne but then hadn't made the journey. Some journalists who did cover the Games also found other accommodation. The end result was that 'many hotels were left with unoccupied rooms, which they claim would not have occurred had the Committee not entered the field,' the committee noted. The point was moot: media organisations needed a central contact point rather than trying to organise accommodation with individual hotels. But the committee's involvement might well have restricted choice and tariff flexibility.

The committee took it upon itself to cover the hotels' revenue shortfall, and it also retained the deposits from booked but unattended rooms. That amounted to £905, which suggested 181 journalists hadn't used the hotel rooms they had been allocated.[3] About 600 overseas journalists, photographers, and broadcasters did attend the Melbourne Olympics, but it's clear that was nowhere near as many as originally expected. The withdrawal of teams certainly hadn't helped.

Tourist numbers were down too. 'Many Melbourne people held somewhat extravagant ideas about the potential number of overseas visitors who could be attracted to the Games,' the committee said in the wash-up. 'A comparatively modest estimate by the organising committee of 10,000 to 15,000 [overseas tourists] proved ultimately to be fairly accurate. The record-breaking crowds ... were mostly Australians and New Zealanders.'[4]

The bid team's pitch to its doubters in Rome seven years earlier that faster jet travel to the faraway capital in the Southern Hemisphere would reduce Australia's remoteness had proved overly optimistic. When part of the world was in disarray, air travel seemed perilous. And as several observers had noted, the Americans had stayed away from London and Helsinki, so they were never going to turn up in big numbers to Australia, which was even further away. The press and publicity committee had identified that issue sufficiently early to avoid committing big money to an overseas publicity and advertising campaign about Melbourne, the Games, and Australia, which would, by all indications, have been wasted.

*

On 18 January 1957 there was a knock on the door of Nina Paranyuk's safe house in Melbourne's northern suburbs. It was Detective Sergeant James Rosengren and two other police. Paranyuk was reassured by the people sheltering her that the police were friendly.

'Instead of the bullying types I saw in the police force in the Ukraine, they treated me like a lady. They were smiling as they opened the door of the police car,' she said.[5] 'I got in to the car, and I knew I had done the best thing in my life when I fled from the *Gruzia*.'

She promised she would lose herself in Australia, change her name, and make a different life for herself. 'As the spotlight fades, I will be able to live normally … If I stay as Nina, I will live in fear always. And the members of the society who gave me freedom would soon become known.'

Detective Sergeant Rosengren took Nina to the Russell Street police headquarters, and from there to the immigration department in Elizabeth Street. No charges were laid against her.

Later that day, Paranyuk applied to become a permanent resident in Australia. Her application was accompanied by a short note, that read: 'I joined the vessel [the *Gruzia*] with the intention of leaving Russia and residing in another country. I therefore apply to remain in Australia and become an Australian citizen in the future.'[6]

She didn't have long to wait. On 25 February 1957 a Commonwealth migration officer wrote her a letter: 'I refer to your application for permission to remain permanently in Australia, and I desire to advise that the application has been approved.'[7] To all intents and purposes, Nina was now free and a legal citizen of Australia. But although the police and immigration department knew where she was staying, no one else did.

The newspapers had been trying to find Paranyuk too. Journalist Lionel Hogg had been on a Queensland holiday when she had gone missing, but when he came back to the Flinders Street offices of *The Herald*, he told his editor he reckoned he could track her down. Hogg knew his way around police headquarters and rang Rosengren, who was reluctant to help. But when Hogg said he didn't need to know where Paranyuk lived, but only to talk to her, Rosengren relented.

Three days later, Hogg took a telephone call from someone speaking in a thick accent: 'You want to see Nina? Maybe we can arrange that.' There were conditions to the interview — no photographs without permission, and even then, Paranyuk would not be captured in any portrait shots. Hogg was not to follow the two Ukrainians who accompanied her, who were part of the network of people who had sheltered her.

After an initial meeting with the Ukrainians, Hogg made his first contact with Paranyuk — at the Melbourne Zoo, ironically enough. A photograph was taken of her standing outside; she could have been anyone. Hogg was surprised to find that she had put on weight, her clothes were modern, and her hair had been cut short. She looked like a local.

For the next four nights, Paranyuk and her two Ukrainian companions visited Hogg at his home in suburban Windsor, where she told her story, from her impoverished life in Ukraine to the day she fled the *Gruzia*.[8] The four-part series in *The Herald* won Hogg the first Walkley Award for Australia's best news story. Paranyuk's tale was an artefact of the Cold War. It played to preconceptions of the Soviet Union and the West, of communism and democracy, of oppression and liberty. And it was a story that happened in Australia at a time when the rest of the world had actually turned up on Melbourne's doorstep.

The story even seemed to have the ultimate happy ending. Just six days after the government told Paranyuk she could stay, she was married. Her husband was a 36-year-old engineer, Wasyl Kuzyk. He was one of 12 men who had sent her a marriage proposal after she came out of hiding. He sent her his photo, and the couple, working through the Ukrainian network that had sheltered her, arranged a meeting. After that, they spent every night of the week together, and Paranyuk told friends she was engaged. 'It was love at first sight,' she said.

She and Kuzyk organised a quiet wedding at St Mark's Anglican church in Fitzroy, with a Polish priest officiating. But word of the ceremony got out and more than a hundred Ukrainians flocked to the church. Paranyuk, still nervous after her ordeal, waited in a black taxi for 25 minutes, hoping the crowd would disperse, before she realised she had to get to the church.[9] A private reception was held at one of her former safe houses, with about a dozen guests.[10] There was no discussion that day about where their marital home would be; there were still some secrets she wanted to keep.

That was just as well. In July 1957 the KGB in Moscow included Nina on its list of Soviet people who were political enemies of the state. The KGB had sentenced her to death.[11]

*

Colin Bednall stuck to his promise: his would be the last of the television stations to launch. It meant he had more time to get it right, and more time to see what his competitors were doing. It was fine to be second, Sir Arthur Warner told his general manager. Sir Arthur's attitude gave Bednall the scope to make his own way and build his own station.[12]

On 18 January GTV-9 formally launched onto the airwaves from its £1 million studios. Bednall had worked assiduously to ensure that he built a headquarters that had room to grow — that translated into a 32-metre-long studio that was the biggest outside the United States. There was scope for live performances, not just quiz and game shows. No wonder the old Heinz factory was dubbed 'Studio City', giving a fair indication of Bednall's distinct vision for television in Australia. The renovation had included another studio that was suitable for cooking demonstrations and retained the old Heinz staff canteen, updated, for the GTV-9 staff.

Bednall had faith that television would grow, and struck out boldly where many of his competitors were conservative and measured. A large part of Bednall's confidence in television was based on what he had seen overseas. He had now been a convert to the medium for years, but he also had the programming skills to make it work in Australia. The station Bednall created was fit for a particular purpose: to show off local product. That was why he had a large studio for live performances. It was why he spent a great deal of time trying to identify and promote local talent. There was still a need for overseas content, though, to lure viewers to the station and provide the programming around the local product.

Bednall and his programming manager, Norm Spencer, had gone overseas to source programs, and returned with a selection designed for family viewing, from comedians Burns and Allen, to crime show *Dragnet*, *Alfred Hitchcock Presents*, and new British shows *The Buccaneers* and *The Adventures of Sir Lancelot*.[13] Bednall made sure he made the right noises: 'GTV Channel 9 will offer every day of the week, programmes of outstanding Australian productions and the cream of American and British programming,' he said on the eve of the opening.[14] But his priority was to find local stars, and for viewers to feel they were watching themselves, or people and places they knew.

As a former newspaper man, Bednall had also invested heavily in news coverage. In the early days he would insist that his small executive team read the morning newspapers before their weekly Monday meeting. 'We need to know what's going on in Melbourne,' he told them.[15] That translated into his approach to news. The publicity blurb, as outlined in one of GTV-9's newsprint partners, *The Argus*, showed some old-fashioned brio:

GTV 9's flying squad of newsreel cameramen will rove Melbourne continuously providing coverage of all outstanding events. On the spot film coverage will give a new dramatic power to the news, supplementing the printed word and radio. As soon as the cameramen shoot their film it will be rushed to Richmond for processing … in addition to regular news bulletins, news breaks occurring during the day will be flashed to viewers.[16]

If viewers had any doubt about how this entertainment and information offering might work, Bednall could point not only to the Olympic Games coverage but also to the network's running of the film of the Australian Davis Cup victory, and also the Christmas carols, which were to become a GTV-9 staple.

All the pomp and promise would be revealed on the opening night, when Victorian governor Sir Dallas Brooks was to drive into the studio in a chauffeured limousine. Bednall wanted to show off the expanse of his studio, and had a team of white ponies lined up for one of the acts. He had sourced coir matting from the Myer's department store to ensure the horses could get traction on the shiny studio floor. Ten minutes before the governor arrived, Bednall was cleaning up after the horses' accidents all over the new floor. He was never afraid to get his hands dirty.

There were celebrity interviews, a variety show featuring singer Toni Lamond and her husband, Frank Sheldon — both just back from overseas — ventriloquist Ron Blaskett, a children's choir, Indigenous singer Harold Blair, Lou Toppano's 23-piece orchestra, and Bob and Dolly Dyer, who were about to migrate their successful radio show, *Pick a Box*, to television.[17] There were 400 people in the audience, all of them agog at the new technology, the buzz, the bright lights, and the noise.

Viewers in lounge rooms and those gazing into shop windows were amazed. The new switchboard at the old soup factory lit up for two hours after the show, with happy viewers from rural and regional Victoria gushing about the quality of the vision they had received that night. Five unnamed countries cabled their congratulations to Bednall and his executive team.[18] Even allowing for the boosterism that came from *The Age* and *The Argus*, there was no doubting the opening night was a success. Bednall's television career was up and running.

*

In February the 25-year-old Rupert Murdoch flew to Giles, and Robert Macaulay once again found himself chauffeuring a newcomer around. Murdoch's interest in the area was piqued by Bill Grayden's committee findings and the films, not by Maralinga.

Murdoch had taken over *The Adelaide News* on his father's death, and with two others he chartered a twin-engine Aero 45 and flew up from Adelaide to Alice Springs, then across the hinterland, stopping at mission stations along the way to find out just how badly Indigenous Australians were faring. Not too bad at all, Murdoch concluded. 'No Aborigines in the Central Australian reserves are dying of thirst or starvation — or disease,' he noted. 'The great nationwide concern over these people has not been necessary.' He went on to warn, however, about the need to 'protect these prime but totally unprepared people' from the incursions of international mining companies.[19] Murdoch's priority might have been to debunk Grayden's claims, but the broader debate about Indigenous Australians' imminent safety was still pertinent because there were another three atomic tests at Maralinga to come in 1957.

Grayden's report had been a slow burn in the eastern states, only becoming newsworthy after the 1957 New Year. It was then that Murdoch decided to jump on the topic. He was at the same time negotiating to buy the ailing *Argus* newspaper in Melbourne from Cecil King. On 16 January *The Argus* ran an impassioned piece from a journalist with a long exposure to Indigenous Australians and northern Australia. Gordon Williams wrote partly in response to the Grayden revelations and partly about the impact of the Maralinga tests:

> These people have been driven from their hunting grounds by the White Man's Progress — such progress as is represented by the Maralinga atomic testing ground and by searches for minerals that will help to stabilise our economy, but won't give the dispossessed one witchetty grub or a single goanna to help

him along his dusty road to death. Well, I suppose it is good that the Parliamentarians HAVE discovered these things, and that, discovering, they have shocked a nation. But what shocks me — and everybody to whom for many, many years the tragedy of the Aborigine has been a tale too plainly written — is that these disclosures and 'revelations' should reach us now, in 1957, with all the impact of one of Maralinga's A-grade explosions. What they record has been going for a long, miserable time.[20]

It was a modern and compassionate response, but its capacity to influence opinion was limited. And *The Argus* couldn't spend any resources or send staff to explore the issue — it was financially bereft. Three days later, after Murdoch bought the paper, he fulfilled the condition of sale by closing *The Argus* after 111 years.[21]

*

In March 1957 the Democratic Labor Party formally came into existence, ending the short-lived Australian Labor Party (Anti-Communist), which Les Coleman had led. The national party brought together the anti-communist elements in the state Labor parties and gave them a single platform. The strength of the new organisation was the two states where the split had been so debilitating for Labor: Victoria and Queensland.

The DLP's arrival gave Coleman an opportunity to weigh into the public debate again. His energies in the latter part of 1956 were consumed by his Olympic role, and he didn't appear to miss the state responsibilities that had come from his bruising time as transport minister. But in 1957 he did have a message to impart about 'Australia's appalling weakness before the growing might of Chinese Communism and the growth of Communist subversion in Australian trade unions'.[22]

Coleman's deeply held aversion to communism had emerged as a key determinant in the final stages of his political career. And his brawling with the union movement over the One-Man Bus dispute had convinced him of the trade union movement's fundamental opposition to what Coleman considered efficiency and progress.

He was elected state president of the DLP in March 1958, and considered himself a good candidate for Senate preselection four months later. Despite presenting a strong case and clearly having the experience to do the job, Coleman was overlooked for a non-Catholic, Jack Little. Although Little was 20 years younger than Coleman, it appeared that Bob Santamaria wanted to ensure the party was not seen as a Catholics-only organisation. Coleman resigned from the party soon after, and then announced he would not be recontesting his seat on the Melbourne City Council. With those two decisions, Les Coleman drew a veil over his political career.

The DLP became the electoral bane of the Australian Labor Party, whittling important preference votes off Labor that locked it out of government. Gough Whitlam's surge to power in 1972 effectively neutralised the DLP bogey, but it wasn't until after the double-dissolution election of 1974 that it was marginalised. It limped along for several years before slipping off the electoral landscape, then emerged like a curio from another time to have a Victorian senator in 2010.

Les Coleman wouldn't live to see the end of the party he had been integral to establishing; he died on 6 October 1974.

*

Only six Hungarian Olympic team members stayed in Melbourne after the Games, including steeplechase silver medallist Sándor Rozsnyói, wrestler Bálint Galántai, kayaker Zoltán Szigeti, and sprinter Géza Varasdi.

Although Andor Mészáros had little money to offer the new refugees, he did what he could. Varasdi needed to do three years' additional study in Australia for his medical degree to be of use, so Mészáros got him working on the pick and shovel to help build the house attached to Mészáros' Kew studio while he studied.

Mészáros remained a proud and homesick Hungarian, and understood how important it was to help newcomers adjust to the Australian way of life. Such support became increasingly important after the federal government increased its initial intake of Hungarian refugees to 14,000. The reputation of previous Hungarian immigrants, such as Mészáros, and the broad sympathy for what had happened to the refugees made adaptation and engagement with Australians somewhat easier than it had been for those of Mészáros' generation.[23]

Varasdi became a GP, lived in Melbourne's northern suburbs, and retained a clear view of why he decided to stay in Melbourne:

[W]hen we were competing in Western countries, our families were at gunpoint. If you don't go back — bang — you know? … Sport was part of the propaganda. We were taken out while the family were at gunpoint and we were there to look happy, so people made the conclusion: 'After all, Communism can't be so bad.' But of course, we looked like that, because how can I send my family to a concentration camp or God knows where?[24]

Mészáros, too, had been won over to Australia, after confronting what he called 'the cultural desert' when he arrived. There were issues with his clients, many of whom he gave short shrift because of their lack of sophistication and cultural vulgarity when it came to dealing with artists. But Mészáros saw that he could, in effect, paint his own canvas, and he became Australia's first and best portrait medallion maker. His son Michael understood that his father came to see the opportunities in Australia, the distance from the scenes of international conflict, and the relaxed approach to life as an inviting contrast to the highly competitive and regimented life he had led in Hungary.[25]

By the time he died in 1972, Mészáros' work in stone and bronze was at Brisbane's Shrine of Remembrance, Darwin's Supreme Court, Sydney's international airport terminal, the King George V Hospital in Sydney, as well as in the trophy cabinet, sock drawer, or pool room of everyone who had played a role in the 1956 Melbourne Olympics.

*

On 21 August 1956 someone had finally noticed that *The Catcher in the Rye* was banned in Australia. Seven months later, the Australian agents for the book's British publisher, Hamish Hamilton, wrote to customs officials to appeal the decision. Part of the argument was that the US edition had been banned in Australia, but the English edition was perhaps more palatable. Certainly, the Hamish Hamilton *Catcher* had been on sale in Australia since 1951. 'We might mention that the sales of the book in Australia have been negligible, and it came as a great surprise to learn that this action had been taken,' the letter read.[26]

Of course, how popular the book was or otherwise wasn't the issue. But when the federal parliamentary library had its copy of the book seized, the issue became news. It was, the press said, a national embarrassment, and the censorship system needed an urgent overhaul. The book was released the following month and a review of the censorship system announced.

*

After hearing the 'Rock Around the Clock' record and seeing the film, the next thing was actually seeing it live. And in January 1957 Bill Haley and the Comets obliged, making their first tour to Australia. Haley did two concerts a night, and the reactions to the band mirrored the film's wild-eyed physical enthusiasm. According to *The Sydney Morning Herald*, 'Couples leapt from their seats and danced in the aisles ... Young people with glassy looks in their eyes swayed in their seats as the bands played ... two girls in the front row wearing matador pants and loose-fitting shirts leapt up and began jiving in the aisle.'[27]

Something had stirred, and Australia would soon get its own rock'n'roll stars: in 1958 a young tearaway from Sydney, Johnny O'Keefe, would have a number one hit song with 'The Wild One'.

*

GTV-9 soon became the powerhouse of Melbourne television. The secret of its success was Colin Bednall's desire to find local talent and use it to best effect. Graham Kennedy was working at radio station 3UZ when Bednall and his programming manager, Norm Spencer, spotted him. They got Kennedy to come in to Bendigo Street for a test.

Bednall was sitting in the radio control room with Spencer when the camera zoomed in on Kennedy's face. The pair were transfixed. 'When a full face of Kennedy alone came on the monitors, Spencer and I turned to one another without exchanging a word and shook hands,' Bednall said. But he would always deny he 'discovered' the man who would go on to be called 'the King of Australian television'. 'A man with a performer's genius as Kennedy possessed, projected himself,' Bednall wrote in his unpublished autobiography. 'I merely saved him from dismissal five times a year for seven years.'[28]

That became a pressing issue when Sir Arthur Warner sold GTV-9 to the Sydney Channel 9, which was owned by Sir Frank Packer, in 1960. Packer was homophobic and constantly harangued Bednall about getting Kennedy off the air. Bednall always resisted. And Kennedy thrived.

Bednall left it all behind in 1965 (operational costs once again got the better of him), and his working life then became a series of stops and starts. He went from working for the United Nations on space communications to managing an English-Chinese TV station in Hong Kong, stood unsuccessfully as a Labor candidate in the 1972 and 1974 federal elections, worked briefly for Gough Whitlam, and then wrote a media column for *The Age*.

Not only had Bednall's political views changed from the days when he'd cultivated Sir Robert Menzies, so had his views about television. With the flawless judgement of hindsight, he admitted: 'Tragically, when applications [for TV licences] were invited, the only ones worth considering, apart from a consortium embracing Sir Arthur Warner, were those of newspaper, radio and cinema interests.' The upshot of that newspaper involvement was that television began 'sliding down into mediocrity the moment a newspaper proprietor ... insisted on making management decisions'.[29] He died on 26 April 1976.

*

Marlene Mathews married Barry Willard in March 1957. For the next 18 months, she was in rare form, free of the expectation of being Australia's number one female sprinter, and relatively injury-free too. At the Empire Games in Cardiff in 1958 she won the sprint double, and it would have been three golds but for another problem with the relay team, this time with the baton change rather than team selection. At the end of 1958, at the national championships in Sydney, Mathews broke Marjorie Jackson's world record for the 100 metres by 0.1 second. The next night she set a new world mark in the 200 metres. These were two days she would never forget.[30]

But Mathews suffered another leg injury in the build-up to the 1960 Rome Olympics, which meant she was not at her best. Australia's only track and field gold came when Herb Elliott smoothly and comprehensively won the 1500 metres title. Rome was hot, uncomfortable, and out of season for the Australians, and the competition was fierce. Although Mathews managed to finish second to the great US sprinter Wilma Rudolph in the post-Olympics meeting, she understood why the Australians could not match their performance from Melbourne. 'The rest of the world was catching up,' Mathews explained.[31]

Mathews never fulfilled her goal of becoming a physical education teacher, but she came pretty close, helping coordinate athletics coaching and promoting athletics through the Rothmans National Sport Foundation. She coached at club level, in schools, and across states. Mathews was appointed to the NSW Women's Advisory Council, and earned numerous honours for her athletic achievements. In January 2018 bronze statutes of Marlene and the recently deceased Betty Cuthbert were unveiled at the Sydney Cricket Ground. The pair were, in Mathews' words, 'polite rivals' who became friends.

*

There were three more 'major' nuclear bomb trials held in Maralinga in 1957, and a further five trials up to April 1963. In 1985 the Australian Labor government established a royal commission, under former Labor senator and judge Jim McClelland, to investigate the nuclear tests. The final report was a fierce denunciation of Australia's subservience to the British demands, and levelled uncompromising criticism against Beale and others in the Menzies government and the British scientific establishment for their utter lack of honesty and care for the Indigenous communities in and around the test zone.

Walter MacDougall continued to patrol the area, although his main work became the recording of Aboriginal sites. He retired to Victoria, but after his death in 1976 his ashes were returned to the Ernabella mission. Robert Macaulay married Jean in Sydney in October 1958, and after his initial posting at Giles spent seven years at Woomera. After that, he joined the department of immigration and continued his working life a long way from Woomera, Giles, or Maralinga.

*

Bruce Howard became a senior photographer at *The Herald*, and wrote a popular book on the 1956 Olympics, which featured many of his photographs. *The Herald* remained Australia's biggest-selling afternoon paper until the 1980s, when circulation started to fall. Rupert Murdoch bought his father's old paper (and the rest of The Herald and Weekly Times stable) in 1987, and three years later merged *The Herald* with its morning stablemate, *The Sun*, to create the nation's biggest-selling daily newspaper.

*

The double scullers Mervyn Wood and Murray Riley went their separate ways in graphic contrast to each other. Wood ultimately became the NSW police commissioner, and Riley a convicted drug trafficker.

Riley had left the police force in 1962. The Moffit royal commission into alleged organised crime connections to licensed clubs found in 1974 that he had gone into business with Raymond Smith sometime after he had become Smith's bodyguard. '[Smith] was apparently engaged with Riley in doubtful or criminal conduct in the financing of poker machines,' the commission reported.[32] Riley went into hiding while Justice Athol Moffit held the hearings for the inquiry, and then turned up a day after the report was tabled in the NSW parliament.[33]

The poker machine business proved to be a huge boon to licensed clubs in New South Wales. In 1967 there were 1,419 clubs in the state, with a total of 19,617 machines, almost four times as many machines as there had been a decade earlier. The other beneficiary was the state government: in the first two years of legalised poker machines, the government raised an extra £1.5 million in tax revenue.[34]

*

Nina Kuzyk declared in 1968 that she 'wasn't frightened any more'. 'They can't touch me. I'm in a free country,' she said.

She had decided in the 12 years since she'd arrived to keep a low profile. She and Wasyl had a son, Wally, who went to Pascoe Vale

North Primary School and helped his mother learn English. Wasyl had a job as a crane operator in Melbourne. On 27 November 1967 Nina had been naturalised in Broadmeadows. The picture of the family published in *The Herald* showed a normal, shy, and happy group. Nina admitted that her elderly mother, married sister, and brother were still in the USSR. 'I haven't seen them since 1954. I hope they're all right. But I know they haven't got in to trouble because of me,' she said.[35] It is hard to know how Nina could be so certain, unless she was in communication with them.

The family were regular attendants at the North Melbourne Ukrainian church, and they had a network of Ukrainians around them. Nina became unwell and, after a time in hospital, left Melbourne. Wasyl and Wally were left behind. Nina went to the Blue Mountains in New South Wales. She appears to have changed her name — as she had always promised. No one has revealed what happened to her. Nina Paranyuk had disappeared for the final time.

*

Seven months after the Games, the Victorian Historical Society hosted an address from Ted Doyle, who had chaired the Melbourne press and publicity committee. It was, on the face of it, an odd forum in which to reflect on the Games, but it suggested Melbourne was already seeing the Games as a moment in a time. Doyle's address gave words to feelings that had swirled around the MCG and the city during the Games, about the advantage of being so far from international turmoil:

> Curiously, Melbourne's very remoteness which had been envisaged as the worst handicap Melbourne faced as the host city for the Games became in this extremity her saving grace. Many of the athletes, their official and supporters, were already here, others arrived in the midst of the tumult to find that in the long sight the shattering events of the other hemisphere slipped

in to a new perspective, took on more correct proportions as proximity faded in to middle distance, middle distance in to the far away.[36]

While there was some truth in the observation about Melbourne's distance, the idea that an athlete took a healthier perspective on the threat to his or her family from Soviet tanks by competing in Melbourne tests credibility.

Doyle was on stronger ground when it came to reflecting on what it took to get Melbourne up and ready for the Olympics:

> We might have lost the Games. Be it said to the everlasting credit of Australian sportsmanship, Australian national sentiment and Australian teamwork — in the treasury as well as one the track — and the civic pride of a great city, we neither defaulted nor, once the honour was ours, did we fail in our determination.[37]

The ultimate consequence of that, Doyle said, was immeasurable. There were stadiums, buildings, visits from VIPs, tourism, publicity, commerce, and the goodwill of thousands of locals in supporting the Games, but no one could know what that all amounted to:

> [No] ... Olympic city stood to gain so much as Melbourne ... from the experience of housing and catering, accommodation and transport which the Games thrust upon its citizens and services, an ordeal intensified by the rapid changes and improvisations created by the alarums and excursions of the international aspect.[38]

This was the official view of the men who had delivered the Games. They were justifiably proud of their achievement.

Earlier in the year, Avery Brundage thanked the city for making the Games a success in a message he sent to Lord Mayor Sir Frank Selleck. 'Everyone in Melbourne, under your leadership, seemed to have captured the Olympic spirit. In this respect the Games were probably the most successful ever staged,' Brundage wrote. 'I am sure Australia has gained thousands of friends as a result.'[39] Brundage's approval was hard-won, and his endorsement had value to those who had endured his bullying and bluster.

There were easy ways to measure the nation's success through individual gold medallists — in the swimming pool, Dawn Fraser, David Theile, Lorraine Crapp, Murray Rose, and Jon Henricks, in addition to Cuthbert and Strickland on the track — and standout Australian performances in a range of disciplines. The Rome Olympics in 1960 was a far harder challenge: many Australian competitors felt that the world had caught up to and gone past Australia by then.

*

In time, *Summer of the Seventeenth Doll* would be regarded as the cornerstone of modern Australian drama. It won the *Evening Standard* award in London for the best play of 1957 after a stellar season in the West End. A New York season went well, but without the awards. Ray Lawler would write more plays, including two that became part of the Doll trilogy, but the original remained the best loved. Its capacity to tell us about ourselves at a particular time in our history became increasingly valuable. '[I]n the 1950s its complex reflection of the nation's confused image of itself made it a central document of Australian culture,' the experienced theatre critic John McCallum observed.[40]

Australia's 'confused image of itself' is central to understanding the importance of 1956. The year ushered in a significant but subtle shift from the most odious of Australia's distinguishing features — the White Australia policy. From July, non-European residents were for the first time allowed to apply for Australian citizenship. It was a pointer to further changes to come, which included the abolition of the dictation test in 1958, and the dismantling of most of the policy in 1966. The policy had signalled to Australia's neighbours that it wasn't interested in engaging with the region but continued to cast an adoring eye halfway around the world to a continent increasingly removed from its daily concerns.

By the end of 1956, Australia had hosted the world's sports men and women, welcomed wartorn refugees, broken some of its cultural conventions, exposed some of its Indigenous communities to the risk of another nation's atomic weapon, and, through its prime minister, been involved in the world's worst crisis since World War II. Taken together, the events and outcomes paint a contradictory picture, capturing a nation in the throes of progress at one moment, and firmly stuck in its history at another. Yet there was no doubting that the international exposure, in all its colours, successes, and failures, had an impact on Australians.

The difficult preparations for the Games might have helped lower expectations among many Australians about Melbourne's capacity to deliver the Olympics, but the end result defied all predictions. The practical manifestation of the Games — the stadiums, the pools, and the infrastructure — were permanent reminders of what had occurred, in case anyone thought it had been a kind of dream. The Games' success became central to Melbourne's conception of itself as the nation's sporting capital, and it would parlay that reputation for generations to come.

A slower, more nuanced impact came from the Olympic chefs who decided to stay in Australia, some opening restaurants in Melbourne, others moving to Sydney. The style and quality of what they produced added another important element to the broadening cultural offerings of European migration. The Games meant Melbourne, and the nation, was exposed to nationalities it had never known from the security of its place in the Empire. It was the city's enthusiasm to embrace the unfamiliar that made the Games a success. 'By being allowed to play the host city we've grown up overnight from a spotty-faced adolescent to something approaching maturity,' *Herald* columnist Douglas Wilkie concluded.[41] Perhaps it was the civilising force of internationalism that had made the difference.

The rest of the nation could bask in the reflection of Melbourne's new-found maturity — or, if you were in Sydney, you could do something about it. In February 1956 the premier of New South Wales, Joe Cahill, released details of a competition to design a national opera house on Sydney's Bennelong Point. Eleven months later, he announced that the competition winner was Danish architect Jørn Utzon. One of the nation's most famous landmarks, which would help define Sydney as an international city, was underway.

The ribbon that runs through Australia in 1956 is the collision of old and new attitudes, the desire for peace among war-weary generations, and the thirst for comfort and a different kind of security among younger Australians. It was a year when the empire of which Australia had been an integral part became less relevant to many Australians, and the United States emerged not only as the nation's best ally but as a cultural touchstone too. Prime Minister Menzies had negotiated the 1950s with adept footwork, but in 1956 his missteps in the Suez Crisis became his biggest foreign policy failure, driven in large part by his trusting of old friends who had too much to lose. The Cold War was an ever-present threat, made more menacing by the secrecy that surrounded it, but for most Australians it became more remote after 1956. Across the nation, new kinds of entertainment emerged from the sedate days of radio serials and 78 rpms. Prosperity was desirable, and cars, fridges, and TV sets were the mark of a comfortable and successful life. Many Australians looked around and saw the emergence of a new world in 1956, and they wanted to be part of it. There would be no turning back.

Acknowledgements

This book has been a far more challenging process than I naively predicted when I started working on the idea. There were a range of reasons for this. One was the passage of time, rendering some sources' memories incomplete. Another was several potential sources being protective of their memories, due to some enduring anxiety. This underlined to me how confronting the era really had been. Thankfully, there were still many people who were happy to reflect on the events of that year and how they intersected with their lives. I'm deeply appreciative of their insights and help; in some cases, they even trusted me with their family records. My thanks go in particular to Marlene Mathews, Michael and Daniel Mészáros, Bruce Howard and Jennifer Howard, Ray and Thelma Kahl, Robert and Jean Macaulay, Les Coleman, and Anne Marsden. A particular thank you to Marta Marot for sharing her story and introducing me to many wonderful Hungarian refugees.

The research involved a range of institutions and people. I'm grateful to Greg Hunter at the National Sports Museum, and Marko Pavlyshyn and Ryna Ordynat at Monash University. Librarians and archivists at the National Library of Australia, the National Archives of Australia, the State Library of Victoria, the Herald & Weekly Times library, the Public Records Office in Victoria, the University of Melbourne Archives, the Noel Butlin Archives, and the Athenaeum Library in Melbourne have all played a significant, if perhaps unwitting, role. And the wonder of Trove remains the first destination in any researcher's travel plan.

I've been fortunate to have the assistance of several people who have provided me with some significant input and brokered important contacts along the way, including Engel Schmidl, Simon Plant, Paul Strangio, Fay Anderson, Nigel Dick, Julie Mack, Bill Cummings of the 56ers Olympic Torchbearers Club, and Sybil Nolan. The works of Harry Gordon and Graeme Davison, despite their differences in style and focus, were not only the foundation texts but, in Graeme's case, also provided some inspiration for the book's subtitle. Special thanks to Wendy Blacklock and Leonie Ginkel for giving me so much texture of the time. In Sweden I was given good assistance by Gunilla Lyden and Marja Von Stedingk.

I was fortunate to have some frank advice from those who read parts of the manuscript — thanks, Helen Elliott, Andrew Rule, and June Senyard (again!). Thanks also to my agent, Jacinta di Mase: an author couldn't ask for a stronger advocate. To the team at Scribe — from Henry Rosenbloom, who provided a calm presence on some occasionally fraught moments, to Kevin O'Brien, an expert managing editor, and Julian Welch, who edited the text with empathy and insight — I'm very grateful. They made this a better book.

I have spent a great deal of time in my bungalow, trooping off to the bottom of the garden, where I remained oblivious to all but the basic requirements of civilised society. Thankfully, my companion for a lot of it was a little black dog called Maggie. She never once quibbled over a turn of phrase, arched an eyebrow at my inconsistent grammar, or questioned my research techniques. Bless her.

My wife, Sue, has carried the weight of this book too, perhaps more than the others I've written. She remained steadfast, encouraged me at the low points, and took care of that most pernickety of jobs: doing the end notes. Thanks. Again.

Notes

Prologue: April 1949

1 *The Honolulu Star*, 15 April 1949.
2 Nick Richardson, *The Game of Their Lives*, Pan Macmillan, Sydney, 2016, p. 211.
3 *The Herald*, 4 June 1946.
4 *The Argus*, 12 June 1946.
5 Shane Cahill, 'Damned Lies and Olympics', *Good Weekend*, 18 September 1993, p. 28.
6 Sir Frank Beaurepaire to R.T. McPherson, Melbourne Invitation Committee, 11 February 1949, Olympic Consolidated Industries Pty Ltd (1987.0079), University of Melbourne Archives.
7 Tanja Luckins, 'Competing for Cultural Honours: cosmopolitanism, food, drink and the Olympic Games, Melbourne, 1956', in Diane Kirby and Tanja Luckins (eds), *Dining on Turtles: food feasts and drinking in history*, Palgrave Macmillan, Basingstoke, 2007, p. 86.
8 David Dunstan, 'Sir Harold Luxton', *Australian Dictionary of Biography*, http://adb.anu.edu.au/biography/luxton-sir-harold-daniel-7264.
9 Sir Raymond Connelly to Sir Frank Beaurepaire, 11 November 1948, Olympic Consolidated Industries, op. cit.
10 A.S. Drakeford letter, 22 March 1949, Olympic Consolidated Industries, op. cit.
11 Ibid.
12 'Buying or Building a House in Australia', http://john.curtin.edu.au/1940s/house/housing.html.
13 Cahill, op. cit.
14 *The Argus*, 28 October 1948, p. 3.
15 *The Argus*, 21 April 1949, p. 5.
16 *The West Australian*, 10 February 1938.
17 Sandra Collins, *The 1940 Tokyo Games: the missing Olympics*, Routledge, Oxford/New York, 2007, p. 166.
18 Ibid.
19 Graham Lomas, *The Will to Win: the story of Frank Beaurepaire*, Heinemann, Melbourne, 1960, p. 156.

20 *The Argus*, 5 May 1949, p. 12.

21 Lomas, op. cit., p. 156.

22 Sir Frank Beaurepaire to R.T. Macpherson, 2 March 1949, Olympic Consolidated Industries, op. cit.

23 Harry Gordon, *Australia and the Olympic Games*, University of Queensland Press, St Lucia, 1994, p. 195.

24 Ibid.

25 *The Sporting Globe*, 16 November 1949, p. 10.

26 *The Detroit Free Press*, 29 April 1949, p. 1.

27 *The Detroit Free Press*, 2 May 1949.

28 *The Sporting Globe*, May 1949.

29 Cahill, op. cit, p. 29.

30 Cablegram from Australian embassy in Tokyo to Prime Minister's Department, 11 May 1949, NAA, A1838, Control Symbol 480/1/3/1 Japan — Olympic Games.

31 Letter to Prime Minister Chifley, 25 May 1949, NAA, A1838, Control Symbol 480/1/3/1, op. cit.

32 *The Sydney Morning Herald*, 16 November 1949, p. 3.

33 *The Sporting Globe*, 16 November 1949, p. 10.

34 *The Sunday Sun*, 26 June 1949, p. 8.

35 Ibid.

36 *The Argus*, 24 November 1949, p. 3.

37 *Geraldton Guardian*, 26 November 1949, p. 2.

38 Lomas, op. cit., p. 159.

Chapter One: A Dame Is Born

1 Barry Humphries, *More Please*, Viking/Penguin, London, 1992, pp. 142–43.

2 John Lahr, *Dame Edna Everage and the Rise of Western Civilization*, Bloomsbury, London, 1991, p. 82.

3 *The Argus*, 4 October 1955, p. 24.

4 Humphries, op. cit., p. 151.

5 *Port Phillip Gazette*, vol. 2, no. 3, Autumn 1956, p. 9.

6 Humphries, op. cit., p. 152.

7 Lahr, op. cit., p. 84.

8 *The Australian Women's Weekly*, 4 January 1956, p. 2.

9 *The Argus*, 2 January 1956, p. 4.

10 Janet McCalman, *Journeyings: the biography of a middle-class generation 1920–1990*, Melbourne University Press, Carlton, 1993, p. 219.

11 A.W. Martin, *Robert Menzies: a life, volume 2 1944–1978*, Melbourne University Press, Carlton, 1993, p. 169.

12 Elizabeth Tynan, *Atomic Thunder: the Maralinga story*, NewSouth, Sydney, 2016, pp. 4–7.

13 Judith Brett, *Robert Menzies' Forgotten People*, Pan Macmillan, Sydney, 1992, p.45.

14 *The Canberra Times*, 10 May 1954.

15 Paul Hasluck (edited by Nicholas Hasluck), *The Chance of Politics*, Text, Melbourne, 1997, p. 73.

16 Frederick Howard, *Kent Hughes: a biography*, Macmillan, South Melbourne, 1972, pp. 180–183.

17 Ibid.

18 Ann Curthoys, 'The Getting of Television: dilemmas in ownership, control and culture', in Ann Curthoys and John Merritt (eds), *Better Dead Than Red: Australia's first Cold War, volume 2*, Allen & Unwin, Sydney, 1986, p. 152.

19 Colin Bednall, unpublished biography, Papers of Colin Bednall, National Library of Australia, MS5546, p. 251.

20 Lyn Gorman, 'Menzies and Television: a medium he "endured"', *Media International Australia*, no. 87, May 1998, p. 54.

21 Nick Richardson, 'In the Box Seat', *Herald Sun*, 15 July 2000, p. 12.

22 Colin Bednall, op. cit., p. 126.

23 Ibid.

24 Ibid.

25 Ibid., p. 249.

26 Ibid., pp. 249–50.

27 Ibid., pp. 235–37.

28 Quoted in Graeme Osborne and Glen Lewis, *Communication Traditions in Twentieth Century Australia*, Oxford University Press, Melbourne, 1995, p. 109.

29 Colin Bednall to Keith Murdoch, 25 November 1952; Keith Murdoch to Colin Bednall, 4 December 1952, NLA, MS5546.

Chapter Two: Rebels, Villains, and Heroes

1 Stephen J. Whitfield, 'Cherished and Cursed: toward a social history of *The Catcher in the Rye*', *The New England Quarterly*, vol. 70, no. 4, December 1997, pp. 567–600.

2 '"The Catcher in the Rye" prohibition lifted', NAA, B13, 1957/10559, p. 34.

3 Nicole Moore, 'Secrets of the Censors: obscenity in the archives', paper presented at the National Archives of Australia, Canberra, 2 May 2005, http://www.naa.gov.au/about-us/grants/margaret-george/moore-paper.aspx.

4 *The Sydney Morning Herald*, 28 August 1953.

5 McCalman, op. cit., p. 208.

6 *The Australian Women's Weekly*, 12 December 1956.

7 *The Central Queensland Herald*, 2 August 1956.

8 Stella Lees and June Senyard, *The 1950s: how Australia became a modern society, and everyone got a house and a car*, Hyland House, South Yarra, 1987, p. 75.

9 Bolton, Geoffrey, *The Oxford History of Australia: the middle way 1942–1988*, Oxford University Press, Melbourne, 1993, p. 106.

10 Murray Goot, 'Newspaper Circulation 1932–1977', in Peter Spearitt and David Walker (eds), *Australian Popular Culture*, George Allen & Unwin, North Sydney, 1979, pp. 210–211.

11 Author interview with Bruce Howard, 23 March 2017.

12 Ibid.

13 *The Argus*, 12 March 1956.

14 Ibid.

15 *The Argus*, 24 November 1949.

16 Letter from George Moir (recipient unclear), 26 January 1951, George Moir Collection, Australian Sports Museum.

17 Gordon, op. cit., p. 196.

18 Graham Lomas, op. cit., p. 160.

19 Letter from Frank Beaurepaire, 28 December 1955, Olympic Consolidated Industries, op. cit.

20 Memo from Graham Lomas, 16 January 1956, Olympic Consolidated Industries, op. cit.

21 *The Argus*, 25 April 1956.

22 For a discussion of this topic, see Richard White, *Inventing Australia: images and identity 1688–1980*, George Allen & Unwin, Sydney, 1980.

23 See, for example, 'Australia and Asia: will the "white" policy survive?', *The Guardian*, 27 May 1949.

24 A.T. Yarwood, 'The White Australia Policy', in James Jupp (ed.), *The Australian People*, Angus & Robertson, North Ryde, 1988, p. 78.

25 Geoffrey Sherington, 'Immigration Between the Wars', in James Jupp (ed.), *The Australian People*, op. cit., p. 96.

26 Ibid.

27 Andor Mészáros, unpublished autobiography, p. II/3.

28 Ibid., p.II/5.

29 Ibid., p. II/10.

30 Author interview with Michael Mészáros, 31 January 2018.

31 Mészáros, op. cit., p. II/21.

32 John Murphy, *Imagining the Fifties: private sentiment and political culture in Menzies' Australia*, UNSW Press, Sydney, 2000, p. 6.

33 A.W. Martin, op. cit., p. 319.

34 *The Argus*, 15 March 1956.

35 Ibid.

36 *The Herald*, 17 March 1955.

37 *The Age*, 27 April 1950.

38 *The Age*, 14 August 1952.

39 *The Argus*, 5 January 1956.

40 McCalman, op. cit., p. 237.

41 *The Argus*, 20 March 1956.

42 *The Vigilante*, 15 March 1956.

43 *The Central Queensland Herald*, 29 March 1956.

44 *The Argus*, 26 March 1956.

Chapter Three: The Enemy Within

1 *The Sunday Herald*, 20 February 1949.

2 *The Fortian* (Fort Street Girls School magazine), August 1950, p. 27.

3 Author interview with Marlene Mathews, 14 October 2018.

4 *The Argus*, 3 April 1956.

5 Tim Rowse, *Nugget Coombs: a reforming life*, Cambridge University Press, Port

Melbourne, 2002, p. 192.

6   *The Sun-Herald*, 8 July 1956.

7   *The West Australian*, 16 March 1948.

8   The Actors and Announcers Equity Association of Australia, Executive Minutes, 1 December 1955, 1984.0044, Actors Equity of Australia, Victorian Division (1936–1992), University of Melbourne Archives.

9   Philip Jones, 'They Still Call Australia *?#X!', *The Age*, 4 March 2006.

10 Ray Lawler, 'Athenaeum Memories', *The Melbourne Athenaeum: 170 years 1839–2009; a journal of the history of a Melbourne institution*, Melbourne Athenaeum, Melbourne, 2009, p. 7.

11 *The Sydney Morning Herald*, 4 February 1954.

12 Howard Manns, 'Posh Accents: discrimination and employment in Australia', *The Conversation*, https://theconversation.com/posh-accents-discrimination-and-employment-in-australia-43527.

13 *The Australian Women's Weekly*, 4 January 1956.

14 John Sumner, *Recollections at Play: a life in the Australian theatre*, Melbourne University Press, Carlton, 1993, p. 64.

15 Julian Meyrick, 'The Great Australian Plays: *The Torrents*, *The Doll* and the critical mass of Australian drama', *The Conversation*, https://theconversation.com/the-great-australian-plays-the-torrents-the-doll-and-the-critical-mass-of-australian-drama-69990.

16 Quoted in Simon Plant, *1956: Melbourne, modernity and the XVI Olympiad*, Museum of Modern Art at Heide, 1996, p. 9.

17 P.L. Coleman, *The Riddle of Les Coleman MP*, Connor Court, Brisbane, 2017, pp. 17–18.

18 *The Argus*, 11 February 1953.

19 Gordon, op. cit., p. 196.

20 *The Argus*, 3 February 1953.

21 Ibid.

22 Stella M. Barber, 'Sir Arthur Coles', *Australian Dictionary of Biography*, http://adb.anu.edu.au/biography/coles-sir-arthur-william-12334.

23 *The Age*, 26 May 1953.

24 *The Age*, 25 May 1954.

25 Ross Fitzgerald, with the assistance of Adam Carr and William J. Dealy, *The Pope's Battalions: Santamaria, Catholicism and the Labor split*, University of Queensland Press, St Lucia, 2003, p. 186.

26 Brenda Niall, *Mannix*, Text, Melbourne, 2015, p. 299.

27 Coleman, op. cit., p. 174.

28 Robert Murray, *The Split: Australian Labor in the fifties*, F.W. Cheshire, Melbourne, 1970, p. 107.

29 Coleman, op. cit., pp. 173–75, 284.

30 Ibid.

31 Graeme Davison, *City Dreamers: the urban imagination in Australia*, NewSouth, Sydney, 2016, p. 168.

32 *The Argus*, 9 April 1955, p. 6.

33 Murray, op. cit., p. 258.

34 Kate White, *John Cain and Victorian Labor 1917–57*, Hale & Iremonger, Sydney, 1982, p. 159.

35 *The Argus*, 10 May 1955.

36 Paul Strangio, *Neither Power nor Glory: 100 Years of political Labor in Victoria, 1856–1956*, Melbourne University Press, Carlton, 2012, p. 342.

37 Murray, op. cit., p. 255.

38 Ibid., p. 256.

39 *The Argus*, 13 March 1956.

Chapter Four: The Bomb in the Outback

1 'Atomic Weapons Test, Monte Bello Islands, Western Australia, 16 May, 1956', https://www.awm.gov.au/collection/C281508.

2 *The Canberra Times*, 26 June 1956.

3 Bolton, op. cit., pp. 94–95.

4 Tynan, op. cit., pp. 86–87. Tynan refers to evidence that indicates the bomb could have been as large as 98 kilotons.

5 *The Canberra Times*, 20 June 1956.

6 *The Canberra Times*, 24 August 1956.

7 Frank Walker, *Maralinga*, Hachette Australia, Sydney, 2016, pp. 66–67.

8 Roger Cross, *Fallout: Hedley Marston and the British bomb tests in Australia*, Wakefield Press, Kent Town, 2001, p. 48.

9 Quoted in Stella Lees and June Senyard, op. cit., p. 95.

10 *The Cairns Post*, 19 October 1951.

11 Lees and Senyard, op. cit., p. 96.

12 Maggie Brady, 'The Politics of Space and Mobility: controlling the Ooldea/Yalata Aborigines, 1952–1982', *Aboriginal History*, vol. 23, 1999, p. 3.

13 Kingsley Palmer, 'Dealing with the Legacy of the Past: Aborigines and atomic testing in South Australia', *Aboriginal History*, vol. 14, no. 2, 1990, pp. 196–97.

14 *The Report of the Royal Commission in to British Nuclear Tests in Australia*, vol. 1, Australian Government Printing Service, Canberra, 1985, p. 152.

15 Ibid., p. 157.

16 Brady, op. cit, p. 4.

17 Ibid., p. 4.

18 Ibid., p. 8.

19 *Royal Commission*, op. cit., p. 311.

20 Author interview and subsequent email exchange with Robert Macaulay, 28 October 2018.

21 *The Argus*, 30 April 1956.

22 *The Argus*, 30 May 1956.

23 Michael McKernan, *Beryl Beaurepaire*, University of Queensland Press, St Lucia, 1999, p. 79.

24 *The Canberra Times*, 30 May 1956.

25 Quoted in Charmaine O'Brien, *Flavours of Melbourne: a culinary biography*, Wakefield Press, Kent Town, 2008, p. 250.

26 *Catering*, June 1956, pp. 24–28.

27 *The Age*, 19 October 1956.

28 Melbourne Olympic Games Organising Committee (Catering Committee) minutes, 17 February 1956, PROV VPR10743, Unit 22.

29 *The Argus*, 22 February 1956.

30 Luckins, op. cit., p. 86.

31 Melbourne Olympic Games Organising Committee (Catering Committee) minutes, op. cit., 1 May and 19 June 1956.

32 *The Age*, 13 November 1956; *The Argus*, 5 October 1956; *The Argus*, 29 November 1956.

Chapter Five: It's a Men's Game

1 *The Canberra Times*, 26 June 1956.

2 Sir Robert Menzies, *Afternoon Light*, Penguin Books, Ringwood, 1970, p. 342.

3 Ibid.

4 Quoted in Gideon Haigh, *The Summer Game*, Text, Melbourne, 1997, p. 20.

5 G.V. Portus, *The Sydney Morning Herald*, 4 February 1954, p. 13.

6 *The Advertiser*, 13 November 1954.

7 *The Courier-Mail*, 26 March 1954.

8 *The Argus*, 9 July 1956.

9 *The Brisbane Telegraph*, 28 November 1952.

10 *The Courier-Mail*, 20 December 1952.

11 Robert Osborne to Sir George Paton, 23 June 1953, 1966.0004, Sir George Whitecross Paton Archive, Royal Commission into Television 1953–1954, University of Melbourne Archives.

12 'Colin Bednall 1913–1976', W.F. Mandle, *Australian Journal of Communication*, vol. 24, no. 3, 1997, p. 5.

13 Ibid.

14 Curthoys, op. cit., p. 143.

15 Ibid., p. 106.

16 *The Adelaide News*, 19 February 1953, p. 4.

17 Mandle, op. cit., p. 6.

18 'The Catcher in the Rye', NAA, op. cit., p. 4.

19 Minutes of the Olympic Press and Publicity Sub-committee, 26 January 1954, PROV 10743/P/000, Unit 17.

20 *The Argus*, 14 January 1955.

21 PROV 10743/P/000, Box 14, 1 April 1954.

22 Ibid., 5 October 1955.

23 *Labor Call*, 9 October 1952.

24 *The Canberra Times*, 12 July 1955.

25 Charles H. Holmes, 'Olympic Games', *Walkabout*, 1 September 1955.

26 *Central Queensland Herald*, 12 May 1955.

27 Oliver Hilmes, *Berlin 1936: sixteen days in August*, The Bodley Head, London, 2018, p. 191.

28 Avery Brundage to Wilfrid Kent Hughes, 2 February 1954, NLA, MS4856, Series 19, 1956 Melbourne Olympic Games, 1952–1968.

29 Wilfrid Kent Hughes to Avery Brundage, 12 March 1954, NLA, MS4856, Series 19, 1956 Melbourne Olympic Games, 1952–1968.

30 Avery Brundage to Wilfrid Kent Hughes, 9 June 1954, NLA, MS4856, Series 19, 1956 Melbourne Olympic Games, 1952–1968.

31 *The Argus*, 12 April 1955.

32 Wilfrid Kent Hughes, undated memo.

33 Interview with Don Chipp, 25 June 1985, Cahill Collection, National Sports Museum.

34 Wilfrid Kent Hughes to George Moir, 24 April 1955, Moir Collection, National Sports Museum.

Chapter Six: One-Armed Bandits

1 *The Argus* (*The Times* reprint), 12 June 1956.

2 A.W. Martin, *Robert Menzies — A Life, Volume 2 1944–1978*, MUP, Carlton, 1999, pp. 332–333.

3 *The Biz*, 15 August 1956.

4 Peter Charlton, *Two Flies Up a Wall: the Australian passion for gambling*, Methuen Hayes, North Ryde, 1987, p. 251.

5 *The Central Queensland Herald*, 23 August 1956.

6 *The Democrat & Chronicle*, 19 November 1956.

7 'Looting Registered Clubs', Sydney Crime Museum, http://www.sydneycrimemuseum.com/crime-stories/looting-registered-clubs/.

8 Nerilee Hing, 'A History of Machine Gambling in the NSW Club Industry: from community benefit to commercialisation', *International Journal of Hospitality and Tourism Administration*, vol. 7, no. 1, 2006, pp. 81–107.

9 Charlton, op. cit., p. 244.

10 John Douglas Pringle, *Australian Accent*, Chatto and Windus, London, 1959, p. 190.

11 Sarah McVeigh, 'Australian Pokies King Len Ainsworth on 70 Years in the Business', *ABC News*, 19 September 2017, https://www.abc.net.au/news/2017–09–19/australias-pokie-king-len-ainsworth-on-70-years-in-the-business/8945524.

12 *The Sydney Morning Herald*, 4 December 1954; *The Sun-Herald*, 5 December 1954; *The Sydney Morning Herald*, 17 December 1954.

13 *The Daily Telegraph*, 11 December 1954.

14 Neil Bennetts, Interview with Mervyn Wood, National Library of Australia, 22 October 1975.

15 ULVA Minutes, 10 January 1956, ULVA Archives, Noel Butlin Archives.

16 Cyril Cahill to Rev. Powell, 27 June 1956.

17 Rowley E. Hodgson to club members, 5 July 1956.

18 *The Australian Women's Weekly*, 8 August 1956, p. 33.

19 Julian Croft, 'Nevil Shute Norway', *Australian Dictionary of Biography*, http://adb.anu.edu.au/biography/norway-nevil-shute-11262.

20 Quoted in David Marr, *Patrick White: a life*, Jonathan Cape, London, 1991, p. 304.

21 Ibid., p. 307.

22 '1956 Celebrations: review of Patrick White's *Tree of Man*', ABC Radio National, https://www.abc.net.au/radionational/programs/archived/book-show/1956-celebrations-review-of-patrick-whites-the/3347494.

23 Ibid., p. 309.

24 A.G. Serle, 'Literature', in *The Arts Festival of the Olympic Games: a guide to the exhibitions with introductory commentaries on the arts in Australia*, Olympic Organising Committee, Melbourne, 1956, pp. 38–39.

25 Minutes of Arts Festival sub-committee, 1 July 1954, 1968.0001, George Whitecross Paton Olympic Fine Arts Festival Archive 1951–63, University of Melbourne Archives.

26 *The Age*, 14 July 1956.

27 Interview with Don Chipp, op. cit., p. 5.

28 Bernard Smith, 'Paintings and Drawings', Olympic Arts Festival catalogue, p. 18.

29 John Berger, 'London Exhibition of Australian Art', *Meanjin*, vol. 12, no. 3, Spring 1953, p. 278.

30 A.V. Cook, 'Sculpture', Olympic Arts Festival catalogue, op. cit., p. 17.

31 *Good Neighbour*, 1 April 1955.

32 Ibid.

33 PROV VPR10743, Unit 22, Melbourne Olympics Catering Committee minutes, 1 August 1956; 21 August 1956.

34 Marcus Marsden, *Carrying the Torch: 1956 Melbourne Olympic Games*, Marsden Publishing, Fitzroy North, 2006, pp. 3–4.

35 Ibid., p. 14.

36 *The Argus*, 27 May 1950.

37 *The Argus*, 31 October 1953.

38 *The Herald*, 7 November 1953.

39 *The Age*, 10 November 1953.

40 Diaries of Richard Casey, NAA, M1153, 507734, p. 1178.

Chapter Seven: With Open Arms

1 *The Record Emerald Hill*, 31 July 1954.

2 *The Australian Women's Weekly*, 19 October 1955.

3 *The Argus*, 2 October 1956; *The Age*, 19 October 1956.

4 Interview with Don Chipp, op. cit.

5 *The Daily Telegraph*, 20 November 1953.

6 Klaus Neumann, 'Fifth Columnists? German and Austrian refugees in Australian internment camps', NAA Frederick Watson Fellowship Paper, 17 April 2002.

7 Ibid.

8 Ibid.

9 *The Australian Women's Weekly*, 21 November 1956, p. 5.

10 Ibid.

11 Ibid.

12 Interview with Don Chipp, op. cit.

13 John Lack, 'Sir David Fletcher Jones', *Australian Dictionary of Biography*, http://adb.anu.edu.au/biography/jones-sir-david-fletcher-10638.

14 University of Melbourne Archives, 'Fletcher Jones: How the 1956 Melbourne Olympic skirt changed everything!', https://blogs.unimelb.edu.au/archives/fletcher-jones-how-the-1956-melbourne-olympics-skirt-changed-everything/.

15 Menzies, *Afternoon Light*, op. cit., p. 156.

16 A.W. Martin, *Robert Menzies: a life, volume 1*, op. cit., p. 396.

17 Quoted in A.W. Martin, 'R.G. Menzies and the Suez Crisis', in J.R. Nethercote (ed.), *A.W. Martin: the 'Whig' view of Australian history and other essays*, MUP, Carlton, 2007, p. 214.

18 Thomas Keneally, *The Australians: flappers to Vietnam*, Allen & Unwin, Sydney, 2014, p. 461.

19 Judith Brett, *Robert Menzies' Forgotten People*, Pan Macmillan, Sydney, 1992, p. 177.

20 Diaries of Richard Casey, op. cit., p. 1150.

21 Menzies, op. cit., p. 158.

22 Ibid.

23 Robert Menzies, 'Nationalization of the Suez Canal', https://menziesvirtualmuseum.org.au/books-overview/contents/105-nationalization-of-the-suez-canal.

24 Martin, op. cit., p. 335.

25 Stan Correy, 'The Suez Crisis 1956', *Background Briefing*, ABC Radio National, https://www.abc.net.au/radionational/programs/backgroundbriefing/the-suez-crisis-1956/3386572.

26 Martin, op. cit., p. 338.

27 Ibid., p. 339.

28 John Hurst, *The Walkley Awards: Australia's best journalists in action*, John Kerr, Richmond, 1988, pp. 22–23.

29 Jon Savage, 'Demonising those teenage dirtbags', *Index on Censorship*, vol. 47, Summer, 2018, p. 67.

30 Simon Hall, *1956: the world in revolt*, Faber & Faber, London, 2016, p. 195.

31 Keith Moore, 'Bodgies and Widgies and Moral Panic in Australia 1955–1959', QUT, 2004.

32 *The Argus*, 22 October 1956.

33 *The Argus*, 29 September 1956.

34 Michael Sturma, 'The Politics of Dancing: when rock 'n' roll came to Australia', *Journal of Popular Culture*, vol. 25, no. 4, Spring 1992.

35 *The Courier-Mail*, 19 September 1954.

36 *The Central Queensland Herald*, 8 March 1956.

37 *People*, 1 August, 1951.

38 John Braithwaite and Michelle Barker, 'Bodgies and Widgies: folk devils of the fifties', in Paul R. Wilson and John Braithwaite (eds), *Two Faces of Deviance: crimes of the powerless and the powerful*, University of Queensland Press, St Lucia, 1978, p. 36.

39 *Journal of Police History*, vol. 2, no. 1, pp. 61.

40 Jon Hewett, 'Aspects of the Bodgies/Widgies Sub-Culture 1948–1960', honours thesis, University of Melbourne, 1983.

41 'Pauline', in Hewett, 'Aspects of the Bodgies/Widgies Sub-Culture 1948–1960', op. cit.

42 *The Argus*, 1 December 1955.

43 Ibid.

44 *Report of Juvenile Delinquency Advisory Committee to A.G. Rylah, MLA, Chief Secretary of Victoria*, 17 July 1956, p. 11.

45 *The Argus*, 19 July 1956.

46 *The Argus*, 25 August 1956.

47 P.L. Coleman, op. cit., p. 220.

48 Ben Collins, 'A Glorious Season', *Grand Finals Volume 2, 1939–1978*, The Slattery Media Group, Richmond, 2012, p. 192.

49 *The Argus*, 17 September 1956.

50 Ibid.

51 *The Argus*, 19 September 1956.

52 Author interview with Bruce Howard, op. cit.

53 *The Argus*, 26 September 1956.

54 Marsden, op. cit., pp. 20–21.

55 Ibid., p. 22.

Chapter Eight: Clouds on the Horizon

1 Bednall, op. cit., p. 209.

2 Ibid., pp. 238–39.

3 C.H. King to Colin Bednall, 25 January 1954, Colin Bednall papers, op. cit.

4 C.H. King to Colin Bednall, 1 July 1955.

5 C.H. King to Colin Bednall, 8 February 1955.

6 C.H. King to Colin Bednall, 18 April 1955.

7 Jim Usher (ed.), *The Argus: life and death of a newspaper*, Australian Scholarly Publishing, North Melbourne, 2007, p. 164.

8 Colin Bednall to C.H. King, 26 October 1954.

9 C.H. King to Colin Bednall, 30 December 1955.

10 Sandra Hall, *Supertoy: 20 years of television*, Sun Books, Melbourne, 1976, pp. 20–21.

11 Author interview with Nigel Dick, 4 May 2017.

12 Quoted in David Kynaston, *Family Britain 1951–1957*, Bloomsbury, London, 2010, p. 125.

13 *Royal Commission*, vol. 1, 1985, op. cit., p. 15.

14 Robert Milliken, *No Conceivable Injury: the story of Britain and Australia's atomic cover-up*, Penguin, Ringwood, 1986, p. 147.

15 Frank Walker, *Maralinga*, Hachette, Sydney, 2014, pp. 157–58.

16 Cross, op. cit., p. 32.

17 *The Argus*, 28 August 1956, p. 4.

18 Sue Rabbit Roff, 'Australia's Nuclear Testing Before the 1956 Olympics in Melbourne Should Be a Red Flag for Fukushima', *The Conversation*, https://theconversation.com/australias-nuclear-testing-before-the-1956-olympics-in-melbourne-should-be-a-red-flag-for-fukushima-in-2020-85787.

19 Milliken, op. cit., pp. 100–101.

20 *Royal Commission*, vol. 1, 1985, op. cit., p. 304.

21 Transcript of proceedings, *Royal Commission British Nuclear Tests in Australia*,

19 October 1984–30 October 1984, NAA, 6448, no. 4, pp. 1587–88.

22 Luckins, op. cit., p. 91.

23 Ibid., p. 92.

24 'TCN Channel 9 First in Australia', http://www.tcnchannel9.com.

25 *Newspaper News*, 1 March 1956.

26 'TCN Channel 9 First in Australia', http://www.tcnchannel9.com.

27 Royal Commission transcript of proceedings, op. cit., pp. 1589–90.

28 *Royal Commission*, vol. 1, 1985, op. cit., p. 316.

29 Ibid., p. 317.

30 Royal Commission transcript of proceedings, op. cit., pp. 8593–94.

31 *Royal Commission*, vol. 1, 1985, op. cit., p. 374.

32 Milliken, op. cit., p. 106.

33 *The Argus*, 28 September 1956.

Chapter Nine: Lighting the Way

1 *The Herald*, 9 February 1957.

2 Ibid.

3 'Consular representatives in Australia — Union of Soviet Socialist Republics — Re: two consular officers', Melbourne Olympic Games, NAA, A1838, Item 551682.

4 Letter from Charles Spry, 11 October 1956, ibid.

5 Ibid.

6 Linda Hungerford, 'Sugar Cane Farming in the Bundaberg District 1945–1985', masters thesis, University of Queensland, 1991, p. 55.

7 *The Sydney Morning Herald*, 18 October 1956.

8 Aleksandr Fursenko and Timothy Naftali, *Khrushchev's Cold War*, W.W. Norton, New York, 2006, p. 111.

9 Menzies, op. cit., p. 166.

10 Martin, op. cit., pp. 342–45.

11 Martin, op. cit., p. 347.

12 *The Age*, 1 January 1987.

13 Harry Blutstein, *Cold War Games*, Echo, Richmond, 2017, pp. 32–35.

14 Martin, op. cit., p. 347.

15 Simon Hall, op. cit., pp. 317–324.

16 Diaries of Richard Casey, op. cit., 20 November 1956, p. 1209.

17 John Howard, *The Menzies Era: the years that shaped modern Australia*, HarperCollins, Sydney, 2014, p. 210.

18 Quoted in Paul Strangio, Paul 't Hart and James Walter, *The Pivot of Power*, Miegunyah Press, Carlton, 2013, pp. 30–31.

19 Kristine Toohey and A.J. Veal, *The Olympic Games: a social science perspective*, CABI, Oxfordshire, p. 97.

20 Andor Mészáros, unpublished autobiography, p. IV/16.

21 Ibid., p. IV/17.

22 Author interview with Bruce Howard, op. cit.

23 Marsden, op. cit., p. 41.

24 Sumner, op. cit., p. 60.

25 *The Australian Women's Weekly*, 19 September 1956.

26 *The Sydney Morning Herald*, 18 October 1956.

27 Sumner, op. cit., p. 61.

28 *The Age*, 20 February 1957.

29 'Chinese Opera Company — visit to Australia', NAA A10302, 1956/1597, p. 5.

30 *The Argus*, 19 October 1956.

31 Ibid.

32 *The Age*, 22 October 1956.

33 *The Sydney Morning Herald*, 19 October 1956.

34 *The Argus*, 11 October 1956.

Chapter Ten: The World Waits

1 *The Herald*, 9 February 1957.

2 Coles Phinizy, 'The 1956 Olympics', *Sports Illustrated*, 19 November 1956.

3 Marsden, op. cit., p. 53.

4 *The Listener-In*, 6–12 December 1956.

5 *The Listener-In*, 27 October–2 November 1956.

6 'TV at 60: HSV first in Melbourne', *Television.au*, 4 November 2016, https://televisionau.com/2016/11/tv-at-60-hsv7-first-in-melbourne.html.

7 *The Argus*, 5 November 1956.

8 Humphries, op. cit., pp. 155–58.

9 'The Dutch Boycott of the 1956 Olympic Games, Part 2: rehabilitation', *The Olympians from 1964 to 2020*, 27 February 2016, https://theolympians.co/2016/02/27/the-dutch-boycott-of-the-1956-olympic-games-part-2-rehabilitation.

10 Ian Jobling, 'Strained Beginnings and Friendly Farewells: the Games of the XVI Olympiad, Melbourne, 1956', *Stadion: International Journal of the History of Sport*, vol. 21/22 (1995–96), p. 258.

11 *The Sydney Morning Herald*, 8 November 1956, p. 4.

12 Phinizy, op. cit.

13 Frederick Howard, *Kent Hughes: a biography*, Macmillan, South Melbourne, 1972, pp. 191–92.

14 *Medford Mail Tribune*, 15 February 1956.

15 Horner, David, *The Spy Catchers: the official history of ASIO 1949–1963*, Allen & Unwin, 2014, p. 456.

16 XVI Olympiad Melbourne 1956 Transport Russian Ship GRUZIJA aka GRUZIA aka GRUZIYA Volume 2, NAA, A6122, 2765.

17 *The Age*, 9 November 1956.

18 Tom Bamforth, 'Green and Pleasant Memories', *Griffith Review*, https://griffithreview.com/articles/green-and-pleasant-memories-1956-olympic-village.

19 Author interview with Marlene Mathews, op. cit.

20 Nikki Henningham, Interview with Marlene Mathews for the Sport Oral History Project, NLA, 1 May 2008.

21 *The Argus*, 15 October 1956.

22 Alexander Wolff, 'Revolution Games', *Sports Illustrated*, 18 June 2012.
23 *The Argus*, 14 November 1956.
24 *The Herald*, 11 February 1957.
25 *The Free Thought*, Issue 47, 25 November 1956, p. 1.
26 Erin Elizabeth Redihan, *The Olympics and the Cold War 1948–1968: sport as a battleground in the US-Soviet rivalry*, McFarland & Co, Jefferson, 2017, pp. 125–127.
27 Wilfrid Kent Hughes to Avery Brundage, 22 June 1954.
28 Stephen R. Wenn, 'Lights! Camera! Little Action: television, Avery Brundage and the 1956 Melbourne Olympics', *Sporting Traditions*, vol. 10, November 1993, pp. 45–46.
29 Graeme Davison, '"Welcoming the World": the 1956 Olympic Games and the re-presentation of Melbourne', in John Murphy and Judith Smart (eds), *The Forgotten Fifties* (MUP/*Australian Historical Studies* Vol. 28, No. 109, October 1997, p. 73).
30 Bednall, op. cit., p. 264.
31 Roy Masters, 'Man Who Brought the Big Event to the Small Screen', *The Sydney Morning Herald*, 29 July 2005.
32 *The Argus*, 21 November 1956.
33 Jobling, op. cit., p. 260.
34 Gerald Stone, *Compulsive Viewing: the inside story of Packer's Nine Network*, Viking/Penguin, Ringwood, 2000, p. 78.
35 Marsden, op. cit., p. 60.
36 Ibid., pp. 68–75.
37 *The Western Herald*, 9 November 1956.
38 *The Herald*, op. cit.
39 Ibid.

Chapter Eleven: Let the Games Begin

1 Nina Paranyuk to Robert Menzies, 26 November 1956, NAA, MP1139/V57/30023.
2 Charles Spry to Robert Menzies, 28 November 1956, NAA, MP1139/V57/30023.
3 For a description of ASIO's preparations for the Olympic Games, see Horner, op. cit., pp. 455–60.
4 *The Argus*, 19 November 1956.
5 Kent, Hilary and Merritt, John, 'The Cold War and the Melbourne Olympic Games', in Curthoys, Ann and Merritt, John (eds), *Better Dead Than Red: Australia's first Cold War: 1945–1959*, vol. 2, Allen & Unwin, North Sydney, 1986, p. 181.
6 *The Argus*, 22 November 1956.
7 *The Argus*, 27 October 1956.
8 *The Sydney Morning Herald*, 22 November 1956.
9 Marsden, op. cit., pp. 125–26.
10 Doug Eales, in Marsden, op. cit., p. 128.
11 Rick Broadbent, *Endurance: the extraordinary life and times of Emil Zátopek*,

Bloomsbury, London, 2016, p. 252.

12 *The Argus*, 1 December 1956, p. 11.

13 *The Ottawa Citizen*, 23 November 1956, p. 17.

14 *The Guardian*, 23 November 1956, p. 8.

15 *The Sydney Morning Herald*, 23 November 1956, p. 3.

16 *The Central Queensland Herald*, 29 November 1956, p. 14.

17 Ibid.

18 Quoted in Broadbent, op. cit., p. 127.

19 Author interview with Bruce Howard, op. cit.

20 *The Tribune*, 5 December 1956, p. 1.

21 'Political Asylum — Nina Paranyuk', NAA, A1838, 1606/3, p. 154.

22 *The Tampa Bay Times*, 14 November 1956, p. 14.

23 Mészáros, op. cit., p. IV/16.

24 Henningham, Interview with Marlene Mathews, op. cit.

25 Keith Donald and Don Selth, *Olympic Saga*, Futurian Press, Sydney, 1957, pp. 186–87.

26 Author interview with Marlene Mathews, op. cit.

27 *The Age*, 28 November 1956.

28 Ibid.

29 *The Central Queensland Herald*, 29 November 1956.

30 Lees and Senyard, op. cit., p. 65.

31 *The Listener-In*, 3–9 March 1956.

32 Ibid.

33 Ibid., 15–21 December 1956.

34 Lees and Senyard, op. cit., p. 66.

35 *The Sydney Morning Herald*, 24 November 1956.

36 Donald and Selth, op. cit., p. 190–91.

37 Author interview with Marlene Mathews, op. cit.

38 *The Argus*, 9 November 1956.

39 *Seamen's Journal*, December 1956.

40 *The Sydney Morning Herald*, 2 December 1956.

41 *The Age*, 4 December 1956.

42 *The Sydney Morning Herald*, 11 December 1956.

43 Blutstein, op. cit., p. 247.

Chapter Twelve: The Worst of Times, the Best of Times

1 Author interview with Marlene Mathews , op. cit.

2 *The Age*, 1 December 1956.

3 Dennis H. Phillips, *Australian Women at the Olympic Games*, Petersham, Walla Walla Press in conjunction with the Centre of Olympic Studies, University of New South Wales, 2001, p. 84.

4 Henningham, Interview with Marlene Mathews, op. cit.

5 *The Argus*, 29 July 1956.

6 Phillips, op. cit.

7 Donald and Selth, op. cit., p.201.

8 Robin Hughes, Interview with Shirley Strickland de la Hunty, *Australian Biography*, http://www.australianbiography.gov.au/subjects/strickland/interview2.html.

9 *The Herald*, 11 February 1956.

10 Ibid.

11 *The Age*, 7 December 1956.

12 Bednall, op. cit., p. 267.

13 *The Argus*, 7 December 1956.

14 Broadbent, op. cit., p. 256.

15 Howard, op. cit., p. 193.

16 James Button, 'Ceremony Born from a Wing and a Prayer', *The Age*, 11 November 2006.

17 David Goldblatt, 'The Most Incredible Moments in Olympic History', 13 July 2016, https://www.panmacmillan.com/blogs/history/history-of-the-olympics.

18 Button, op. cit.

19 Donald and Selth, op. cit., p. 62.

20 Ibid., p. 68.

21 *The Herald*, 10 December 1956; *The Argus*, 10 December 1956.

22 Ibid.

23 *The Herald*, op. cit.

24 Broadbent, op. cit., p. 262.

25 'Consular representatives in Australia — Union of Soviet Socialist Republics — Re: two Consular Officers', Melbourne Olympic Games, NAA, A1838, 551682.

26 'Nina Paranyuk — political asylum', op. cit.

27 *The Herald*, op. cit.

28 Donald and Selth, op. cit., p. 224.

29 *The Argus*, 17 November 1956.

30 *Democrat and Chronicle*, 6 December 1956.

31 *The Argus*, 10 December 1956.

32 *The Canberra Times*, 6 December 1956.

33 *The Argus*, ibid.

34 *The San Francisco Examiner*, 8 December 1956.

35 Author interview with Marlene Mathews, op. cit.

36 *The Argus*, 13 December 1956.

37 Parliament of Western Australia, *Hansard*, 15 August 1956, p. 207.

38 Ibid., 17 October 1956, pp. 1417–18.

39 Ibid.

40 Peter Morton, *Fire Across the Desert: Woomera and the Anglo-Australian Joint Project 1946–1980*, Defence Science Technology, Canberra, 1989, p. 88.

41 Parliament of Western Australia, Select Committee Report, Native Welfare Conditions in the Laverton-Warburton Range Area, 12 December 1956, p. 17.

42 Ibid, p. 14.

43 Robert Manne, *The Petrov Affair*, Pergamon Press, Sydney, 1987, pp. 257–58.

44 'Vladimir and Evdokia Petrov — Naturalisation', NAA, A4940, C1293.

45 Ibid.

46 Blutstein, op. cit., pp. 242–43.

47 Matthew Engle, *Tickle the Public: one hundred years of the popular press*, Indigo, London, 1997, p. 166.

48 *The Canberra Times*, 19 December 1956, p. 6.

Finale

1 'A Review of the Activities of the Olympic Civic Committee and the Olympics (special) Committee, performed on behalf of the council of the City of Melbourne', December 1956, p. 19, PROV VPRS 10743/PO, Unit 17.

2 *The Herald*, 7 December 1956, quoted in Davison, op. cit., p. 75.

3 1956 Melbourne Olympics, Press and Publicity Committee, undated statement, PROV VPRS 10743/PO, Unit 17.

4 Ibid.

5 *The Herald*, 13 February 1957.

6 Nina Paranyuk, 18 January 1956, NAA, MP1139.

7 Ibid.

8 Hurst, op. cit., pp. 23–25.

9 *The Herald*, 4 March 1957.

10 *The Age*, 4 March 1957.

11 David Binder, 'Détente Is Said to Give the KGB a Bigger Workload', *The New York Times*, 2 June 1975.

12 Stone, op. cit., p. 76.

13 *The Argus*, 18 January 1956.

14 *The Argus*, 18 January 1956.

15 Author interview with Nigel Dick, 4 May 2017.

16 *The Argus*, 18 January 1956.

17 'TV at 60: The viewing's fine on GTV 9', https://televisionau.com/2017/01/tv-at-60-viewings-fine-on-gtv9.html.

18 *The Age*, 21 January 1957.

19 Quoted in William Shawcross, *Murdoch*, Pan, London, 1993, p. 99.

20 *The Argus*, 16 January 1957.

21 Usher (ed.), op. cit., pp. 7–8.

22 Coleman, op. cit., p. 224.

23 Egon F. Kunz, *Blood and Gold: Hungarians in Australia*, F.W. Cheshire, Melbourne, 1969, pp. 195–96.

24 Liz Minchin and Peter Ker, 'Police Still Searching for Absent Athletes', *The Age*, 23 March 2006.

25 Author interview with Michael Mészáros, op. cit.

26 E.C. Harris to Collector of Customs, 18 April 1957, NAA B13, 1957/10559.

27 *The Sydney Morning Herald*, 18 January 1957.

28 Nick Richardson, 'Power Behind the Throne', *Herald Sun*, 21 June 2000.

29 Bednall, op. cit., p. 272.

30 Interview with Marlene Mathews, NLA, op. cit.

31 Author interview with Marlene Mathews, op. cit.

32 *Royal Commission of Inquiry in Respect of Certain Matters Relating to Allegations of Organised Crime in Clubs 1973–74*, Government Printer, Sydney, 1974, p. 73.

33 Alfred W. McCoy, *Drug Traffic: narcotics and organized crime in Australia*, Harper & Row, Sydney, 1980, p. 242.

34 Charlton, op. cit., p. 244.

35 *The Herald*, 28 May 1968.

36 E.A. Doyle, 'The XVIth Olympiad, Melbourne 1956', *Victorian Historical Magazine*, December 1957, vol. 28, no. 1, p. 7.

37 Ibid., p. 10.

38 Ibid., p. 11.

39 *The Age*, 23 January 1957.

40 John McCallum, '*The Summer of the Seventeenth Doll*', in Philip Parsons (ed.), *Companion to Theatre in Australia,* Currency Press, Sydney, 1995, p. 565.

41 Wilkie in Davison, op. cit. pp. 75–76.

Select Bibliography

Archives

National Archives of Australia

'The Catcher in the Rye', NAA, B13, 1957/10559

'Chinese Opera Company — Visit to Australia', NAA, A10302, 1956/1597

'Consular Representatives in Australia — Union of Soviet Socialist Republics — Re: two Consular Officers, Melbourne Olympic Games', NAA, A1838, 551682

'Japan — Olympic Games', NAA, A1838, 480/1/3/1

'Political Asylum — Nina Paranyuk', NAA, A1838, 1606/3

'Nina Paranyuk', NAA, MP1139, V57/30023

'Selected Appendices of Unpublished History of ASIO (Intelligence Aspects of 1956 Olympic Games Melbourne)', NAA, A6122, 1414/1067037

'Vladimir and Evdokia Petrov — Naturalisation', NAA, A4940, C1293

'XVI Olympiad Melbourne 1956 Transport Russian Ship GRUZIJA aka GRUZIA aka GRUZIYA Volume 2', NAA, A6122, 2765

National Library of Australia

Colin Bednall, MS 5546, including unpublished autobiography

Bruce Howard papers, MS Acc09/117

Sir Wilfrid Kent Hughes papers, MS4856

Audio

Neil Bennetts, Interview with Marlene Mathews, 28 August 1981

Neil Bennetts, Interview with Mervyn Wood, 22 October 1975

Nikki Henningham, Interview with Marlene Mathews, 1 May 2008

Noel Butlin Archives, Australian National University

Australian Hotels Association New South Wales Branch deposit, Z195

University of Melbourne Archives

Actors Equity of Australia, Victorian Division (1936–1992), 1984.0044

Sir Frank Beaurepaire (Olympic Consolidated Industries Ltd), 1987.0079

Sir George Whitecross Paton, 1966.0004

National Sports Museum

George Moir papers

Shane Cahill collection

Public Record Office of Victoria

Minutes of the Melbourne Olympics Organising Committee (Catering Committee), PROV VPR 10743/P/000, Unit 22

Minutes of the Melbourne Olympics Organising Committee (Press and Publicity Committee), PROV VPR 10743/P/0000, Unit 17

Articles/Chapters

Brady, Maggie, 'The Politics of Space and Mobility: controlling the Ooldea/Yalata Aborigines, 1952–1982,' *Aboriginal History*, vol. 23, 1999, pp. 1–14

Braithwaite, John and Barker, Michelle, 'Bodgies and Widgies: folk devils of the fifties', in Paul R. Wilson and Braithwaite, John (eds), *Two Faces of Deviance: crimes of the powerless and the powerful*, University of Queensland Press, St Lucia, 1978, pp. 26–45

Cahill, Shane, 'Damned Lies and Olympics', *Good Weekend*, 18 September 1993, pp. 23–34

Curthoys, Ann, 'The Getting of Television: dilemmas in ownership, control and culture, 1941–1956', in Curthoys, Ann and Merritt, John (eds), *Better Dead Than Red: Australia's first Cold War: 1945–1959*, vol. 2, Allen & Unwin, North Sydney, 1986, pp. 123–154

Doyle, E.A., 'The XVIth Olympiad, Melbourne 1956', *The Victorian Historical Magazine*, vol. 28, no. 1, December 1957, pp. 1–15

Goot, Murray, 'Newspaper Circulation 1932–1977', in Spearritt, Peter and Walker, David (eds), *Australian Popular Culture*, George Allen & Unwin, North Sydney, 1979, pp. 210–221

Gorman, Lyn, 'Menzies and Television: a medium he "endured"', *Media International Australia*, no. 87, May 1998, pp. 49–67

Hing, Nerilee, 'A History of Machine Gambling in the NSW Club Industry: from community benefit to commercialisation', *International Journal of Hospitality and Tourism Administration*, vol. 7, no. 1, pp. 81–107

Jobling, Ian, 'Strained Beginnings and Friendly Farewells: the Games of the XVI Olympiad, Melbourne, 1956', *Stadion: International Journal of the History of Sport*, vol. 21/22, 1995–96, pp. 251–66

Kent, Hilary and Merritt, John, 'The Cold War and the Melbourne Olympic Games', in Curthoys, Ann and Merritt, John (eds), *Better Dead Than Red: Australia's first Cold War: 1945–1959*, vol. 2, Allen & Unwin, North Sydney, 1986, pp. 170–85

Laguerre, Andre, 'Down a Road Called Liberty', *Sports Illustrated*, 17 December 1956

Luckins, Tanja, 'Competing for Cultural Honours: cosmopolitanism, food, drink and the Olympic Games, Melbourne, 1956', in Kirkby, Dianne and Luckins, Tanja, *Dining on Turtles: food feasts and drinking in history*, Palgrave Macmillan, Basingstoke, 2007, pp. 82–100

Mandle, W.F., 'Colin Bednall 1913–1976', *Australian Journal of Communication*, vol. 24, no. 3, 1997, pp. 129–44

Moore, Keith, 'Bodgies and Widgies and Moral Panic in Australia 1955–1959', QUT, ePrint, conference paper, 29 October 2004

Neumann, Klaus, 'Fifth Columnists? German and Austrian refugees in Australian internment camps', NAA Frederick Watson Fellowship Paper, 17 April 2002

Palmer, Kingsley, 'Dealing with the Legacy of the Past: Aborigines and atomic testing in South Australia', *Aboriginal History*, vol. 14, no. 2, 1990, pp. 197–207

Phinizy, Coles, 'The 1956 Olympics', *Sports Illustrated*, 19 November 1956

Scalmer, Sean, 'Crisis to Crisis: 1950–1966', in Faulkner, John and Macintyre, Stuart (eds), *True Believers: the story of the federal parliamentary Labor Party*, Allen & Unwin, Crows Nest, 2001, pp. 90–104

Stratton, Jon, 'Bodgies and Widgies: just working-class kids doing working-class things', in White, Rob (ed.), *Youth Sub Cultures: theory, history and the Australian experience*, ACYS Publishing, Hobart, 2012, pp. 185–92

Sturma, Michael, 'The Politics of Dancing: when rock 'n' roll came to Australia', *Journal of Popular Culture*, vol. 25, no. 4, Spring 1992, pp. 123–42

Wenn, Stephen R., 'Lights! Camera! Little Action: television, Avery Brundage and the 1956 Melbourne Olympics', *Sporting Traditions*, vol. 10, November 1993, pp. 38–53

White, Richard, 'The Shock of Affluence: the fifties in Australia', in O'Callaghan, Judith and Pickett, Charles (eds), *The Australian Dream: design and the home of the 1950*, Powerhouse Publishing, Sydney, 1992, pp. 11–26

Whitfield, Stephen J., 'Cherished and Cursed: toward a social history of *The Catcher in the Rye*', *The New England Quarterly*, vol. 70, no. 4, December 1997, pp. 567–600

Wolff, Alexander, 'Revolution Games', *Sports Illustrated*, 18 June 2012

Books

Arnold, Lorna, *Britain, Australia and the Bomb: the nuclear tests and their aftermath*, Palgrave, Basingstoke, 2006

Arrow, Michelle, *Friday on Our Minds: popular culture in Australia since 1945*, UNSW Press, Sydney, 2009

Barber, Noel, *Seven Days of Freedom: the Hungarian uprising, 1956*, Stein and Day, New York, 1974

Bashford, Alison and Macintyre, Stuart, *The Cambridge History of Australia, Volume 2: The Commonwealth of Australia*, Cambridge University Press, Port Melbourne, 2013

Beckett, Francis and Russell, Tony, *1956: the year that changed Britain*, Biteback Publishing, London, 2015

Blutstein, Harry, *Cold War Games*, Echo, Richmond, 2017

Bolton, Geoffrey, *The Oxford History of Australia: the middle way 1942–1988*, Oxford University Press, Melbourne, 1993

Brett, Judith, *Robert Menzies' Forgotten People*, Pan Macmillan, Sydney, 1992

Broadbent, Rick, *Endurance: the extraordinary life and times of Emil Zátopek*, Bloomsbury, London, 2016

Brown, Nicholas, *Governing Prosperity: social change and social analysis in Australia*, Cambridge University Press, Oakleigh, 1995

Bunting, Sir John, *R.G. Menzies: a portrait*, Allen & Unwin, North Sydney, 1988

Carroll, Brian, *The Menzies Years*, Cassell Australia, Stanmore, 1977

Charlton, Peter, *Two Flies Up a Wall: the Australian passion for gambling*, Methuen Haynes, North Ryde, 1987

Coleman, Peter, *Australian Civilization*, F.W. Cheshire, Melbourne, 1962

Coleman, P.L., *The Riddle of Les Coleman MP: the life and political times of the DLP's first leader*, Connor Court, Brisbane, 2017

Collins, Sandra, *The 1940 Tokyo Games: the missing Olympics*, Routledge, Oxford/New York, 2007

Costar, Brian, Love, Peter and Strangio, Paul (eds), *The Great Labor Schism: a retrospective*, Scribe Publications, Melbourne, Carlton, 2005

Cox, Peter, *On the Box: great moments in Australian television, 1956–2006*, Powerhouse Publishing, Sydney, 2006

Cross, Roger, *Fallout: Hedley Marston and the British bomb tests in Australia*, Wakefield Press, Kent Town, 2001

Davie, Michael, *Anglo-Australian Attitudes*, Secker & Warburg, London, 2000

Davison, Graeme, *City Dreamers: the urban imagination in Australia*, NewSouth, Sydney, 2016

Donald, Keith and Selth, Don, *Olympic Saga: the track and field story, Melbourne 1956*, Futurian Press, Sydney, 1957

Espy, Richard, *The Politics of the Olympic Games*, University of California Press, Los Angeles, 1979

Finder, Henry (ed.), *The 50s: the story of a decade*, The New Yorker, Random House, New York, 2015

Fitzgerald, Ross (with Adam Carr and William J. Dealy), *The Pope's Battalions: Santamaria, Catholicism and the Labor split*, University of Queensland Press, St Lucia, 2003

Frame, Tom, *The Life and Death of Harold Holt*, Allen & Unwin, Crows Nest, 2005

Fursenko, Aleksandr and Naftali, Timothy, *Khrushchev's Cold War*, W.W. Norton, New York, 2006

Goldblatt, David, *The Games: a global history of the Olympics*, Macmillan, London, 2016

Golding, Peter, *Black Jack McEwen: political gladiator*, MUP, Carlton, 1996

Gordon, Harry, *Australia and the Olympic Games*, University of Queensland Press, St Lucia, 1994

Grattan, Michelle (ed.), *Australian Prime Ministers*, New Holland, Sydney, 2000

Griffen-Foley, Bridget, *Sir Frank Packer: the young master*, HarperCollins, Sydney, 2000

Halberstram, David, *The Fifties*, Villard Books, New York, 1993

Hall, Sandra, *Supertoy: 20 years of Australian television*, Sun Books, South Melbourne, 1976

Hall, Simon, *1956: the world in revolt*, Faber & Faber, London, 2016

Hasluck, Nicholas (ed.), *Paul Hasluck: the chance of politics*, Text, Melbourne, 1997

Henderson, Gerard, *Menzies' Child: the Liberal Party of Australia, 1944–1994*, Allen & Unwin, St Leonards, 1994

Hilmes, Oliver, *Berlin 1936: sixteen days in August*, The Bodley Head, London, 2018

Horner, David, *The Spycatchers: the official history of ASIO 1949–1963*, Allen & Unwin, Crows Nest, 2014

Howard, Bruce, *15 Days in '56: the first Australian Olympics*, Angus & Robertson, Pymble, 1995

Howard, Frederick, *Kent Hughes: a biography*, Macmillan, South Melbourne, 1972

Howard, John, *The Menzies Era: the years that shaped modern Australia*, HarperCollins, Sydney, 2014

Hudson, W.L., *Casey*, Oxford University Press, Melbourne, 1986

Hudson, W.L., *Blind Loyalty: Australia and the Suez crisis, 1956*, MUP, Carlton, 1989

Humphries, Barry, *A Nice Night's Entertainment*, Granada, London, 1981

Humphries, Barry, *More Please: an autobiography*, Viking, Ringwood, 1993

Hurst, John, *The Walkley Awards: Australia's best journalists in action*, John Kerr, Richmond, 1988

James, G.F., *The Arts Festival of the Olympic Games Melbourne: a guide to the exhibitions and introductory commentaries on the arts in Australia*, The Olympic Civic Committee of the Melbourne City Council for the Olympic Organisation Committee, Melbourne, 1956

Jones, Benjamin, T., Bongiorno, Frank, and Uhr, John (eds), *Election Matters: ten federal elections that shaped Australia*, Monash University Publishing, Clayton, 2018

Jupp, James (ed.), *The Australian People: an encyclopedia of the nation, its people and their origins*, Angus & Robertson, North Ryde, 1988

Keneally, Thomas, *Australians: flappers to Vietnam*, Allen & Unwin, Crows Nest, 2014

Kiernan, Colm, *Calwell: a personal and political biography*, Thomas Nelson, West Melbourne, 1978

Kingston, Beverley, *Basket, Bag and Trolley: a history of shopping in Australia*, Oxford University Press, South Melbourne, 1994

Kunz, Egon F., *Blood and Gold: Hungarians in Australia*, F.W. Cheshire, Melbourne, 1969

Kynaston, David, *Family Britain 1951–1957*, Bloomsbury, London, 2009

Lahr, John, *Dame Edna Everage and the Rise of Western Civilisation*, Bloomsbury, London, 1991

Lees, Stella and Senyard, June, *The 1950s: how Australia became a modern society, and how everyone got a house and a car*, Hyland House, South Yarra, 1987

Lomas, Graham, *The Will to Win: the story of Sir Frank Beaurepaire*, Heinemann, Melbourne, 1960

Macintyre, Stuart, *Australia's Boldest Experiment: war and reconstruction in the 1940s*, NewSouth, Sydney, 2015

McCalman, Janet, *Struggletown: public and private life in Richmond 1900–1965*, MUP, Carlton, 1985

McCalman, Janet, *Journeyings: the biography of a middle-class generation 1920–1990*, MUP, Carlton, 1993

McCoy, Alfred W., *Drug traffic: narcotics and organised crime in Australia*, Harper & Rowe, Sydney, 1980

McKernan, Michael, *Beryl Beaurepaire*, University of Queensland Press, St Lucia, 1999

McMullin, Ross, *The Light on the Hill: the Australian Labor Party 1891–1991*, Oxford University Press, South Melbourne, 1991

Mandle, W.F., *Going It Alone: Australia's national identity in the twentieth century*, Allen Lane, London, 1977

Manne, Robert, *The Petrov Affair*, Pergamon Press, Rushcutters Bay, 1987

Marr, David, *Patrick White: a life*, Jonathan Cape, London, 1991

Marsden, Marcus, *Carrying the Torch: 1956 Melbourne Olympic Games*, Marsden Publishing, Fitzroy North, 2006

Martin, A.W., *Robert Menzies: a life, Volume 1, 1894–1943*, MUP, Carlton, 1993

Martin, A.W., *Robert Menzies: a life, Volume 2, 1944–1978* MUP, Carlton, 1999

Menzies, Sir Robert, *Afternoon Light*, Penguin, Ringwood, 1970

Menzies, Sir Robert, *The Measure of the Years*, Cassell Australia, North Melbourne, 1970

Miller, David, *The Official History of the Olympic Games and the IOC: Athens to London 1894–2012*, Mainstream Publishing, Edinburgh, 2012

Milliken, Robert, *No Conceivable Injury*, Penguin, Ringwood, 1986

Mitchell, Susan with Dyer, Ken, *Winning Women: challenging the norms in Australian sport,* Penguin, Ringwood, 1985

Morton, Peter, *Fire Across the Desert: Woomera and the Anglo-Australian Joint Project 1946–1980*, Defence Science Technology, Canberra, 1989

Murphy, John and Smart, Judith (eds), *The Forgotten Fifties*, MUP/*Australian Historical Studies*, vol. 28, no. 109, October 1997

Murphy, John, *Imagining the Fifties: private sentiment and political culture in Menzies' Australia*, UNSW Press, Sydney, 2000

Murray, Robert, *The Split: Australian Labor in the fifties*, F.W. Cheshire, Melbourne, 1970

Murray, Robert, *Labor and Santamaria*, Australian Scholarly Publishing, North Melbourne, 2016

Nethercote, J.R. (ed.), *A.W. Martin: the 'Whig' view of Australian history*, MUP, Carlton, 2007

Neumann, Klaus, *In the Interest of National Security: civilian internment in Australia during World War II,* National Archives of Australia, Parkes, 2006

Neumann, Klaus, *Across the Seas: Australia's response to refugees*, Black Inc., Collingwood, 2015

Newnham, W.H., *Melbourne: the biography of a city*, F.W. Cheshire, Melbourne, 1956

Niall, Brenda, *Mannix*, Text, Melbourne, 2015

O'Brien, Charmaine, *Flavours of Melbourne: a culinary biography*, Wakefield Press, Kent Town, 2008

Osborne, Graeme and Lewis, Glen, *Communication Traditions in 20th Century Australia*, Oxford University Press, Melbourne, 1995

Perkins, Kevin, *Menzies: last of the Queen's men*, Rigby Limited, Adelaide, 1968

Phillips, A.A., *On the Cultural Cringe*, MUP, Carlton, 2006

Phillips, Dennis, *Australian Women at the Olympic Games*, Walla Walla Press, Petersham, 2001

Prasser, Scott, Nethercote, J.R. and Warhurst, John, *The Menzies Era: a reappraisal of government, politics and policy*, Hale & Iremonger, Sydney, 1995

Pringle, John Douglas, *Australian Accent*, Chatto and Windus, London, 1959

Reynolds, P.L., *The Democratic Labor Party*, The Jacaranda Press, Milton, 1974

Richardson, Nick, *The Game of Their Lives*, Pan Macmillan, Sydney, 2016

Rowse, Tim, *Nugget Coombs: a reforming life*, Cambridge University Press, Port Melbourne, 2002

Sandbrook, Dominic, *Never Had It So Good: a history of Britain from Suez to the Beatles*, Abacus, London, 2006

Shaw, A.G.L., *The Story of Australia*, Faber and Faber, London, 1955

Stone, Gerald, *Compulsive Viewing: the inside story of Packer's Nine Network*, Viking, Ringwood, 2000

Strangio, Paul, *Neither Power nor Glory: 100 years of political Labor in Victoria, 1856–1956*, MUP, Carlton, 2012

Strangio, Paul, 't Hart, Paul and Walter, James, *The Pivot of Power*, Miegunyah Press, Carlton, 2017

Stratton, Jon, *The Young Ones*, Black Swan Press, Perth, 1992

Sumner, John, *Recollections at Play: a life in the Australian theatre*, MUP, Carlton, 1993

Tavan, Gwenda, *The Long Slow Death of White Australia*, Scribe, Carlton North, 2005

Tynan, Elizabeth, *Atomic Thunder: the Maralinga story*, NewSouth, Sydney, 2016

Usher, Jim (ed.), *The Argus: life & death of a newspaper*, Australian Scholarly Publishing, North Melbourne, 2007

Walker, Frank, *Maralinga*, Hachette, Sydney, 2014

White, Kate, *John Cain and Victorian Labor 1917–1957*, Hale & Iremonger, Sydney, 1982

White, Richard, *Inventing Australia: images and identity 1688–1980*, George Allen & Unwin, Sydney, 1981

Williams, Ron, *Born in 1956? What else happened?*, Boom Books, Wickham, 2016

Newspapers and Magazines

Catering
Meanjin
The Age
The Argus
The Australian Women's Weekly
The Canberra Times
The Detroit Free Press
The Guardian
The Herald (Melbourne)
The Listener-In
The New York Herald Tribune
The Sporting Globe
The Sun
The Sydney Morning Herald
The Vigilante
Walkabout

Online Resources

'Atomic Weapons Test, Monte Bello Islands, Western Australia, 16 May, 1956', https://www.awm.gov.au/collection/C281508

Bamforth, Tom, 'Green and Pleasant Memories', *Griffith Review*, https://griffithreview.com/articles/green-and-pleasant-memories-1956-olympic-village

'The Dutch Boycott of the 1956 Olympic Games, Part 2: rehabilitation', *The Olympians from 1964 to 2020*, https://theolympians.co/2016/02/27/the-dutch-boycott-of-the-1956-olympic-games-part-2-rehabilitation

McVeigh, Sarah, 'Australian Pokies King Len Ainsworth on 70 Years in the Business', ABC News, 19 September 2017, https://www.abc.net.au/news/2017–09–19/australias-pokie-king-len-ainsworth-on-70-years-in-the-business/8945524

Manns, Howard, 'Posh Accents: discrimination and employment in Australia', *The Conversation*, https://theconversation.com/posh-accents-discrimination-and-employment-in-australia-43527

Meyrick, Julian, 'The Great Australian Plays: *The Torrents*, *The Doll* and the critical mass of Australian Drama', *The Conversation*, https://theconversation.com/the-great-australian-plays-the-torrents-the-doll-and-the-critical-mass-of-australian-drama-69990

Moore, Nicole, 'Secrets of the Censors: obscenity in the archives', 2 May 2005, http://www.naa.gov.au/about-us/grants/margaret-george/moore-paper.aspx

'Nationalization of the Suez Canal', https://menziesvirtualmuseum.org.au/books-overview/contents/105-nationalization-of-the-suez-canal

Rabbit Roff, Sue, 'Australia's Nuclear Testing before the 1956 Olympics in Melbourne Should Be a Red Flag for Fukushima', *The Conversation*, https://theconversation.com/australias-nuclear-testing-before-the-1956-olympics-in-melbourne-should-be-a-red-flag-for-fukushima-in-2020-85787

State Library of Victoria and the 1956 Olympics, https://www.slv.vic.gov.au/search-discover/explore-collections-theme/sport-games/melbourne-olympics

State Parliament of Victoria and the 1956 Olympics, https://www.parliament.vic.gov.au/publications/research-papers/download/36-research-papers/13610–2016–3-olympics-hn

'The Suez Crisis', *Background Briefing*, ABC Radio National, https://www.abc.net.au/radionational/programs/backgroundbriefing/the-suez-crisis-1956/3386572#transcript

Official Reports

Parliament of Western Australia, Select Committee Report, Native Welfare Conditions in the Laverton-Warburton Range Area, 12 December 1956

Report of Juvenile Delinquency Advisory Committee to A.G. Rylah, MLA, Chief Secretary of Victoria, 17 July 1956

Report of the Royal Commission in to the British Nuclear Tests in Australia, Australian Government Publishing Service, Canberra, 1985

Royal Commission of Inquiry in Respect of Certain Matters Relating to Allegations of Organised Crime in Clubs 1973–74, Government Printer, Sydney, 1974

Catalogues and Ephemera

1956 Melbourne, Modernity and the XVI Olympiad, Museum of Modern Art at Heide, Bulleen, 1997

The Games of the Sixteenth Olympiad, Melbourne MCMLVI, The Argus and Australasian Limited, Melbourne, 1956

The Olympic Games, Melbourne 1956, Colorgravure, Melbourne, 1956

Opening Ceremony, Olympic Games, Melbourne 1956, Melbourne Olympic Games Organisation Committee, Melbourne, 1956

Theses

Hewett, John, 'Aspects of the Bodgies/Widgies Sub-Culture 1948–1960', honours thesis, University of Melbourne, 1983

Hungerford, Linda, 'Sugar Cane Farming in the Bundaberg District 1945–1985', masters thesis, University of Queensland, 1991